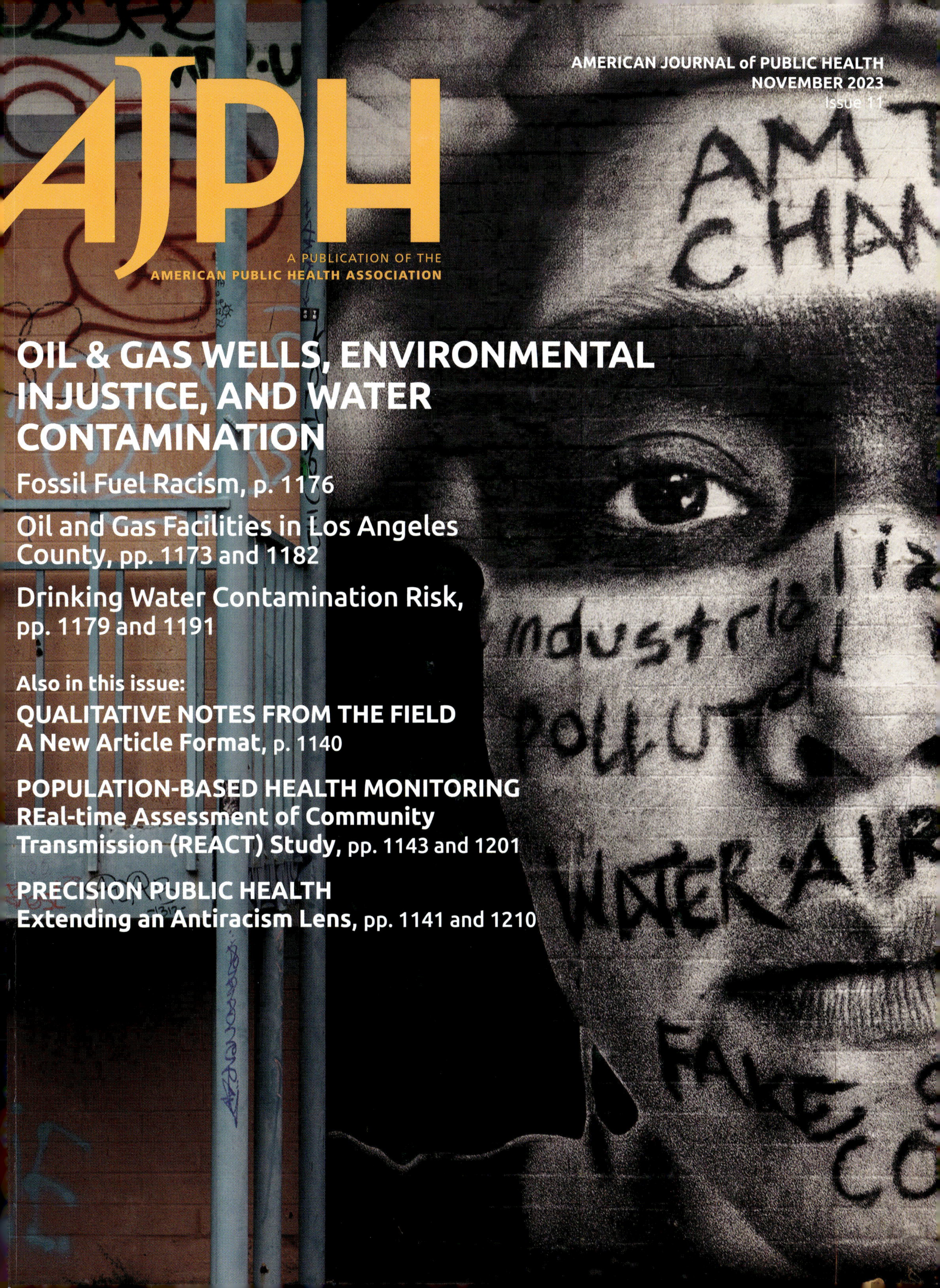

AMERICAN JOURNAL of PUBLIC HEALTH
NOVEMBER 2023
Issue 11

AJPH

A PUBLICATION OF THE
AMERICAN PUBLIC HEALTH ASSOCIATION

OIL & GAS WELLS, ENVIRONMENTAL INJUSTICE, AND WATER CONTAMINATION

Fossil Fuel Racism, p. 1176

Oil and Gas Facilities in Los Angeles County, pp. 1173 and 1182

Drinking Water Contamination Risk, pp. 1179 and 1191

Also in this issue:

QUALITATIVE NOTES FROM THE FIELD
A New Article Format, p. 1140

POPULATION-BASED HEALTH MONITORING
REal-time Assessment of Community Transmission (REACT) Study, pp. 1143 and 1201

PRECISION PUBLIC HEALTH
Extending an Antiracism Lens, pp. 1141 and 1210

When It Comes To Health, Never Compromise. Choose Quality Rubber Medical Devices.

Good health is not something money can buy. However, choosing high-quality, reliable medical devices certainly is. **Made in Malaysia** quality rubber medical devices are produced to meet stringent international standards and are exported worldwide. Malaysian manufacturers have esteemed reputations, using modern manufacturing facilities to produce a wide range of quality rubber medical devices such as examination gloves, surgical gloves, condoms, foley catheters, dental dams, breathing bags, and medical tubing at competitive prices. When it comes to rubber, **No One Knows Rubber Like Malaysia Does.**

Reach Malaysian manufacturers via Marketplace at **www.myrubbercouncil.com**

NO ONE KNOWS RUBBER LIKE MALAYSIA DOES

Conform to International Standards	World's No. 1 in Natural Rubber Gloves & Nitrile Gloves	Made in Malaysia Quality Rubber Products	Wide Range of Rubber Medical Devices

www.myrubbercouncil.com @MYrubbercouncil @MYrubbercouncil @MYrubbercouncil

MRC MALAYSIAN RUBBER COUNCIL

APHA
AMERICAN PUBLIC HEALTH ASSOCIATION
For science. For action. For health.

AJPH®, published monthly, is the official Journal of the American Public Health Association®, 800 I St NW, Washington, DC 20001-3710; (202) 777- APHA; TDD (202) 777-2500. APHA is a nongovernmental professional society founded in 1872, representing all disciplines and specialties in public health.

APHA OFFICERS

Chris Chanyasulkit, PhD, MPH
President

Kaye Bender, PhD, RN
Immediate Past-President

Ella Greene-Moton
President-Elect

Mary Wooley, MA
Vice President (USA)

Vamini Selvanandan, MD, MPH
Vice President (Canada)

Rosana Teresa Onocko-Campos, PhD
Vice President (Latin America and the Caribbean)

Benjamin H. Hernandez, MBA
Treasurer

M. Aaron Guest, PhD, MPH
Speaker, Governing Council

Georges C. Benjamin, MD
Executive Director/Secretary

APHA EXECUTIVE BOARD

E. Oscar Alleyne, DrPH, MPH (2024)
Moose Alperin, EdD, MPH (2025)
Kaye Bender, PhD, RN (2023)
Immediate Past-President

Georges C. Benjamin, MD
Executive Director/Secretary

Apryl Renee Brown, MD, MPH (2023)
Chair, Science Board

Bryan O. Buckley, DrPH, MPH (2025)
Charlene Cariou, MHS, CPH, CHES (2023)
Chair, Executive Board

Chris Chanyasulkit, PhD, MPH (2024)
President

Shontelle Dixon, MPH, CHES (2026)
Sarah Gareau, DrPH, MEd (2023)
Ella Greene-Moton (2025)
President-Elect

M. Aaron Guest, PhD, MPH, MSW (2023)
Speaker, Governing Council

Benjamin H. Hernandez, MBA (2025)
Treasurer

Sandy-Asari Hogan, DrPH, MPH (2023)
Chair, Intersectional Council

Claude A. Jacob, MPH (2026)
Amy Lee, MD, MPH, MBA (2025)
Brittany Marshall, DrPH (2023)
Nandi A. Marshall, DrPH, MPH (2024)
Shirley A. Orr, MHS, APRNA (2023)
Chair, Action Board

Lauren Ray, MPH (2023)
Chair, Student Assembly

David Reyes, DNP, MN/MPH, RN (2024)
Sarah A. Rines (2023)
Chair, Council of Affiliates

Gopal Sankaran, MD, DrPH (2026)
Kusuma K. Schofield, MSEd, MPH (2023)
Chair, Education Board

The *American Journal of Public Health*® (*AJPH*) (print ISSN: 0090-0036; electronic ISSN: 1541- 0048), first published in 1911, is the official journal of the American Public Health Association® (APHA). The oldest and largest organization of public health professionals in the world, APHA represents approximately 30 000 members from more than 50 occupations of public health.

Submissions: Visit www.editorialmanager.com/ajph or ajph.edmgr.com for online manuscript preparation and submission guidelines. Contributions of original unpublished research, social science analyses, scholarly essays, critical commentaries, departments, and letters to the editor are welcome. Questions? Write ajph.submissions@apha.org or call APHA at (202) 777-2469.

Print plus online subscriptions: Institutional price (print copy with online access for a single institution and all authorized users, regardless of geographic location) varies by size of organization and ranges from $993–$1445 for US organizations, and $1073–$1526 for international organizations (air delivery); multiple campuses not permitted without special arrangement. Details of the tiered pricing system at https://subscriptionoffice.com/pages/apha-landing-page. To order, write apha.subscriptions@apha.org.

Online-only subscriptions: Institutional price for one institution and its authorized users (regardless of geographic location) is $878–$1307. To order, write apha.subscriptions@apha.org. For academic consortia or multisite corporate subscriptions, contact apha.subscriptions@apha.org.

Print-only subscriptions: Institutional price is US $701, $782 international.

Back print issues: A limited number of print issues are for sale. Single copies are US $49, $55 international (air delivery). Shipping included; prepay only. To order, write apha.subscriptions@apha.org.

Reprints: For prices and ordering information on 50 or more reprints, check the Reprints section at www.ajph.org. To order smaller quantities of reprints (rush delivery), use the "Purchase Article" link on the article site itself.

Electronic access: Online articles more than 10 years old are available free for personal use at www.ajph.org. Recent articles are available through pay-per-view: single PDF article for $24, single issue access for 24 hours for $33, or entire site access for 24 hours for $38.

Postal information: Periodicals postage paid at Washington, DC, and additional mailing offices. Postmaster: Send address changes to American Journal of Public Health, 800 I St NW, Washington, DC 20001-3710.

Address changes: Send to AJPH, Membership Department (members) or AJPH Subscriptions (subscribers), APHA, 800 I St NW, Washington, DC 20001-3710. Or write to membership.mail@apha. org (members) or apha.subscriptions@apha.org (subscribers).

Advertising: For pricing and other information, see www.ajph.org. Please write to ashell.alston@ apha.org or call (202) 777-2470 for other advertising opportunities. Ask about special exhibit packages and sponsorships. Acceptance of advertising by the *Journal* does not imply endorsement of products.

Copyright: Copyright © 2023 by the American Public Health Association. Opinions expressed by authors of articles summarized, quoted, or published in full in this *Journal* represent only the opinions of the authors and do not necessarily reflect the official policy of the American Public Health Association or the institution with which the author(s) is (are) affiliated, unless so specified.

Any report, article, or paper prepared by employees of the US government as part of their official duties is, under the Copyright Act, a "work of the United States Government" for which copyright protection under Title 17 of the US Code is not available. However, the *Journal* format is copyrighted and pages may not be photocopied, except in limited quantities, or posted online, without permission of APHA. Copying done for other than personal or internal reference use—such as copying for general distribution, for advertising or promotional purposes, for creating new collective works, or for resale—without the expressed permission of APHA is prohibited. Requests for special permission should be sent to permissions@apha.org.

Indexes: Publications that index or abstract articles from AJPH include the following: Ageline, Assia (Applied Social Science Index and Abstracts), Biological Abstracts, Chemical Abstracts, CINAHL, Criminal Justice Abstracts, EMBASE, EMCare, Environmental Abstracts, e-psyche, ERIC, ETOH (Alcohol and Alcohol Problems Science Database), Excerpta Medica, Food Science and Technology, General Science Index, Grateful Med, Hospital Literature Index, Human Resources Abstracts, International Pharmaceutical Abstracts (IPA), Medline, Physical Education Index, Pollution Abstracts, Psychological Abstracts, PsychINFO, Safety Science Abstracts, Sage Family Studies Abstracts, Sage Human Resources Abstracts, Science Citation Index, SCOPUS, SIIC Data Bases, Social Work Research and Abstracts, and Statistical Reference Index (SRI)/LexisNexis.

Medscape Publishers' Circle

AJPH

A PUBLICATION OF THE
AMERICAN PUBLIC HEALTH ASSOCIATION

COVER: An abandoned hotel is covered with paintings by street artists who were supported by the Painted Desert Project on September 12, 2022 on the Navajo Nation near Cameron, Arizona. Murals and graffiti are scattered across the Navajo Nation on buildings abandoned and often vandalized and tagged by outsiders driving through the reservation. Most address issues important to the Navajo people such as COVID-19, which devastated the Navajo Nation early in the pandemic, and radiation cancers and other health problems from decades of uranium and coal mining on Navajo land. Other topics include tribal stories and ceremonies and the loss of sacred sites. Numerous murals on US Route 89 were commissioned by the privately funded public art initiative, Painted Desert Project. Navajo Nation is a sovereign Native American nation and is the largest reservation for indigenous people in the United States.

Cover concept and image selection by Aleisha Kropf, Image Editor. Photo by David McNew/Getty Images. Printed with permission.

APHA
AMERICAN PUBLIC HEALTH ASSOCIATION
For science. For action. For health.

Promoting public health research, policy, practice, and education is the *AJPH* mission. As we widen our scope to embrace global issues, we also sharpen our focus to support the needs of public health practitioners. We invite contributions of original unpublished research, opinion and commentary, and letters to the editor.

The *Journal* is printed on acid-free recycled paper.

EDITOR-IN-CHIEF
Alfredo Morabia, MD, PhD

SENIOR DEPUTY EDITOR
Michael C. Costanza, PhD

DEPUTY EDITOR
Farzana Kapadia, PhD

DEPUTY STATISTICAL EDITOR
Hua He, PhD

DEPUTY EDITOR FOR OPEN ACCESS SUPPLEMENTS
Steven C. Fiala, MPH

IMAGE EDITOR
Aleisha Kropf

ASSISTANT EDITOR
Erica J. Carter, BS

STUDENT EDITOR
Katherine M. Anderson, MPH

EDITORS
Luisa Borrell, DDS, PhD
Lisa Bowleg, PhD, MA
Theodore M. Brown, PhD
Nabarun Dasgupta, PhD, MPH
Paul C. Erwin, MD, DrPH
Laura Ferguson, PhD, MSc, MA
Daniel M. Fox, PhD
Robert J. Kim-Farley, MD, MPH
Stewart J. Landers, JD, MCP
Tanya Telfair LeBlanc, PhD
Jonathan I. Levy, ScD
Jihong Liu, ScD
Evan Mayo-Wilson, DPhil
Marian Moser Jones, PhD, MPH
Wendy Parmet, JD
Kenneth Rochel de Camargo Jr, MD, PhD
Lorna Thorpe, PhD
Roger Vaughan, DrPH, MS
Eric R. Walsh-Buhi, PhD, MPH

EDITORIAL BOARD
Moya L. Alfonso, PhD, MSPH (2024)
Heather M. Brandt, PhD (2023), Chair
Amy Hagopian, PhD, MHA (2024), Vice Chair
Michael T. Halpern, MD, PhD, MPH (2024)
Kenneth Hoekstra, PhD (2024)
Amar Kanekar, PhD, MPH, MB (2023)
Shawn M. Kneipp, PhD, RN, ANP (2024)
Laura A. Nabors, PhD, MA (2024)
A.G. Palladino, MPH, MJ, MS (2023)
Laura Schwab Reese, PhD, MA (2023)
Gulzar H. Shah, PhD, MStat, MS (2024)
Mark A. Strand, PhD, MS (2023)
Joseph Telfair, DrPH, MSW, MPH (2024)
Cynthia Williams, PhD, MHA, PT (2025)
Samantha H. Xu, MPH (2023)

FORMER EDITORS-IN-CHIEF
Mary E. Northridge, PhD, MPH (Editor Emerita)
Mervyn Susser
Michel Ibrahim
Alfred Yankauer
George Rosen
Abel Wolman
Charles-Edward A. Winslow
Harry S. Mustard
Mazÿck Ravenel

STAFF
Georges C. Benjamin, MD
Executive Director/Publisher
Ashell Alston
Director of Publications
Brian Selzer
Deputy Director of Publications
Michael Henry
Associate Production Editor (Sr)
Avery Ferguson, MA
Associate Production Editor
Shokhari Tate, MPH
Journal Project Liaison
Kristin Crocker, MFA
Journal Production Coordinator
Emily Dalton
Digital Publications Specialist

FREELANCE
Kelly Burch
Greg Edmondson
Aisha Jamil
Gary Norton
Michelle Quirk
Sarah Cook
Copyeditor
Aisha Jamil
Sinéad Schenk
Proofreader
Vanessa Sifford
Graphic Designer
Michelle Sarah Livings, MPH
Data Presentation Specialist

OPEN ACCESS ONLINE ONLY PODCAST DATA SUPPLEMENT AVAILABLE

EDITOR'S CHOICE

1140 Introducing *AJPH*'s Newest Manuscript Format: Qualitative Notes From the Field
L. Bowleg

OPINIONS, IDEAS, & PRACTICE

EDITORIALS

1141 A Call for Course Correction: Applying an Antiracism Lens to Precision Public Health
S. A. Choate

1143 Designing Surveillance at a Population Level
S. Tancredi and A. Chiolero

1146 *AJPH* Peer Reviewers: Thank You for Your Services
M. Henry, B. Selzer, A. Ferguson, and K. Crocker

PERSPECTIVES

1153 Two-Spirit Identity and Adolescent Survey Measures: Considerations of Appropriation, Transparency, and Inclusion
L. Hayes, A. LaFrinier-Ritchie, N. Matthews, B. O'Keefe, N. Perrote, G. N. Rider, C. Brown, M. Filoteo, K. Johnston-Goodstar, B. J. McMorris, and L. Martin

1157 Training Latinx Community Health Workers as Clinical Research and Health Care System Navigators
G. Plasencia, K. Kaalund, and A. Thoumi

1160 Homelessness Is a Form of Structural Violence That Leads to Adverse Obstetrical Outcomes
M. Walsh, A. Varshneya, E. Beauchemin, L. Rahman, A. B. Schick, M. Goldberg, and V. Ades

NOTES FROM THE FIELD

1163 Impact of a Permitless Concealed Firearm Carry Law in West Virginia, 1999–2015 and 2016–2020
E. W. Lundstrom, J. K. Pence, and G. S. Smith

1167 Impact of the Choose Well Initiative on Contraceptive Access at Federally Qualified Health Centers in South Carolina: A Midline Evaluation
K. Beatty, M. G. Smith, J. de Jong, A. Weber, R. Adelli, and A. Khoury

OIL AND GAS: ENVIRONMENTAL JUSTICE

1173 Environmental Injustice and Cumulative Environmental Burdens in Neighborhoods Near Oil and Gas Development: Los Angeles County, California, and Beyond
N. C. Deziel

1176 Fossil Fuel Racism: The Ongoing Burden of Oil and Gas Development in the Shadows of Regulatory Inaction
M. D. Willis and J. J. Buonocore

1179 The Imperative of Equitable Protection: Structural Racism and Oil Drilling in Los Angeles
B. Shamasunder and J. E. Johnston

RESEARCH & ANALYSIS

OIL AND GAS: ENVIRONMENTAL JUSTICE

1182 Social and Environmental Stressors of Urban Oil and Gas Facilities in Los Angeles County, California, 2020
M. Chan, B. Shamasunder, and J. E. Johnston

1191 Race, Racism, and Drinking Water Contamination Risk From Oil and Gas Wells in Los Angeles County, 2020
A. G. Berberian, J. Rempel, N. Depsky, K. Bangia, S. Wang, and L. J. Cushing

SURVEILLANCE

1201 Design and Implementation of a National Program to Monitor the Prevalence of SARS-CoV-2 IgG Antibodies in England Using Self-Testing: The REACT-2 Study
H. Ward, C. Atchison, M. Whitaker, B. Davies, D. Ashby, A. Darzi, M. Chadeau-Hyam, S. Riley, C. A. Donnelly, W. Barclay, G. S. Cooke, and P. Elliott

OPEN-THEMED RESEARCH

1210 Extending an Antiracism Lens to the Implementation of Precision Public Health Interventions
C. G. Allen, D. L. Olstad, A. R. Kahkoska, Y. Guan, P. S. Ramos, J. Steinberg, S. A. S. Staras, C. Y. Lumpkins, L. V. Milko, E. Turbitt, A. K. Rahm, K. W. Saylor, S. Best, A. Hatch, I. Santangelo, and M. C. Roberts

1219 Examining Excess Mortality Among Critical Workers in Minnesota During 2020–2021: An Occupational Analysis
H. Karnik, E. Wrigley-Field, Z. Levin, Y.-H. Chen, E. W. Zabel, M. Ramirez, and J. P. Leider

BACKMATTER

ERRATA

1223 Erratum In: "*AJPH* Global News"

OTHER DEPARTMENTS

1231 Statement of Ownership

1232 Subscription Form

Introducing *AJPH*'s Newest Manuscript Format: Qualitative Notes From the Field

Introducing Qualitative Notes From the Field (QNFTF). Each year, *AJPH* receives hundreds of submissions documenting novel and innovative programs and public health approaches; findings from small-scale studies conducted with members of understudied, underrepresented, or historically marginalized communities; or perspectives on public health issues of the day from people with leadership positions in the field, such as health commissioners and departments of public health. Often, these submissions describe the use of qualitative methods, such as individual interviews or focus groups, or qualitative methodologies, such as PhotoVoice or ethnography.

As is the case with qualitative approaches writ large, these articles often provide rich, local and community-specific, and contextually grounded insights about important topics in public health. Yet, because these articles often describe projects that were not specifically developed as research, they do not meet the requirements for *AJPH*'s research article format, and thus, we have not been able to consider them for publication in *AJPH*. That is, until now with our new QNFTF section.

In triaging many of these submissions from our regular review process, primarily because they did not meet our research article format, we recognized a major missed opportunity for the field and *AJPH*. Namely, the submissions evinced a rich and vital showcase of qualitative public health approaches and programs by highlighting novel and innovative strategies and approaches, advancing and enhancing knowledge, sparking new ideas, and laying the foundation for larger-scale qualitative, quantitative, or mixed methods research projects. To this end, we have designed QNFTF to be the dedicated space for notes about new or noteworthy public health programs and projects that use qualitative approaches. Note, however, that this does not include interventions. *AJPH*'s Notes from the Field (NFTF) is still the designated place to submit notes about the implementation and evaluation of local interventions that have implications for the practice of public health. We are aware that eligibility for NFTF or QNFTF may overlap sometimes. Notwithstanding, we hope that you will find QNFTF to be the ideal site for brief qualitative reports from the field, and we invite submissions using the guidelines provided here.

QNFTF are used to share the perspective of selected members of understudied, underrepresented, or historically marginalized communities or persons with specific public health leadership positions (e.g., health commissioners) that have been obtained using qualitative methods (e.g., individual interviews, focus groups). These notes have a maximum of 1500 words, with an 80-word abstract, up to 15 references, and up to 2 tables and figures.

QNFTF submissions should use the following subheadings. If an element of the subheading is not relevant for your study, simply write "Not applicable" next to the subheading. (For detailed descriptions of each heading, see our author instruction page at https://ajph.aphapublications.org/authorinstructions.)

1. Study Objective;
2. Research Question(s);
3. Participants, Sample, Geographic Location, Setting, and Year of Study;
4. Methods;
5. Key Findings;
6. Evaluation, Transferability, and Adverse Effects;
7. Scalability; and
8. Public Health Significance. AJPH

Lisa Bowleg, PhD, MA
AJPH Associate Editor and
Department of Psychological and Brain Sciences
The George Washington University, Washington, DC

DOI: https://doi.org/10.2105/AJPH.2023.307436

12 Years Ago

The Rush to Drill for Natural Gas

[In Pennsylvania], there are more than 350 000 active and inactive gas wells. . . . [O]ver the next 20 to 30 years an additional 300 000 new wells could be drilled by using fracking technology. As drilling companies are not legally required to list the chemical compounds used in fracking, it is difficult to assess the full scope of the contents of fracking fluids. However, toxic mud and fluid byproducts from the drilling and fracking as well as spills of oil and gas wastes are not uncommon. . . . Post-mineral extraction cleanup costs are substantial, including restoration of damaged or contaminated streams and soil, improper handling of wastewater disposal, and improper disposal of radioactive material and hazardous waste. . . . We hope that before drilling in the Marcellus Shale becomes harmful, legislators and the natural gas industry will . . . pause to reflect on recent and past oil and gas disasters by agreeing to a moratorium on hydraulic fracturing.

From AJPH, May 2011, pp. 784–785.

81 Years Ago

Fuel Oil Rationing Protects Public Health

The public health officer and the medical profession are in a position to contribute importantly in passing on specific advice to consumers about ways of getting optimum health conditions from their fuel oil rations. Insulation, storm windows and doors, and weather stripping will aid greatly. . . . An efficient burner properly adjusted, a carefully checked chimney, and a boiler or furnace, and heating pipes that are properly insulated will do much to get the most out of a limited ration. . . . Unused rooms, such as extra bedrooms, . . . can be shut off completely. Radiators and registers should be shut off when windows are opened. Window shades can be lowered when light is not needed. Keeping draperies, or anything that interferes with circulation, away from radiators will greatly increase the efficiency of the heating plant. . . . Great fuel economy results from lowering the temperature for at least 8 hours during the night. Many of these improvements and adjustments cost little or nothing except care and thought.

From AJPH, December 1942, p. 1342.

A Call for Course Correction: Applying an Antiracism Lens to Precision Public Health

Sara A. Choate, PhD, MSEd

ABOUT THE AUTHOR

Sara A. Choate is with the Department of Health Promotion and Behavioral Sciences, University of Louisville School of Public Health and Information Sciences, Louisville, KY.

See also Allen et al., p. 1210.

Precision public health (PPH) has captivated the public health field in recent years on the premise that by tailoring preventive interventions for individuals who are considered high risk, the overall health of the population will ultimately improve. In this issue of *AJPH*, Allen et al. (p. 1210) apply an antiracism lens to this work, highlighting evidence-based, equity-minded approaches to the development, implementation, and evaluation of PPH interventions. As such, the authors illuminate potential opportunities for researchers and practitioners to apply a critical framework to PPH mental health interventions and, in doing so, strengthen PPH's promise of achieving greater health equity for all.

The concept of PPH emerged nearly a decade ago as an extension of precision medicine, presenting the possibility of personalized clinical approaches to population health via big data and new genomics tools to predict, detect, and treat people exhibiting the greatest risk of disease.[1,2] Elevated by President Obama in his 2016 State of the Union address, the initiative quickly captured the public's attention, inspiring global conferences and attracting major federal funding dollars.[3] However, despite the excitement surrounding it, many in the field have questioned its potential impact on population health. Bayer and Galea have argued that PPH's individualized clinical focus distracts from the more pressing need for comprehensive social policy to address the social determinants of health that negatively affect millions of Americans across the lifespan.[4]

In recent years, focus has shifted to include greater emphasis on the structural determinants of health, with proponents arguing for more social and economic policies aimed at uprooting the social inequities that drive health disparities.[5,6] In the wake of COVID-19, the field of public health has acknowledged that greater attention is needed to comprehensively address the mental health crisis that has affected millions of Americans, especially those lacking adequate social and financial support.

THE PROBLEM WITH PRECISION PUBLIC HEALTH

The enthusiasm surrounding PPH simultaneously reflects our national appetite for shiny new things and avoidance of doing the hard work of addressing the staggering inequality that drives the majority of negative health outcomes experienced by communities that have been systematically disenfranchised by US economic and social policies. Moreover, critics have correctly highlighted that PPH fails to mitigate the real challenges these individuals face in accessing routine medical screenings and care. These include, but are not limited to, a historical mistrust of medicine (e.g., Tuskegee, Henrietta Lacks, Sara Baartman),[7] perceived discrimination by medical providers,[8] and limited standardization of curricula on implicit bias, antiracism, and diversity, equity, and inclusion in health professional degree programs.[9,10] People with low socioeconomic status (SES) are also more likely to be uninsured or underinsured, and consequently are less likely to opt for expensive health testing and treatment. Even for those who are insured, individuals with low SES are more often faced with the decision of paying rent or purchasing food, pushing health care further down their list of priorities.[11]

Although PPH does offer some measure of promise to prevent disease from occurring in the first place, this premise proves tenuous at best because it fails to fundamentally address the social and structural determinants of health that disproportionately affect communities with low SES and diverse identities. When applying these challenges to mental health interventions, we must also highlight the additional stigma faced by Black, Latinx, and Indigenous communities that disincentivizes individuals from seeking professional support for themselves and loved ones.[12] This ultimately begs the question: what is the value of modernizing technologies to pinpoint the next big outbreak or genomic marker if individuals who are the most vulnerable to its potential impact are wary of getting screened—or unable to do so—because of systemic barriers to care?

NOTHING ABOUT US WITHOUT US

Coined during the 1990s disability rights movement in South Africa, "Nothing About Us Without Us" provides a common rallying call for scholars to evolve their efforts in dismantling systemic oppression.[13] A critical first step invites us to center communities at greatest risk of disease in the research and development of interventions that they stand to directly benefit from. In doing so, researchers and community members become cocreators of knowledge, which in turn cultivates engagement and, over time, consistent opportunities to sow seeds of trust. When applying this critical framework to PPH interventions, community-based participatory research provides useful guidance, inviting the engagement of community members through community advisory boards to participate in all stages of the research, translation, and dissemination processes.[14] Moreover, PPH interventions that implement a person-centered design may also mitigate another challenge posed by PPH—specifically, biases in big data created in the collection and analysis stages of research that serve to undermine equitable practices in health care delivery.[15]

As public health practitioners and researchers, we are called on to be more inclusive and thoughtful in our collective efforts to achieve greater health equity for all. This can only occur through thoughtful praxis, requiring vigilance and critical questioning of all new public health initiatives that claim to improve population health. In response to the fundamental challenges PPH presents, Allen et al. have effectively redirected researchers and practitioners to center people, not technology, at the heart of this work. And in doing so, they invite future PPH research and innovation to make good on its original promise. AJPH

CORRESPONDENCE

Correspondence should be sent to Sara A. Choate, PhD, MSEd, Assistant Professor, Department of Health Promotion and Behavioral Sciences, University of Louisville School of Public Health and Information Sciences, 485 E. Gray St, Suite 203, Louisville, KY 40202 (e-mail: sara.choate@louisville.edu). Reprints can be ordered at http://www.ajph.org by clicking the "Reprints" link.

PUBLICATION INFORMATION

Full Citation: Choate SA. A call for course correction: applying an antiracism lens to precision public health. *Am J Public Health*. 2023;113(11):1141–1142.

Acceptance Date: August 16, 2023.

DOI: https://doi.org/10.2105/AJPH.2023.307424

ACKNOWLEDGMENTS

I wish to acknowledge the support of Brian P. Schaefer and Monica L. Wendel and thank them for their mentorship.

CONFLICTS OF INTEREST

The author has no conflicts of interest to disclose.

REFERENCES

1. Khoury M. Precision public health and precision medicine: two peas in a pod. Centers for Disease Control and Prevention. 2015. Available at: https://blogs.cdc.gov/genomics/2015/03/02/precision-public. Accessed July 14, 2023.
2. Weeramanthri TS, Dawkins HJS, Baynam G, Bellgard M, Gudes O, Semmens JB. Editorial: precision public health. *Front Public Health*. 2018;6:121. https://doi.org/10.3389/fpubh.2018.00121
3. National Archives and Records Administration. Fact sheet: President Obama's Precision Medicine initiative. January 30, 2015. Available at: https://obamawhitehouse.archives.gov/the-press-office/2015/01/30/fact-sheet-president-obama-s-precision-medicine-initiative. Accessed July 14, 2023.
4. Bayer R, Galea S. Perspective: public health in the precision-medicine era. *N Engl J Med*. 2015;373(6):499–501. https://doi.org/10.1056/NEJMp1506241
5. Dawes DE. *The Political Determinants of Health*. Baltimore, MD: Johns Hopkins University Press; 2020. https://doi.org/10.56021/9781421437903
6. Yearby R. Structural racism and health disparities: reconfiguring the social determinants of health framework to include the root cause. *J Law Med Ethics*. 2020;48(3):518–526. https://doi.org/10.1177/1073110520958876
7. Akpan AM. Dark medicine: how the national research act has failed to address racist practices in biomedical experiments targeting the African-American community. *Seattle J Soc Justice*. 2013;11(3). https://digitalcommons.law.seattleu.edu/sjsj/vol11/iss3/11
8. Hausmann LR, Jeong K, Bost JE, Ibrahim SA. Perceived discrimination in health care and health status in a racially diverse sample. *Med Care*. 2008;46(9):905–914. https://doi.org/10.1097/MLR.0b013e3181792562
9. Johnson-Mallard V, Jones R, Coffman M, et al. The Robert Wood Johnson nurse faculty scholars diversity and inclusion research. *Health Equity*. 2019;3(1):297–303. https://doi.org/10.1089/heq.2019.0026
10. Dandar V, Fair M, Steinecke A, Sweeney N, Mallery T. The power of collective action: assessing and advancing diversity, equity, and inclusion efforts at AAMC medical schools. Association of American Medical Colleges. 2022. Available at: https://store.aamc.org/downloadable/download/sample/sample_id/578. Accessed July 14, 2023.
11. Garfield R, Orgera K, Damico A. The uninsured and the ACA: a primer—key facts about health insurance and the uninsured amidst changes to the Affordable Care Act. Kaiser Family Foundation. 2019. Available at: https://www.kff.org/report-section/the-uninsured-and-the-aca-a-primer-key-facts-about-health-insurance-and-the-uninsured-amidst-changes-to-the-affordable-care-act-how-does-lack-of-insurance-affect-access-to-care/#:~:text=Health%20insurance%20makes%20a%20difference,care%20or%20forgo%20it%20altogether. Accessed July 16, 2023.
12. Eylem O, de Wit L, van Straten A, et al. Stigma for common mental disorders in racial minorities and majorities: a systematic review and meta-analysis [erratum in *BMC Public Health*. 2020;20(1):1326]. *BMC Public Health*. 2020;20(1):879. https://doi.org/10.1186/s12889-020-08964-3
13. Charleton JI. Nothing about us without us: disability, oppression and empowerment. 1998. Available at: https://www.jstor.org/stable/10.1525/j.ctt1pnqn9. Accessed July 14, 2023.
14. Minkler M, Garcia AP, Rubin V, Wallerstein N. Community-based participatory research: a strategy for building healthy communities and promoting health through policy change. Policy Link. University of California-Berkeley School of Public Health. 2012. Available at: https://www.policylink.org/sites/default/files/CBPR.pdf. Accessed July 18, 2023.
15. Crawford K. The hidden biases in big data. Harvard Business Review. 2013. Available at: https://hbr.org/2013/04/the-hidden-biases-in-big-data. Accessed July 14, 2023.

Designing Surveillance at a Population Level

Stefano Tancredi, MD, and Arnaud Chiolero, MD, PhD

ABOUT THE AUTHORS

Stefano Tancredi and Arnaud Chiolero are with the Population Health Laboratory (#PopHealthLab), University of Fribourg, Switzerland. Arnaud Chiolero is also with the School of Population and Global Health, McGill University, Montreal, QC, Canada.

See also Ward et al., p. 1201.

As a core activity of public health, surveillance is paramount for managing crises such as the COVID-19 pandemic. Efficient surveillance systems are needed for disease monitoring, timely intervention, and informed decision-making, so that public health officials can track the spread of the virus, identify hotspots, assess population-level immunity and vaccinations, inform the population, and evaluate the impact of control measures. Ideally, these systems would capture high-quality data in a timely manner for proactive and evidence-based responses. However, during the COVID-19 pandemic, especially in its early phases, surveillance systems were insufficient in many jurisdictions; they were not timely and had poor data accuracy. As a result, information needs were only partially fulfilled.[1] How can we build more robust and efficient surveillance systems for future outbreak preparedness and response?

One problem with surveillance during the pandemic was that it relied essentially on data from health care providers and not on data designed primarily for surveillance. This is not surprising, because health care providers are the first to track emerging diseases and are key players in rapid identification, especially at the start of an epidemic. Furthermore, with basic information systems, it can be relatively easy to count the number of diagnosed or hospitalized cases.

However, these numbers are difficult to interpret because they are exposed to a large "surveillance bias": they are influenced by differences in screening, diagnosis, and treatment strategies and cannot be used directly to assess the true disease burden in populations, over time, and across areas.[2] For instance, trends in the number of cases based on diagnosis might be biased by variations in health care–seeking behaviors, testing availability, and changes in reporting rates. As a case in point, there were roughly eight times more cases in the second than the first wave of the pandemic in Switzerland, but this huge difference was explained by much more frequent testing during the second wave, rather than a massive spread of the virus in the population.[3] And currently, most cases are missed because people are no longer getting tested.

To overcome the low accuracy of diagnosis-based surveillance, it is better to have data collected primarily for surveillance purposes at a population level. The REal-time Assessment of Community Transmission-2 (REACT-2) study, conducted in England and presented in detail in this issue of *AJPH* (p. 1201), along with studies like ENE-COVID in Spain and Corona Immunitas in Switzerland, exemplify the benefits of this approach.[3,4] Using randomly selected population-based samples, these studies aim to capture the true disease dynamics and the extent of virus spread and give information on the evolution of population-level immunity. These studies are much less exposed to a surveillance bias. Hence, using population-based seroprevalence estimates as a proxy for virus spread in the population (before people were vaccinated),[3] the severity of the second wave was estimated to be slightly higher (roughly 1.5 times) than the first wave in Switzerland; this is in sharp contrast with severity estimates using the number of diagnosed cases.

However, like any other surveillance method, these population-based surveillance strategies come with limitations, such as difficulties acquiring representative samples of the general population or lack of timeliness (Box 1).[5–8] Therefore, they should be integrated with other surveillance strategies to create multilayer surveillance systems that ensure timeliness, comprehensiveness, and accuracy.[9] The basic layer of this system can be provided by health care provider diagnoses, for example, using sentinel surveillance to track new cases as early as possible. But the main layer should consist of population-level tools, such as surveys based on random sampling using antigenic or PCR (polymerase chain reaction) tests, wastewater surveillance, and population-based seroprevalence studies.

The diversity of these approaches ensures comprehensiveness, and the use of population-based methods improves accuracy, which reduces surveillance bias. To improve decision-making, population-based methods

AJPH November 2023, Vol 113, No. 11

BOX 1— Advantages and Disadvantages of Diagnosis- and Population-Based Surveillance

	Advantages	Disadvantages
Diagnosis-based surveillance		
Diagnosed cases	• Timely • Relatively easy to collect • Useful for identifying local spreads and clusters in specific populations (e.g., pregnant women, nursing homes residents)	• Strongly influenced by differences in screening and diagnostic strategies, test availability, care-seeking behaviors, and reporting rate • Burdened by standardization and interoperability issues
Hospitalizations	• Less prone to surveillance bias than cases • Relatively easy to collect • Useful for assessing the severity of the epidemic and pressure on health care systems • Useful for identifying local spreads and clusters	• Influenced by changes in admission criteria, hospital bed capacity, and availability of effective in-hospital treatments • Less timely than diagnosed cases • Burdened with standardization and interoperability issues
COVID-19 deaths	• Less prone to surveillance bias than cases or hospitalizations • Useful for assessing the severity of the epidemic	• Influenced by differences in COVID-19 death definition, testing availability, and test practices at death[5] • Not timely owing to the lag between diagnosis and death • Not timely because data can be provisional or incomplete for months or years
Population-based surveillance		
Population-based seroprevalence studies	• Less prone to surveillance bias than diagnosis-based surveillance • Useful for providing information on population-level immunity	• Not timely[6] • Burdened by possible low representativeness • Not designed to reach underprivileged and other at-risk populations • Prone to underestimation because of waning immunity[7]
Population-based surveys of infections	• Less prone to surveillance bias than diagnosis-based surveillance • Not dependent on care-seeking behaviors or reporting test results	• Not timely • Burdened by possible low representativeness • Not designed to reach underprivileged and other at-risk-populations[8]
Wastewater surveillance	• Less prone to surveillance bias than diagnosis-based surveillance • Not dependent on care-seeking behaviors or reporting test results[8,9]	• No individual-level information • Burdened by lack of information on the specific location of the epidemic or subpopulation[8]
Excess mortality	• Useful for estimating the global impact of COVID-19[5]	• Not timely • Burdened by differences in registration and reporting practices of deaths between countries

must be made more timely. This could be achieved by, for example, establishing quickly scalable surveillance teams with ad hoc infrastructures and preplanned protocols, creating pipelines that could work for more than one pathogen, or exploring new testing methods (as in the case of the REACT-2 study, in which, using at-home self-administered tests, information on seroprevalence was produced within days).

We believe that giving more weight to population-based surveillance systems is needed. As countries continue to navigate the challenges of the COVID-19 pandemic and prepare for future outbreaks, designing integrated and comprehensive surveillance strategies with a focus on populations is essential for accurate monitoring and better management of future epidemics. AJPH

CORRESPONDENCE

Correspondence should be sent to Prof. Arnaud Chiolero, MD, PhD, Population Health Laboratory, University of Fribourg, Route des Arsenaux 41, 1700 Fribourg, Switzerland (e-mail: achiolero@gmail.com). Reprints can be ordered at http://www.ajph.org by clicking the "Reprints" link.

PUBLICATION INFORMATION

Full Citation: Tancredi S, Chiolero A. Designing surveillance at a population level. *Am J Public Health*. 2023;113(11):1143–1145.

Acceptance Date: August 15, 2023.

DOI: https://doi.org/10.2105/AJPH.2023.307425

CONTRIBUTORS

The authors contributed equally to this editorial.

CONFLICTS OF INTEREST

The authors have no conflicts of interest to report.

REFERENCES

1. Brownson RC, Burke TA, Colditz GA, Samet JM. Reimagining public health in the aftermath of a pandemic. *Am J Public Health*. 2020;110(11):1605–1610. https://doi.org/10.2105/AJPH.2020.305861
2. Tancredi S, Anker D, Rosella L, Chiolero A. Elimination of COVID-19: beware of surveillance bias. *BMJ*. 2021;374(2126):n2126. https://doi.org/10.1136/bmj.n2126
3. West EA, Anker D, Amati R, et al. Corona Immunitas: study protocol of a nationwide program of SARS-CoV-2 seroprevalence and seroepidemiologic studies in Switzerland. *Int J Public Health*. 2020;65(9):1529–1548. https://doi.org/10.1007/s00038-020-01494-0

4. Pérez-Gómez B, Pastor-Barriuso R, Fernández-de-Larrea N, et al. SARS-CoV-2 infection during the first and second pandemic waves in Spain: the ENE-COVID study. *Am J Public Health*. 2023;113(5):533–544. https://doi.org/10.2105/AJPH.2023.307233
5. Msemburi W, Karlinsky A, Knutson V, Aleshin-Guendel S, Chatterji S, Wakefield J. The WHO estimates of excess mortality associated with the COVID-19 pandemic. *Nature*. 2023;613(7942):130–137. https://doi.org/10.1038/s41586-022-05522-2
6. Donnici C, Ilincic N, Cao C, et al. Timeliness of reporting of SARS-CoV-2 seroprevalence results and their utility for infectious disease surveillance. *Epidemics*. 2022;41:100645. https://doi.org/10.1016/j.epidem.2022.100645
7. Accorsi EK, Qiu X, Rumpler E, et al. How to detect and reduce potential sources of biases in studies of SARS-CoV-2 and COVID-19. *Eur J Epidemiol*. 2021;36(2):179–196. https://doi.org/10.1007/s10654-021-00727-7
8. Dean N. Tracking COVID-19 infections: time for change. *Nature*. 2022;602(7896):185. https://doi.org/10.1038/d41586-022-00336-8
9. Mello MM, Meschke JS, Palmer GH. Mainstreaming wastewater surveillance for infectious disease. *N Engl J Med*. 2023;388(16):1441–1444. https://doi.org/10.1056/NEJMp2301042

SOFTCOVER,100 PAGES, 2021
ISBN 978-0-87553-312-6

Landesman's Public Health Management of Disasters: The Practice Guide, 5th Edition

By: Linda Young Landesman, DrPH, MSW; Robyn R. Gershon, DrPH, MT, MHS; Eric N. Gebbie, DrPH, MIA, MA; Alexis A. Merdjanoff, PhD, MA

This new edition is both a comprehensive textbook and an essential tool for those who have a role in disaster management. Every chapter now includes extensive sections on Covid-19 covering all of public health's responsibility as it relates to a pandemic.

APHABOOKSTORE.ORG

APHA PRESS
AN IMPRINT OF AMERICAN PUBLIC HEALTH ASSOCIATION

AJPH Peer Reviewers: Thank You for Your Services

Michael Henry, BS, Brian Selzer, BS, Avery Ferguson, MA, and Kristin Crocker, MFA

ABOUT THE AUTHORS

The authors are with the American Public Health Association.

Peer review is the backbone of any publication operation; experts volunteer their time and expertise to evaluate and provide feedback on submitted papers. Without these dedicated individuals, *AJPH* would not have its track record of publishing high-quality research and commentary each month. The current peer review system has become overburdened—record numbers of papers have flooded all journals, and the demand for peer review is at an all time high. We realize that peer reviewers are inundated with requests to review papers. At *AJPH*, we are very grateful to those who continue to accept review invitations and subsequently set aside their personal time to read through assigned papers and submit quality, thoughtful, and impactful evaluations. Your contributions are essential, and we sincerely thank you.

Interested in joining our stellar group of *AJPH* peer reviewers and helping to advance the science of public health? Please visit our information for authors and reviewers page at https://ajph.aphapublications.org/page/authors.html. AJPH

CORRESPONDENCE

Correspondence should be sent to Michael Henry, American Public Health Association, 800 I St, NW, Washington, DC 20001 (e-mail: michael.henry@apha.org). Reprints can be ordered at http://www.ajph.org by clicking the "Reprints" link.

PUBLICATION INFORMATION

Full Citation: Henry M, Selzer B, Ferguson A, Crocker K. *AJPH* peer reviewers: thank you for your services. *Am J Public Health*. 2023;113(11): 1146–1152.

Acceptance Date: August 19, 2023.

DOI: https://doi.org/10.2105/AJPH.2023.307432

CONTRIBUTORS

Michael Henry drafted the initial version. All authors reviewed the article and approved final proof.

CONFLICTS OF INTEREST

The authors have no conflicts of interest to report.

YEAR 2022–2023 PEER REVIEWERS

Pamela M. Aaltonen
Shawn D. Aaron
Erika Nayeli Abad-Vivero
Rosliza Abdul Manaf
Demetrius Abshire
Maria E. Acosta
Pauline S. Acosta
Saudat Adamson Fadeyi
Durre Aden
Elizabeth Ann Omoluyi Adesanya
Avanti Adhia
Chandana Adhikarla
Nelson Videnyi Agbodo
Bruce Agins
Jon Agley
Maria del Pilar Aguinaga
Eileen M. Ahlin
Kathryn Ahnger-Pier
Emily Quinn Ahonen
Sarah H. Ailey
Bolajoko Ajoke Aina
Behnaz Akbari
Suzanne Akuley
Nadia Al-Amin
Sirry Alang
Cinthya K. Alberto
Jennifer S. Albrecht
Philip Alcabes
Apostolos Alexander Alexandridis
Bradley L. Allen
Chenoa D. Allen
Christopher T. Allen
Kristi L. Allgood
Kirk C. Allison
Jenifer E. Allsworth
Danny Alon
Karen A. Alroy
Heidi M. Altman
Jennifer Alvidrez
Richard Alweis
Reza Amini
Andrew Anderson
Carley Anderson
Gerard Anderson
Katherine M. Anderson
Katerina Andreadis
Kristin L. Andrejko
Wyndham Kent Anger
Antoinette Angulo
George Annas
Izabela E. Annis
Md Abu Yusuf Ansari
Nadav Antebi-Gruszka
James C. Anthony
Armand H. Matheny Antommaria
Jacob M. Appel
Allen Archer
Thomas A. Arcury
Taiwo Opeyemi Aremu
Young Argyris

Shoshana Aronowitz
Deana Around Him
Sabrina S. Arredondo Mattson
Sonya Arreola
Marc S. Atkins
Paavani Atluri
Rania Abdelkader Mohamed Attia
Amanda Aubel
Anna E. Austin
Mona AuYoung
Lenore S. Azaroff
Karan Babbar
Anisah B. Bagasra
Yeonsoo Baik
Jay Bainbridge
Marissa G. Baker
Nazsa S. Baker
Ethan Balk
Elizabeth D. Ballard
Devin Banks
Rita Gabriela Barajas-Gonzalez
Rita Barradas Barata
Amanda Barefield
Mason S. Barnard
Joshua T. Barnett
Sherry L. Baron
Lisa C. Barrios
Karsten Bartels
Marilyn M. Bartholmae
Michael L. Bartholomew
Kimberly Baskette
Amy R. Baugher
Jeannette Michele Beasley
Kate Beatty
David Becker
Stella Beckman
Raman Bedi
Tishra Beeson
Leslie M. Beitsch
Betty Bekemeier
Jennifer K. Bello
John F. Beltrami
Nanette Benbow
Anna Elisabeth Bender
Kaye Bender
Georges C. Benjamin
Sara E. Benjamin-Neelon
Joel Bennett
Julia C. Bennett
Sadie Bergen
Blair Berger
Jennifer Berliner
Natasha Bernstein Bunzl
Janet M. Berreman
John Berrigan
Amanda L. Berry
Carolyn Berry
Amarnath Bhat
Cedric Bien-Gund
Rachael Billock
Emine Bircan
Danae Bixler
Christine Crudo Blackburn
Thomas R. Blair
Etienne Blais
John R. Blosnich
Stephen J. Blumberg
Evelyn Blumenberg
Claire Bodkin
Michele Kines Bohm
Danielle Boothe
Michel Boudreaux
Anne Boustead
Elizabeth Anne Bowen
Angie Boyce
Donte Boyd
Benjamin Robert Brady
Marie Bragg
Charles C. Branas
Allan M. Brandt
Heather M. Brandt
Cole Brokamp
Andrea Danielle Brown
Clare C. Brown
Joseph Dov Bruch
Doug Brugge
Katia J. Bruxvoort
Alexander Brzezny
Omonigho Michael Bubu
Pierre Buekens
Sheana Bull
Kristen Lagasse Burke
Marshall Burke
Scott Burris
James P. Byrne
R. Jean Cadigan
Timothy Callaghan
Angela Gale Campbell
Wangnan Cao
Ariadna Capasso
Felicia Caples
Joseph N. Cappella
Ana W. Capuano
Gabriela Capurro
Alan J. Card
Patrick Carley
Amy Carroll-Scott
Billie F. Castle
Delivette Castor
Brian C. Castrucci
Paola Cecchi Dimeglio
Jessica Cerdeña
Paulette Cha
Sara B. Chadwick
Rosette Chakkalakal
Howard Chang
Ji Eun Chang
Shu-Sen Chang
Susan Chapman
Melissa Charlie
Daniel Li Chen
Jieru Chen
Ya-Ting Chen
Zhuo Chen
Zijing Cheng
Sophia K. Chiu
Sara A. Choate
Jamie F. Chriqui
Melissa A. Clark
Yolanda Wilson Clarke
John Clemens
David H. Cloud
Jasney Cogua
Alyssa Cohen
David Cohen
Jennifer Cohen
Nevin Cohen
James Colgrove
Laura T. Colman
Elena Conis
Kristin Conner

Theodora Consolacion
Kathleen Conte
Nicole Cook
Glenn. E. Copeland
B. Ethan Coston
Hannah Covert
Tori L. Cowger
Kenneth L. Cox
Mari Crabtree
Meghan A. Crabtree
Natalie D. Crawford
Pamela Cromer
Chrysan Cronin
Mary A. Crossley
Humberto Alexis Cruz Esparra
Joanne Csete
Alison J. Culyba
K. Michael Cummings
Kevin Cummins
Brian Custer
William Dab
Laura Dague
Clarissa Damaso
Valerie Danesh
Blair Darney
Nabarun Dasgupta
Corey Davis
John W. Davis
W. Sumner Davis
Jamie R. Daw
Shuva Dawadi
Natalie Dean
Raisa B. Deber
Emily J. Decker
Dorly J. H. Deeg
Susan Dentzer
Abhijit Dey
Biswadeep Dhar
Nicholas Diamond
Melissa E. Dichter
Julia Dickson-Gomez
Charles Doarn
Marnie Dobson
Elizabeth Dodson
Elaine Doherty
Irene Doherty
Margaret K. Doll
Elisabeth A. Donaldson
Emily Donovan
Benjamin Doty
Julia Ana-Rivera Drew
Pete Driezen
Michelle Edwards
William H. Eger
David P. Eisenman
Lacreisha Ejike-King
Agatha Eke
Ulf Ekelund
Erica Linn Eliason
Michele Eliason
Amity Eliaz
Matthew S. Ellis
Olivier Epaulard
Elizabeth Erdman
Temitope Erinosho
Karl Eschbach
W. Douglas Evans
James P. Fabisiak
Daniel Falkstedt
Heather R. Farmer
William Feigelman
Dylan Felt
Andrew Fenelon
Qiushi Feng
Jose Manuel Fernandez
Mary Figgatt
Mary Findling
Theresa Monahan Fiorito
Melanie Firestone
Kate Vinita Fitch
Eric W. Fleegler
Paul J. Fleming
Ryan E. Flinn
Michael Dolan Fliss
Jane Fornoff
Seirra Fowler
Gwendolyn Suzanne Roberts Francavillo
Michael R. Fraser
Amy L. Freeman
Marcelo Freitas
Alexa Friedman
Seth E. Frndak
Edward A. Frongillo
Thomas Fuller-Rowell
Jane Galvao
Emmanuel E. Garcia Morales
Jennifer A. Garner
Karie Gaska
Antonio Gasparrini
Loretta Gavin
Moriah Gendelman
Adrienne Ghorashi
Norman Giesbrecht
Melissa B. Gilkey
Gary David Gilmore
Margaret Giorgio
Frenki Gjika
Kristin Nicole Gmunder
Shelley Diane Golden
Tamar Goldenberg
Sarah Gonzalez-Nahm
Julia M. Goodman
Rachel Anne Gordon
Wendi Gosliner
Mark A. Gottlieb
Mark Grabowsky
Dina N. Greene
Lisa Greenwell
Joan M. Griffin
Christian Grov
Kate Guastaferro
Vikas S. Gupta
Ann P. Haas
Samantha Hack
Cathy Moran Hajo
Jeffrey Erwin Hall
Wayne D. Hall
Evelynn Hammonds
Xuesong Han
Dennis J. Hand
Arden Handler
Katherine J. Harmon
Graham Harriman
Jenine K. Harris
John Harris
Rebecca J. Hart
Cole Haskins
Ahmed Hassan
Lee Hasselbacher
Sarah M. Hatcher

Susan Marie Havercamp
Sara Elizabeth Heins
Frances C. Henderson
Sandra R. Henley
Kevin A. Henry
Owen Henry
Tina Batra Hershey
Jeremy Hess
Jessie Hill
Lisa Hitch
Harry Hochheiser
Lee Hoffer
Beth L. Hoffman
Jennifer Hoffmann
Louisa M. Holmes
Deborah Holtzman
Chenglin Hong
Ickpyo Hong
Diane Joy Horvath
Aila Hoss
Jason N. Houle
Claire Houtsma
Jeffrey T. Howard
Jason Hsia
Xiaoning Huang
Randolph D. Hubach
Phillip Hughes
Morgan Hughey
Ayaz Hyder
Ronaldo Iachan
Fahmeeda Idrees
Sally Ann Iverson
Andrew Ivsins
Laurie M. Jacobs
Peter Jacobson
Susan Jenkins
Leah Jennings
Steven A. John
O'Dell Johnson
Brenda Joly
Tiffany Jones
Nkenge Jones-Jack
Fabrice Jotterand
Adrian Xavier Juarez Cuellar
Amy C. Justice
Andrew T. Kaczynski
Jonathan Kahn
Saurabh Kalra
Debora Kamin Mukaz
Emiko Kamitani
Megan Kang
Farzana Kapadia
Joanne M. Kaufman
Rachel Kaufmann
Megan L. Kavanaugh
Roger Keller Celeste
Lee Kennedy-Shaffer
Kathleen S. Kenny
Anthony Kerbage
Paula M. Kett
Alex S. Keuroghlian
Ali Shan Khan
Melanie Kiechle
Andrea Kim
Heeun Kim
Youngsung Kim
Keith Dennis King
Work M. King
David Joshua Kinitz
Norik Kirakosian
Claas Kirchhelle
Marte Kjøllesdal
Melissa Klapper
Elizabeth S. Knaster
Shawn M. Kneipp
Joanna Kobza
Christopher Koller
Michelle C. Kondo
Bob R. Konrad
David Ethan Koren
Maya Rom Korin
Melissa A. Kowalski
Katy Backes Kozhimannil
Stephanie A. Kraft
Douglas S. Krakower
Ashley M. Kranz
Noah T. Kreski
Kimberly Krytus
Paul Kuehnert
Evelyn Kumoji
Stewart Landers
Bethany Lanese
Caillin Langmann
Colleen Lanier
Judith W. Leavitt
MinJae Lee
Yong Gun Lee
Daniel Lefkowitz
Jami Leichliter
Frances R. Lendacki
Stephanie A. Leonard
Laura Marie Lessard
Charles Levenstein
Carly Rose Levy
Taylor Lewis
Tené T. Lewis
Mingfei Li
Alex C. Liber
Shengjie Lin
Stacy T. Lindau
Kriste Lindenmeyer
Erin Linnenbringer
Sabriya Linton
Hester J. Lipscomb
Marc Lipsitch
Lu Liu
Martha Livingston
Joseph Llobrera
Judith A. Long
Paulo A. Lotufo
Sarah R. Lowe
Bryce Christopher Lowery
Chenyi Ma
John MacDonald
Hannah MacDougall
Alexandria Macmadu
Dana Madigan
Lauren A. Magee
Sanne Magnan
Julie E. Maher
Malia Maier
Shannon E. Majowicz
Hadii M. Mamudu
Lisa Mansfield
Elise Mara
Steven Markowitz
Fatma E. Marouf
Mohammad Ainul Maruf
Duduzile Phindile Mashinini
Leah E. Masselink
Gene Matthews

Yuri Matusov
Randy Mayer
Stephanie Mazzucca
Corinne McDaniels-Davidson
Ian K. McDonough
Mike McEvoy
Marjorie McGee
Laura McGough
Lynn McIntyre
Patrick McLaughlin
Kellie McLean
Samara McPhedran
Meredith C. Meacham
Seth A. Meador
Michael Meit
Valeria Cristina Menendez
Jerry Menikoff
Jeremy Mennis
Maria Michaels
Sarah Michels
Diana Miconi
Norweeta Milburn
Gabrielle Ferro Miller
Greg Millett
Mohammed Umer Mir
Patricia Y. Miranda
Supriya Misra
Marik Moen
Celeste Monforton
Mauda Monger
Jose T. Montero
J. Henry Montes
Katherine A. Moon
Graham Mooney
Justin B. Moore
Carlos M. Morales Rodriguez
Meghan Bridgid Moran
Ellen S. More
Kenneth L. Morford
Rebecca Moritz
Taryn W. Morrissey
Krysia Mossakowski
Jonetta Johnson Mpofu
Jewel Mullen
Zachary Munn
Philip Murphy
Sarah Murray
Aviva A. Musicus
Clarice Myers
Kevin Naaman
Ismail Nabeel
Laura Nabors
Mona Nasser
Maury Nation
Rosalyn Negron
Joni D. Nelson
Mary Spink Neumann
Becca Newman
Kevin H. Nguyen
Len M. Nichols
Victoria M. Nielsen
Fareha Nishat
Justin Nix
Robert Sayoc Nocon
Priscilla Novak
Emmanuel Obeng-Gyasi
Allyson B. O'Connor
Tabatha N. Offutt-Powell
Sumie Okazaki
Olihe Okoro
Sigrun Olafsdottir
Mark Olfson
Antonio Olivas-Martinez
Elyse Olshen Kharbanda
Steven J. Ondersma
Yotam Ophir
Christopher Owens
Jessica L. Owens-Young
Deborah Padgett
Romulo Paes de Sousa
Elina Tselepidakis Page
John R. Pamplin II
Lukas Parker
Tiffany L. Parr
Deesha Patel
Neil Pearce
Stephanie Russo Perniciaro
Chris Perrone
Julie M. Petersen
Mark A. Peterson
Darcy Phelan-Emrick
Celeste Philip
Julie A. Phillips
Jennifer Piatt
Matthew W. Pierce
Francesco Pierri
Natasha V. Pilkauskas
Ana-Catarina Pinho-Gomes
Stacey Plichta
Mathieu Poirier
Harold A. Pollack
Keshia M. Pollack Porter
Austin Porter
Christina Potter
Robyn Powell
Franklin Pratt
Michael Russell Privitera
Robert Proctor
Wayne Psek
David Pyrooz
Tianchen Qian
Christina Ramirez
Athena K. Ramos
David Enrique Rangel
Colleen Ray
Geoffrey L. Ream
Sara Kathleen Redd
Colleen E. Reid
David Relman
Jenny Rempel
Susan M. Reverby
Taeho Greg Rhee
Jesse Rhodes
Eric Rice
Aaron Richterman
Lorinda Riley
William J. Riley
Eric T. Roberts
Megan Roberts
Brendaly Rodriguez
Jose F. Rodriguez Orengo
Roger Rosa
Lisa Goldman Rosas
Molly Rosenberg
Jason Rosenfeld
Asher Rosinger
Philip M. Rosoff
Thomas Lee Rotering
Sebastian Rowland
Laurence Roy
Kara E. Rudolph

Richard E. Rupp
Andrea Rusnock
Darpun Sachdev
Ryan Saelee
Goleen Samari
Jonathan Samet
Sara Jane Samuel
Alycia Santilli
Mohima Sanyal
Mark Savage
Dennis Savaiano
Nadia Sawicki
Lawrence M. Schell
Barbara Schillo
Kristine Schmitz
Benjamin Schram
Jason L. Schwartz
Marlene B. Schwartz
Lara Schwarz
Suzanne Selig
Katie Sellers
Rafael M. Semansky
Eric Sergienko
Carmel Shachar
Paul Shafer
Ellen R. Shaffer
Gulzar H. Shah
Megha D. Shah
Mariam A. Shalaby
Bhavna Shamasunder
Joshua Sharfstein
Leah C. Shaw
Rachel C. Shelton
Bryan E. Shepherd
Dallas Shujing Shi
Ruth Shim
Riti Shimkhada
Marybeth Shinn
Tiffiny Shockley
Glenn Shor
Mina Silberberg
Richard Singer
Samer Singh
Susan B. Sisson
Patricia Skuster
Jason A. Smith
Joyce A. Smith
Karen Lee Smith
Ning Smith
Rhet A. Smith
Todd D. Smith
Reinaldo Antonio Silva Sobrinho
Aparna Soni
Susan B. Sorenson
Paulina Sosa
Brian Southwell
June T. Spector
Katherine Speirs
Emily A. Spieler
Giancarlo Spizzirri
Gerald J. Stahler
Stephen Stansfeld
Jacob Steere-Williams
Matthew Stefanak
Jane Steinberg
Sandra Steiner
Thomas E. Stenvig
Cara S. Stephenson-Hunter
Jim P. Stimpson
Shana D. Stites
Albin Stjernbrandt
Robert Stout
Julia Strasser
Carl Streed
Pamela K. Strohfus
Andrew Makoto Subica
Divya S. Subramaniam
Dianjun Sun
Jing Sun
Gregory Sunshine
Christy Sutherland
Monica E. Swilley-Martinez
Carolyn Swope
Peter G. Szilagyi
Amanda Taffy
Michael S. Taitel
Nandi L. Taylor
Richard Taylor
Kevin Rui-Han Teoh
Linda A. Teplin
Mishka Terplan
Alexander Testa
Christine M. Thomas
Sasha Thomas
Mieke Beth Thomeer
Stephen L. Thompson
Lorna Thorpe
Walker Tisdale
Andrea Titus
Lori Tremmel Freeman
Amber Trueblood
Jack Tsai
Toru Tsuboya
Emma K. Tsui
Sharon Tucker
Mary Tucker-Mclaughlin
Jack L. Turban
Jennifer B. Unger
Lesley Uttley
Danny Valdez
Thomas W. Valente
Gerrit Van Schalkwyk
Mark Vander Weg
Maria Vignau Loria
Alana Marie Vivolo-Kantor
Colby Vorland
Elle Wadsworth
Chastity L. Walker
Haowei Wang
Jianing Wang
Liana Washburn
Rachel Washburn
Linda J. Washington
Jaimee L. Watts Isley
Emily Webster
Shelly Weizman
Brian M. Wells
Ashley Wennerstrom
Suzanne L. Wenzel
Benjamin W. Weston
Mary Kristina Wharton
Kari White
Lindsay F. Wiley
Augusta A. Williams
Joshua Williams
Natasha Williams
Megan Winkler
Michael Wittie
Mary Woinarowicz
Hill Wolfe
Mitchell David Wong

Leila Wood
Tyler Woods
Angie R. Wootton
Eric R. Wright
Robert R. Wright
Elwin Wu
Matthew Wynia
Nan Xiao
Wubin Xie
Jiaquan Xu
Xuewen Yan
Nava Yeganeh
Irene H. Yen
Li Yi
Stella Sun-Young Yi
Youngmin Yi
Xiangji Ying
Jane C. Yoon
Sean D. Young
Jessica Yu
James Zhang
Jingwen Zhang
Zhiyang Zhou
Emily Zimmerman
Matthew Zimmerman
Jane R. Zucker
Rachael B. Zuckerman

Public Health **Career**Mart

#1 job site for **Public Health Professionals**

- **Career Coaching:** Work with one of our experienced and certified coaches to better manage, plan, and develop your career goals.
- **Résumé Writing:** Take advantage of professional résumé writing for all professional levels.
- **Résumé Critiques:** Our expert résumé writer provides helpful feedback.
- **Career Tips:** Search by career stages or services you need using keywords or phrases.
- **Salary and Benefits:** Negotiation techniques and salary analysis. Learn how to negotiate effectively and confidently for a job offer or raise!
- **Reference Checking/Employment Verification:** Identify questionable references before they talk to prospective employers.
- **Social Networking/Profile Development:** Make the right connections and open up job opportunities you never knew existed.
- **You can find it all here:** careers.apha.org/jobseekers/resources/

APHA
AMERICAN PUBLIC HEALTH ASSOCIATION
For science. For action. For health.

Two-Spirit Identity and Adolescent Survey Measures: Considerations of Appropriation, Transparency, and Inclusion

Lenny Hayes, MA, Anne LaFrinier-Ritchie, BA, Nicole Matthews, BS, Beth O'Keefe, Nigel Perrote, MA, G. Nic Rider, PhD, Camille Brown, RN, PhD, Montana Filoteo, BA, Katie Johnston-Goodstar, PhD, MSW, Barbara J. McMorris, PhD, and Lauren Martin, PhD

ABOUT THE AUTHORS

Lenny Hayes, Anne LaFrinier-Ritchie, Nicole Matthews, Beth O'Keefe, and Nigel Perrote are members of the Minnesota Youth Sex Trading (MYST) project's Native+ community advisory board, Minneapolis, MN. G. Nic Rider is with the Institute for Sexual and Gender Health, Department of Family, Medicine and Community Health, University of Minnesota Medical School, Minneapolis. Katie Johnston-Goodstar is with the School of Social Work, University of Minnesota-Twin Cities, St. Paul. Camille Brown, Montana Filoteo, Barbara J. McMorris, and Lauren Martin are with the School of Nursing, University of Minnesota, Minneapolis.

The Minnesota Youth Sex Trading (MYST) project is a collaborative of faculty, staff, and students at the University of Minnesota working in partnership with nonprofit organizations and service providers, government entities, and people with lived experience. This commentary is written by various members of the collaborative across many professional and personal identities, including members of our Native American community advisory board.

The MYST team conducts actionable research to identify prevention opportunities, guide systems change, and promote wellness among youths. In particular, the team analyzes self-report data from youths who completed the Minnesota Student Survey (MSS), a triennial, anonymous, statewide school-based survey conducted in collaboration with local schools and four State of Minnesota agencies. In 2019, the MSS added a new question: "Have you ever traded sex or sexual activity to receive money, food, drugs, alcohol, a place to stay or anything else?" Our team has produced some of the first school-based prevalence estimates of youth sex trading. Sexual exploitation and trafficking of youths cause myriad harms. MYST's research shows disproportionate and intersectional impacts of these harms for youths of color; Indigenous youths; youths experiencing homelessness and poverty; lesbian, gay, bisexual, transgender, queer, or questioning (LGBTQ+) youths; and youths in foster care (https://bit.ly/44GoBiH).[1,2]

NATIVE+ COMMUNITY RESEARCH ADVISORY BOARD

In 2020, the MYST project established a number of community advisory processes to assist researchers, including an intertribal, Native American community advisory board, which consists of six tribally identified service providers working in the field of sexual violence and exploitation. This engagement was particularly meaningful to the research team, given Native youths are often represented by hyper-deficit research narratives[3] or dismissed as statistically insignificant or what Garland refers to as "an asterisk" on a data table.[4] Cautious of this, the collaborative engaged in intense consultation to establish an accurate prevalence rate of sex trading for Native youths that was contextually informed and could guide policy and practice in meaningful ways.

Using available self-reported data on students' race and ethnicity from the 2019 MSS, we cocreated two unique variables to better understand prevalence among Native youths. First, we expanded our definition of Native American youths to "Native+," including those students who selected that they identified as "only" American Indian or Alaska Native (AIAN), AIAN plus an additional race (+), "only" Native Hawaiian or Pacific Islander (NHPI), and NHPI+.

This community-designed definition honors the sovereignty of Indigenous nations to determine community membership that recognizes individuals of mixed racial background and lineal descent. It further reflects the racial diversity present in American Indian communities in our geographic area, and

AJPH November 2023, Vol 113, No. 11

it includes the shared experiences of Indigenous peoples with colonialism, which has been linked to sexual exploitation.[5] This aligns with recommendations in statewide discussions with tribal representatives. These decisions resulted in more than a threefold increase in our sample size.

Second, we created a related variable that was intended to capture Two-Spirit/2-Spirit identity, history, and community-based definitions. To do so, we combined the Native+ variable, gender modality, and sexual orientation to create a dichotomized variable (Two-Spirit/2-Spirit or not Two-Spirit/2-Spirit). This variable was labeled "LGBTQ+2S." Specifically, Native+ youth who self-reported identifying as "transgender, genderqueer, or genderfluid" or unsure of their gender identity (inclusive of all sexual orientations) and those who reported identifying as bisexual, gay or lesbian, questioning, pansexual, queer, or using a different sexual orientation label but not identifying as "transgender, genderqueer, or genderfluid" were included in LGBTQ+2S. We aimed to make this variable inclusive but recognized it was dependent on the pre-established Western conceptualizations of gender and sexuality that informed what questions are typically asked of students on the MSS.

Separate from our collaborative work, a decision was made at the state level to add Two-Spirit as a response option for their item asking about gender identity in the 2022 MSS. This decision contributed to significant discussion among our community advisory members who were appreciative of the inclusive intention but expressed concerns over a lack of understanding of the term Two-Spirit, its history, and the potential for appropriation and harm. When the MYST project team began data analyses of the 2022 MSS data, we followed up on the community advisory board's concerns. Of the 395 students who selected Two-Spirit as their gender identity, less than a quarter (24.1%) were Native+. In comparison, among students who selected Two-Spirit as their gender identity, 45.8% identified their racial identity as exclusively White, and 26.2% identified their racial identity as neither exclusively White nor Native+ (in total 72% of those identifying as Two-Spirit were non-Native+). These response rates provided support for the concerns and led us to write this commentary; yet, we wish to recognize that this is not an effort to criticize our state partners, who have been positively responsive to these findings and have committed to engaging with them. Rather, we use this commentary to advance awareness and scholarly discussion in the field and among our fellow researchers.

TWO-SPIRIT DEFINITION AND APPROPRIATION

While an expansive history of colonialism in the Americas is beyond the scope of this commentary, it is without question that Indigenous peoples were, and still are, subject to a series of colonial acts of violence, treaty-making (and breaking), laws, and policies[6] that sought or seek to dispossess Native people of land and erase cultural, spiritual, political, and intellectual presence. Lewis Meriam, author of the federal report, *The Problem of Indian Administration* (https://bit.ly/3Kgk3Hu), declared that Indians must be advanced "along the white man's road" (p. 552) so that they may be "absorbed into the prevailing civilization or be fitted to live in the presence of that civilization at least in accordance with a minimum standard" (p. 554). These civilizing efforts were based on assumptions of European racial, religious, and economic superiority and included the heteropaternal organization of citizens "into nuclear families, each expressing a 'proper,' modern sexuality."[7(p13)] This forced assimilation sought to erase complex notions of gender and sexuality and their associated cultural, spiritual, and familial roles. As Lugones described, "[g]ender itself is a colonial introduction, a violent introduction consistently and contemporarily used to destroy peoples, cosmologies, and communities."[8(p186)] This construct and subsequent marginalization contributes to disproportionate rates of substance use disorder and mental health challenges because of multiple minority oppressed status and exposure to stress and trauma.[9]

The term Two-Spirit is a direct reflection of this history and refers to a person of a culturally and spiritually distinct gender exclusively recognized by Native American Nations (Lenny Hayes, e-mail communication, October 18, 2021). It affirms the "interrelatedness of all aspects of identity including sexuality, gender, culture, community and spirituality."[10(p304–305)] Two-Spirit people were "seen as being neither men nor women, but as belonging to genders of their own within cultural systems of multiple genders"[11(p114)] and often occupied highly respected social and ceremonial roles.[12] Organizations, such as Gay American Indians, which was founded more than 48 years ago, were started to build safe circles, support one another, and reclaim these roles and relations. By 1990, Native American community members coined the term, Two-Spirit, with a clear intention to distance themselves from non-Native gays and lesbians and historically inaccurate and insulting terminology used by non-Native researchers.[13]

The reclamation of gender(s), sexuality, and Indigenous people's traditional knowledge about gender(s) and sexuality roles and practices is a political, cultural, and spiritual act to define one's self and one's experience. Two-Spirit is a "term of resistance to colonization and non-transferable to other cultures."[14(p125)] Furthermore, "It is part of our counter hegemonic discourse and reclamation of our unique histories. Aboriginal people coined the term Two-Spirit and are using it to reflect our past, and the direction of our future. We are using the term. It is ours."[14(p123)] For additional discussion of the distinction and relationship between Two-Spirit and Native LGBTQ+ communities, please refer to Indigenizing Love: A Toolkit for Native Youth to Build Inclusion (https://bit.ly/3Qew9oc).

CONSIDERATIONS FOR RESEARCH MOVING FORWARD

The addition of the Two-Spirit response option on the 2022 MSS provided an unexpected opportunity to gather empirical evidence that supports community-based concerns. Given this history, one can understand how an appropriation of the term Two-Spirit is problematic within the context of society and particularly within the context of research, which includes an extensive history of extraction and harm in Indigenous communities.[15] As researchers, we ask the following questions: How do we balance our desire to build measurement tools that are expansive and inclusive but also take heed of these critical histories and definitions? What is our responsibility if respondents lack the information or prudence to take heed themselves? How do the "discursive and material practices of [the] academy writ large participate in the dispossession of Indigenous peoples' lands, livelihoods, and futures" and how can we "divest from these practices"[7(p25)] and avoid perpetuating epistemological violence?

Using data based on a significant cultural term poses a number of considerations that are social and scientific in nature, including the generalizability of results, confusion over whom the results are applicable to, and continued harm to communities who have claimed exclusive use of a term that has deep spiritual and cultural significance. Additional limitations are that Native+ people may prefer to use their own distinct tribal terms to define themselves, which may not necessarily be the term, Two-Spirit. As Indigenous peoples recover language, notions of gender, and associated roles, health researchers must be flexible and continue to exercise caution. This requires ongoing consultation in regard to identity (e.g., our lead author often uses "Do you know the word in your language that would identify someone like me?" in his practice) and commitment to nuance and flexibility.

We use this commentary to shine a light on our constructs and engage in scholarly dialogue at the intersection of inclusion and marginalization. We recognize that these considerations do not map well onto the landscape of survey research and perhaps present more questions than answers, but we believe they are critical to consider nonetheless. As we navigate data analyses and future survey and research designs, we encourage careful use of the term Two-Spirit and that researchers use a community-engaged approach. It is crucial to partner with community advisory boards to explore and develop better practices for using survey design tools (e.g., conditional branching) to ensure that only Native American and Indigenous respondents have the option to select this identity. AJPH

CORRESPONDENCE

Correspondence should be sent to Katie Johnston-Goodstar, PhD, School of Social Work, University of Minnesota-Twin Cities, 1404 Gortner Ave, St. Paul, MN 55108 (e-mail: john1906@umn.edu). Reprints can be ordered at https://ajph.org by clicking the "Reprints" link.

PUBLICATION INFORMATION

Full Citation: Hayes L, LaFrinier-Ritchie A, Matthews N, et al. Two-spirit identity and adolescent survey measures: considerations of appropriation, transparency, and inclusion. *Am J Public Health*. 2023;113(11):1153–1156.

Acceptance Date: July 2, 2023.

DOI: https://doi.org/10.2105/AJPH.2023.307387

CONTRIBUTORS

L. Hayes, G. N. Rider, C. Brown, M. Filoteo, K. Johnston-Goodstar, B. J. McMorris, and L. Martin contributed to the conceptualization and design of this opinion editorial and drafted, reviewed, and revised the article and approved the final version to be published. A. LaFrinier-Ritchie, N. Matthews, B. O'Keefe, and N. Perrote contributed to the conceptualization of this opinion editorial, reviewed and revised the article, and approved the final version to be published.

ACKNOWLEDGMENTS

MYST research was supported by the World Childhood Foundation USA and Carlson Family Foundation.

This commentary resulted from ongoing efforts associated with the MYST project and includes authors who are academic researchers with the University of Minnesota and expert community members who make up the MYST Native+ community advisory board. The work reported in this opinion editorial was derived from research projects combined with community expertise and wisdom. The authors thank *AJPH* reviewers and editors.

This editorial is following community-engaged principles where we have a community–university partnership, and this is reflected in the authorship team. We would like to honor the multiple sources of knowledge that our team uses and comes from—all of which are important to us.

CONFLICTS OF INTEREST

The authors report no conflicts of interest.

REFERENCES

1. Martin L, Rider GN, Johnston-Goodstar K, Menanteau B, Palmer C, McMorris BJ. Prevalence of trading sex among high school students in Minnesota: demographics, relevant adverse experiences, and health-related statuses. *J Adolesc Health.* 2021;68(5):1011–1013. https://doi.org/10.1016/j.jadohealth.2020.08.021
2. Rider GN, McMorris BJ, Brown C, et al. Mental health and protective factors for transgender and gender-diverse youths who trade sex: a Minnesota statewide school-based study, 2019. *Am J Public Health.* 2022;112(3):499–508. https://doi.org/10.2105/AJPH.2021.306623
3. Tuck E. Suspending damage: a letter to communities. *Harv Educ Rev.* 2009;79(3):409–428. https://doi.org/10.17763/haer.79.3.n0016675661t3n15
4. Garland JL. Foreword. In: Shotton HJ, Lowe SC, Waterman SJ, eds. *Beyond the Asterisk: Understanding Native Students in Higher Education.* New York, NY: Stylus Publishing; 2013.
5. Smith A. *Conquest: Sexual Violence and American Indian Genocide.* Durham, NC: Duke University Press; 2015.
6. Dunbar-Ortiz R. *An Indigenous Peoples' History of the United States.* Boston, MA: Beacon Press; 2014.
7. Arvin M, Tuck E, Morrill A. Decolonizing feminism: challenging connections between settler colonialism and heteropatriarchy. *Fem Form.* 2013;25(1):8–34. https://doi.org/10.1353/ff.2013.0006
8. Lugones M. Heterosexualism and the colonial/modern gender system. *Hypatia.* 2007;22(1):186–209. Available at: https://www.jstor.org/stable/4640051. Accessed January 1, 2023.
9. Elm JHL, Lewis JP, Walters KL, Self JM. "I'm in this world for a reason": resilience and recovery among American Indian and Alaska Native Two-Spirit women. *J Lesbian Stud.* 2016;20(3-4):352–371. https://doi.org/10.1080/10894160.2016.1152813
10. Wilson A. How we find ourselves: identity development and Two Spirit people. *Harv Educ Rev.* 1996;66(2):303–318. https://doi.org/10.17763/haer.66.2.n551658577h927h4
11. Lang S. Various kinds of Two-Spirit people: gender variance and homosexuality in Native American communities. In: Jacobs S-E, Thomas W, Lang S, eds. *Native American Gender Identity, Sexuality, and Spirituality.* Champaign, IL: University of Illinois Press; 1997:100–118.
12. Walters KL, Evans-Campbell T, Simoni JM, Ronquillo T, Bhuyan R. "My spirit in my heart": identity experiences and challenges among American Indian Two-Spirit women. *J Lesbian Stud.* 2006;10(1-2):125–149. https://doi.org/10.1300/J155v10n01_07
13. Jacobs S-E, Thomas W, Lang S, eds. *Two-Spirit People: Native American Gender Identity, Sexuality, and Spirituality.* Champaign, IL: University of Illinois Press; 1997.
14. Cameron M. Two-Spirited aboriginal people continuing cultural appropriation by non-aboriginal society. *Can Woman Stud.* 2005;24(2):123–127. Available at: https://cws.journals.yorku.ca/index.php/cws/article/view/6129. Accessed January 1, 2023.
15. Smith LT. *Decolonizing Methodologies: Research and Indigenous Peoples.* London, UK: Zed Books; 1999.

2021, SOFTCOVER,
350 PP, 978-087553-3155

APHABOOKSTORE.ORG

Healthy Aging Through The Social Determinants of Health

Edited by Elaine T. Jurkowski, PhD, MSW and M. Aaron Guest, PhD, MPH, MSW

This new book examines the link between social determinants of health and the process of healthy aging. It provides public health practitioners and others interacting with the older population with best practices to encourage healthy aging and enhance the lives of people growing older.

Healthy Aging: Through The Social Determinants of Health gives insight into the role each of these plays in the healthy aging process: health and health care; neighborhood and built environment; social support; education; and economics and policy.

APHA PRESS
AN IMPRINT OF AMERICAN PUBLIC HEALTH ASSOCIATION

Training Latinx Community Health Workers as Clinical Research and Health Care System Navigators

Gabriela Plasencia, MD, MAS, Kamaria Kaalund, BA, and Andrea Thoumi, MPP, MSc

ABOUT THE AUTHORS

Gabriela Plasencia and Kamaria Kaalund are with the Duke–Margolis Center for Health Policy, Duke University, Durham, NC. Gabriela Plasencia and Andrea Thoumi are with the Department of Family Medicine and Community Health, Duke University. Andrea Thoumi is also with Duke–Margolis Center for Health Policy, Washington, DC.

Community health workers (CHWs), or *promotores de salud*, form the spider's web of attachments between community members, families, community-based organizations, academic centers, health care systems, and public health institutions. CHWs are often from the communities they serve and improve health by providing culturally appropriate health information, facilitating system navigation, and building trust with individuals and communities, among other roles.[1] The greater emphasis on awareness, navigation, and dissemination of culturally sensitive resources results in improved institutional trust, decreased barriers to care, and increased health care utilization.[2] The roles CHWs play are especially important when working with marginalized and minoritized populations, such as the Latino/Hispanic populations (hereafter "Latinx").

Because of their ability to increase trust and engagement, CHWs have been increasingly involved in community-based participatory research in various roles, including research question development; intervention design and implementation; and data collection, analysis, and dissemination.[3] Despite this increased involvement in research coupled with lived experiences, CHWs typically lack formal research training in needs assessment, qualitative and quantitative evaluation of programmatic or public data, and policy analysis.

Developing and providing research training to CHWs can strengthen bidirectional information sharing and community-based problem-solving while increasing CHW capacity to inform policy changes and increase community member trust in research participation. We propose key policy steps to advance the inclusion of CHWs in research programs through increased research capacity building.

RESEARCH TRAINING AND OPPORTUNITIES

Studies show that although effective and cost saving, CHW inclusion in community-informed research and community-based health interventions is precarious because of limited training opportunities,[2,4] CHWs' lack of uniformity in core competency skills or certification requirements,[4] inconsistent supervision,[2] or unclear pathways for advancement.[5] Furthermore, other than protocol-driven trainings, there is a general lack of research training available for CHWs, despite their knowledge and lived expertise in minoritized and marginalized communities.[4,6]

INNOVATIVE STRATEGIES

Evidence-based strategies for community-engaged CHW research–training development, implementation, dissemination, and translation include the following:

1. Creation of a CHW research training curriculum. Existing research discusses the need for increased training overall for CHWs, but specifically research training.[2,4,6] Research training may include learning best practices to identify, develop, and evaluate research questions; engage stakeholders; conduct qualitative and quantitative analysis; and disseminate results. Additionally, research training can include translation of research to policy and how to communicate findings to policymakers. Although there has been evaluation of the interests, experience, and training of CHWs in research,[6,7] few trainings for CHWs specifically focus on research fundamentals[7] and instead focus on specific research protocols,[8] research ethics,[9] or other specific topics. Therefore, there is a need to directly address this gap by creating a standardized CHW research training curriculum

AJPH November 2023, Vol 113, No. 11

based on recommendations from the literature, trainings from other research teams conducting community-based participatory research in collaboration with CHWs, and focus groups of local CHWs to tailor training to community interests and goals.

2. Innovative community-informed codevelopment process. For maximum CHW buy-in, it is critical that curricula be developed in partnership with community partners experienced in training CHWs as well as by conducting focus groups with CHWs to understand the topics of most interest, the topics of most and least familiarity, and the preferred method of education. In this way, curricula would be codeveloped and informed by both research and community expertise. Codevelopment processes ensure that CHWs shape the direction of research, increasing the trust-building relationships between communities and researchers.
3. CHW research engagement toolkit. Given a general lack of published research training programs for CHWs, this process of codeveloping the curriculum, barriers and facilitators throughout the process, and lessons learned should be summarized in a CHW research engagement toolkit. This will aid in the adaptation of research curricula for CHWs from other minoritized or marginalized populations, in other geographic locations, or focused on other health-related topics.
4. Embedding CHWs' bicultural and community expertise in population health improvement. CHW knowledge and expertise are often used for individual or family benefit, but they are not aggregated for a better understanding of population health needs. This type of codeveloped research training, therefore, is innovative in that it proposes the application of CHW collective knowledge, experience, and relationships not only for the improvement of the health of individuals but also for the community at large. For example, CHWs can provide expertise on community perspectives and cultural norms, including the development and implementation of culturally and linguistically appropriate service standards.[10]
5. CHWs' strategic engagement in policy and advocacy. Bilingual and bicultural research teams composed of Latinx experts in research, policy, and advocacy, in addition to Latinx community-based organization leaders that have previously engaged in research partnerships, are critical to developing and sustaining a CHW research curriculum. This combination of community and academic expertise will strengthen the ability to translate community-informed CHW research training to the development of evidence-based policy recommendations and advocacy strategies for Latinx population health improvement through research collaboration and authentic partnership.

IMPACT OF RESEARCH TRAINING

Hiring local CHWs and providing them with increased capacities improve local economies, especially for already minoritized and marginalized populations. Community-informed capacity building and retaining CHWs maintain the CHW workforce for continued improvements in long-standing health disparities and in preparation for future public health crises. Additionally, improving CHW capacity for more bidirectional involvement in research will also improve Latinx communities' understanding of the risks and benefits associated with participation in research, which can increase engagement in and access to clinical trials, cohort studies, and other forms of research.

Finally, the community-informed research training of CHWs will enhance public health efforts by enabling more timely identification of community-level problems, review of publicly available data and existing community resources, understanding of tools to translate research to policy, and development of evidence-based community-driven approaches to solving complex problems that can be disseminated to community and institutional leaders for improved population health impact.

Furthermore, CHW training can be adapted to the needs of local communities or other marginalized or minoritized populations facing similar disparities in health care outcomes. CHWs employ the skills and expertise necessary for more trusted and equitable evidence-generation processes and thus are essential to addressing systemic barriers and improved population health. AJPH

CORRESPONDENCE

Correspondence should be sent to Gabriela Plasencia, MD, MAS; 701 Main Street, Durham, NC, 27701 (e-mail: gmp17@duke.edu). Reprints can be ordered at http://www.ajph.org by clicking the "Reprints" link.

PUBLICATION INFORMATION

Full Citation: Plasencia G, Kaalund K, Thoumi A. Training Latinx community health workers as clinical research and health care system navigators. *Am J Public Health*. 2023;113(11): 1157–1159.

Acceptance Date: August 12, 2023.

DOI: https://doi.org/10.2105/AJPH.2023.307418

CONTRIBUTORS

G. Plasencia wrote the first draft of the editorial and provided project administration. G. Plasencia and A. Thoumi conceptualized the editorial. A. Thoumi provided supervision. All authors wrote and edited the editorial.

ACKNOWLEDGMENTS

G. Plasencia was supported by the National Center for Advancing Translational Sciences, National Institutes of Health (NIH; award TL1 TR002555).

Our team would like to thank the community health workers and community-based organizations and their leaders that worked so tirelessly during the pandemic to serve the Latinx communities in Durham, North Carolina, and elsewhere. We would also like to thank the Latinx Advocacy Team and Interdisciplinary Network for COVID-19 (LATIN-19) for their ongoing support of research to support community, advocacy, and policy interventions to improve health equity for Latinx individuals in North Carolina. We would like to thank all members of the Comunidad Latina in North Carolina who have contributed to LATIN-19. Finally, we would like to thank the Duke National Clinician Scholars Program for providing the financial and administrative support to make the corresponding author's research possible.

Note. The content is solely the responsibility of the authors and does not necessarily represent the official views of the NIH.

CONFLICTS OF INTEREST

The authors have no conflicts of interest to declare.

REFERENCES

1. Duhl L. Guide to community preventive services: a commentary. Available at: https://www.thecommunityguide.org/media/pdf/duhl.pdf. Accessed August 24, 2023.
2. Ignoffo S, Margellos-Anast H, Banks M, Morris R, Jay K. Clinical integration of community health workers to reduce health inequities in overburdened and under-resourced populations. *Popul Health Manag.* 2022;25(2):280–283. https://doi.org/10.1089/pop.2021.0376
3. Coulter K, Ingram M, McClelland DJ, Lohr A. Positionality of community health workers on health intervention research teams: a scoping review. *Front Public Health.* 2020;8:208. https://doi.org/10.3389/fpubh.2020.00208
4. Tucker CM, Smith TM, Hogan ML, Banzhaf M, Molina N, Rodríguez B. Current demographics and roles of Florida community health workers: implications for future recruitment and training. *J Community Health.* 2017;43(3):552–559. https://doi.org/10.1007/s10900-017-0451-3
5. Thoumi A, Kaalund K, Bond S, et al. Scaling up equitable access to community-based COVID-19 testing: strategies from the RADx-UP initiative. 2022. Available at: https://healthpolicy.duke.edu/sites/default/files/2022-05/Scaling%20Up%20Equitable%20Access%20RADX.pdf. Accessed August 24, 2023.
6. Klein KG, Tucker CM, Ateyah WA, et al. Research interests, experience, and training of community health workers: a mixed method approach. *J Community Health.* 2022;47(6):949–958. https://doi.org/10.1007/s10900-022-01122-3
7. Varma D, Samuels E, Piatt G, et al. Community health workers and promotoras' perspectives of a research best practice course: a focus group study. *J Clin Transl Sci.* 2022;6(1):e137. https://doi.org/10.1017/cts.2022.464
8. Terpstra J, Coleman K, Simon G, Nebeker C. The role of community health workers (CHWs) in health promotion research: ethical challenges and practical solutions. *Health Promot Pract.* 2011;12(1):86–93. https://doi.org/10.1177/1524839908330809
9. Solomon S, Piechowski P. Developing community partner training: regulations and relationships. *J Empir Res Hum Res Ethics.* 2011;6(2):23–30. https://doi.org/10.1525/jer.2011.6.2.23
10. Community Health Worker Core Consensus (C3) Project. C3 project CHW roles and competencies review checklist. Available at: https://www.c3project.org/_files/ugd/7ec423_cb744c7b87284c75af7318614061c8ec.pdf. Accessed August 24, 2023.

JONES & BARTLETT LEARNING

APHA PRESS

www.essentialpublichealth.com

Homelessness Is a Form of Structural Violence That Leads to Adverse Obstetrical Outcomes

Madeleine Walsh, Avni Varshneya, Esther Beauchemin, MPH, Lameya Rahman, Anna Beth Schick, Madeleine Goldberg, and Veronica Ades, MD, MPH

ABOUT THE AUTHORS

Madeleine Walsh and Madeleine Goldberg are with the New York University (NYU) Grossman School of Medicine, New York, NY. Avni Varshneya and Esther Beauchemin are with the NYU School of Global Public Health. Lameya Rahman is with the School of Arts and Sciences at Hunter College of the City University of New York, New York, NY. Anna Beth Schick is with the NYU Steinhardt School of Culture, Education, and Human Development. Veronica Ades is with the Department of Obstetrics and Gynecology at NYU Grossman School of Medicine.

AJPH November 2023, Vol 113, No. 11

In the United States, homelessness has increased every year for the last four years. In 2020, 39% of those expe-riencing homelessness were women and girls.[1] The US Code defines homelessness as those who

1. lack a fixed, regular, and adequate nighttime residence;
2. reside in a public or private place not designed for or ordinarily used as a sleeping accommodation;
3. live in supervised temporary living arrangements;
4. reside in a place not meant for human habitation;
5. are at imminent risk of housing loss; or
6. are fleeing violence with no alternative residence.[2]

People who are homeless have less access to prenatal care and are at increased risk for pregnancy complications, including hemorrhage, preterm labor, and placental abnormalities.[3] Their babies are at greater risk of being born at low birth weight and have a higher likelihood of newborn intensive care stays.[3,4]

BACKGROUND

An examination of homelessness within a framework of structural violence is essential to understanding how the stress of navigating homelessness while pregnant can lead to adverse obstetrical and neonatal outcomes. Structural violence is "the social arrangements that put people and populations in harm's way," and considers the economic, political, and legal systems that cause harm and shape interpersonal violence.[5] This concept highlights social forces beyond the control of patients and broadens one's perception of violence to include larger entities actively causing harm, like political systems.[5] Thus, the lens of structural violence examines systemic causes of disparities. Contributors to adverse obstetrical outcomes include racism, unequal access to health care, unemployment, exploitation, and gender-based violence, all of which can be exacerbated through homelessness.[5]

The American College of Obstetricians and Gynecologists considers lack of access to safe and stable housing to be a social determinant of health.[6] It recommends that obstetricians recognize and understand the ways that environmental conditions, including homelessness, affect health outcomes.[6] This opinion editorial, in which we seek to describe the effects and challenges of homelessness during pregnancy and better understand how structural violence contributes to adverse birth outcomes, is informed by professional experience and review of the available literature.

LITERATURE SEARCH

We searched PubMed for peer-reviewed articles and white papers with qualitative and quantitative data between May 2021 and July 2023. Search criteria included "homelessness and maternal health" and "pregnant and homeless." To be more inclusive of the range of identities of those who experience pregnancy and homelessness while also highlighting the dramatic gender disparity this issue reflects, we use person-first language whenever possible given space limitations, and gender-neutral terms ("pregnant people") as well as gendered terms ("women" and "mothers"). The literature we reviewed almost exclusively examined women, revealing the need for further research to explore how homelessness in pregnancy affects transgender and gender-nonconforming individuals.

FINDINGS

Pregnant people experiencing homelessness navigate an oppressive cycle, as their ability to access necessary shelter and health care is obstructed by structural violence, leading to avoidance of these systems that should provide support. Homelessness requires pregnant women to navigate a bewildering shelter system that does not meet their needs and adds barriers to prenatal care access.[4]

Families entering shelters report 14-hour intake appointments, insurmountable documentation requirements, and being sent back to homes where they are not welcome.[7]

Obtaining shelter often requires a series of applications and interviews, which can include lengthy interrogations and multiple reapplication attempts to justify the applicant's vulnerability.[7] For example, New York City's Department of Homeless Services employs "fraud investigators" to attempt to "divert" families from shelter by demonstrating lack of need for housing assistance.[7] But the disruptive, demanding, and retraumatizing process of seeking shelter is not limited to a particular state. For many, a history of intergenerational homelessness and past trauma exposure alters their sense of safety and normalcy, making women who are homeless especially vulnerable when entering shelter systems that tend toward a skeptical, punitive approach.[7]

Within the health care system, logistical barriers, hospital culture, and provider biases create an unwelcome prenatal care environment for individuals experiencing homelessness. Women experiencing homelessness are less likely to initiate prenatal care during their first trimester and tend to have fewer prenatal visits than those who are not homeless.[8] In one study, only half of women experiencing homelessness enrolled in prenatal care received an adequate number of prenatal visits.[9] Transportation presents a barrier to attending prenatal care appointments, especially for women with children and those who lack social support.[9,10] While public transportation may be feasible for individuals, it is less practical for women with children, given one study found that 63% of homeless women with children had no childcare options during prenatal appointments.[9]

Other logistical barriers to care include long wait times, high costs, and lack of care coordination.[9] Particularly for individuals with histories of substance use disorder, clashing appointment times and inadequate eligibility for necessary services restricts care access. In one study, pregnant women with substance use disorder were deemed ineligible for addiction programs if they were not actively using drugs.[10]

For those able to access care, many find the health care system inhospitable. Poor treatment from providers was cited as a barrier to accessing and continuing with pre- and postnatal care.[10,11] This violence exists on both interpersonal and structural levels, as institutions incentivize discharging patients before adequate supportive planning.[12] Pregnant women experiencing homelessness report stigmatization and feeling like a "number" rather than a human.[10] Negative past experiences create further barriers to care. From undesired tubal ligations and unexpected cesarean sections to stillbirths, many women recall unsettling experiences in health care settings that contribute to widespread fear of lost agency.[11] Although laws regarding reproductive health care continue to change, impacts of historical policies and current practices reverberate, adding to fear of stolen autonomy.[10,11]

Intersecting identities compound structural violence for pregnant women of color experiencing homelessness.[13] Structural violence and racism place racial and ethnic minorities at greater risk of experiencing both homelessness and pregnancy complications.[13] Overtly racist policies such as Jim Crow laws and redlining, as well as discrimination in housing rental and home buying, have led to generations of disenfranchisement and housing obstacles for Black communities and other ethnic minority populations. This compounds the adverse effects of poverty and unstable housing within those populations and worsens existing maternal health disparities.[13]

Interactions with health care systems can lead to increased surveillance by child protective services, further dissuading women, especially those experiencing homelessness, from accessing care.[10] In a study looking at child custody loss among African American mothers, women who lost custody of their children had higher rates of homelessness in the year preceding the loss of custody when compared with women who did not lose custody.[14] Intersecting structural violence in the form of racism, classism, and sexism can create an unwelcome health care environment for women experiencing homelessness, resulting in avoidance and fear of accessing services.

CONCLUSIONS

Unreliable support from shelter and health care systems sends families back to unsafe households and permits dismissive experiences with prenatal care providers.[7,9,12] These experiences exacerbate trauma and discourage seeking care. A self-perpetuating cycle of barriers to and fear of accessing services, reduction of health care usage, and reinforcement of provider stigma ensues. We argue that this combination of structural violence, shelter factors, and hospital factors contributes to the increased risk of pregnancy and birth complications seen among women experiencing homelessness when compared with housed women.[4] The increased rates of hemorrhage, hypertension, and preterm labor, among other complications, confirms the need to treat homelessness as an individual risk factor during pregnancy.[3,4]

Key interventions for women and families experiencing homelessness start with supportive shelter. Housing instability is a public health issue that must be tackled alongside improvement of prenatal care services. In a study that provided housing resources for women with children, regardless of whether shelter staff and service providers approved a woman's "readiness" for transition beforehand, access to affordable housing reduced their mental distress.[15]

Within care settings, institutions should incorporate person-centered practices to provide coordinated and sensitive care.[10] Such sensitivity requires adaptable service provision for pregnant women experiencing homelessness, allowing for more individualized care.[10] Cognizance of the past traumas that many of these patients have faced and universal trauma-informed care create a prenatal care environment that women feel safe returning to.[11] However, person-centered care requires more than change on the individual level. The health outcomes of homeless pregnant women expose structural weaknesses in our systems, requiring large-scale changes to housing and health care.

Hospital systems should design prenatal and postnatal care programs that better meet the needs of women who are homeless, introducing flexibility in location and timing of visits and additional outreach support. Cities should examine women's trajectories holistically to provide stable housing through pregnancy, postpartum, and child rearing. In addition, a standard definition of homelessness in pregnancy and utilization of *International Classification of Diseases, 10th Revision* (Geneva, Switzerland: World Health Organization; 1992) codes for homelessness in medical records may facilitate identification of patients in need, allowing for quality improvement initiatives and further research.

Our current systems contribute to, rather than alleviate, stress during homelessness and pregnancy. As we seek to improve birth outcomes for pregnant individuals experiencing homelessness, it is vital that we examine the structural violence within our health care and shelter systems and seek to improve the accessibility and quality of services. Better support for those experiencing homelessness while pregnant will have undeniable downstream effects on future generations by providing stability to mothers and children. AJPH

CORRESPONDENCE

Correspondence should be sent to Madeleine Walsh, 550 1st Ave, New York, NY 10016 (e-mail: madeleine.walsh@nyulangone.org). Reprints can be ordered at https://ajph.org by clicking the "Reprints" link.

PUBLICATION INFORMATION

Full Citation: Walsh M, Varshneya A, Beauchemin E, et al. Homelessness is a form of structural violence that leads to adverse obstetrical outcomes. *Am J Public Health*. 2023;113(11):1160–1162.

Acceptance Date: August 15, 2023.

DOI: https://doi.org/10.2105/AJPH.2023.307421

CONTRIBUTORS

All authors contributed substantially to the conceptualization, design, research, and article. M. Walsh and M. Goldberg were involved in the origination of this narrative review and performed the literature scoping and review. A. Varshneya conducted the writing as well as the literature search and review and organized the preparation of this article. M. Walsh also oversaw the preparation of the article. E. Beauchemin, L. Rahman, and A. B. Schick contributed to the writing, editing, and literature review. V. Ades provided guidance on the project's literature analysis and manuscript review. All authors have reviewed and approved this article for submission.

ACKNOWLEDGMENTS

The work will be presented at FIGO World Congress of Gynecology and Obstetrics in October 2023.

CONFLICTS OF INTEREST

All authors have no conflicts of interest, financial or nonfinancial, regarding the submitted work.

REFERENCES

1. Henry M, de Sousa Y, Roddey C, Gayen S, Bednar TJ. The 2020 Annual Homeless Assessment Report (AHAR) to Congress. Washington, DC: US Department of Housing and Urban Development; 2021.
2. General Definition of Homeless Individual. 42 USC §11302 (2014).
3. DiTosto JD, Holder K, Soyemi E, Beestrum M, Yee LM. Housing instability and adverse perinatal outcomes: a systematic review. *Am J Obstet Gynecol MFM*. 2021;3(6):100477. https://doi.org/10.1016/j.ajogmf.2021.100477
4. Clark RE, Weinreb L, Flahive JM, Seifert RW. Homelessness contributes to pregnancy complications. *Health Aff (Millwood)*. 2019;38(1):139–146. https://doi.org/10.1377/hlthaff.2018.05156
5. Montesanti SR, Thurston WE. Mapping the role of structural and interpersonal violence in the lives of women: implications for public health interventions and policy. *BMC Womens Health*. 2015;15(1):100. https://doi.org/10.1186/s12905-015-0256-4
6. Ades V, Goddard B, Ayala SP, Bach SC, Wu SX. ACOG Committee Opinion No. 729: importance of social determinants of health and cultural awareness in the delivery of reproductive health care. *Obstet Gynecol*. 2018;131(6):1162–1163. https://doi.org/10.1097/AOG.0000000000002660
7. Silva J, Teminsky C, Yager J. *Improving PATH: Dismantling Barriers to Shelter for Homeless Families with Children*. WIN Policy Brief Series. New York, NY: WIN NYC; 2021.
8. Richards R, Merrill RM, Baksh L. Health behaviors and infant health outcomes in homeless pregnant women in the United States. *Pediatrics*. 2011;128(3):438–446. https://doi.org/10.1542/peds.2010-3491
9. Bloom KC, Bednarzyk MS, Devitt DL, Renault RA, Teaman V, Van Loock DM. Barriers to prenatal care for homeless pregnant women. *J Obstet Gynecol Neonatal Nurs*. 2004;33(4):428–435. https://doi.org/10.1177/0884217504266775
10. McGeough C, Walsh A, Clyne B. Barriers and facilitators perceived by women while homeless and pregnant in accessing antenatal and or postnatal healthcare: a qualitative evidence synthesis. *Health Soc Care Community*. 2020;28(5):1380–1393. https://doi.org/10.1111/hsc.12972
11. Cronley C, Hohn K, Nahar S. Reproductive health rights and survival: the voices of mothers experiencing homelessness. *Women Health*. 2018;58(3):320–333. https://doi.org/10.1080/03630242.2017.1296060
12. Richter S, Caine V, Kubota H, Chaw-Kant J, Danko M. Delivering care to women who are homeless: a narrative inquiry into the experience of health care providers in an obstetrical unit. *Divers Equal Health Care*. 2017;14(3):122–129. https://doi.org/10.21767/2049-5471.1000102
13. Huang K, Waken RJ, Luke AA, Carter EB, Lindley KJ, Maddox KEJ. Risk of delivery complications among pregnant people experiencing housing insecurity. *Am J Obstet Gynecol MFM*. 2023;5(2):100819. https://doi.org/10.1016/j.ajogmf.2022.100819
14. Harp KLH, Oser CB. Factors associated with two types of child custody loss among a sample of African American mothers: a novel approach. *Soc Sci Res*. 2016;60:283–296. https://doi.org/10.1016/j.ssresearch.2016.06.007
15. Samuels J, Fowler PJ, Ault-Brutus A, Tang DI, Marcal K. Time-limited case management for homeless mothers with mental health problems: effects on maternal mental health. *J Soc Social Work Res*. 2015;6(4):515–539. https://doi.org/10.1086/684122

Impact of a Permitless Concealed Firearm Carry Law in West Virginia, 1999–2015 and 2016–2020

Eric W. Lundstrom, PhD, MPH, Jacob K. Pence, DO, and Gordon S. Smith, MD, MBChB, MPH

We used firearm mortality and sales data to assess the impact of HB 4145, a May 2016 law that legalized concealed firearm carry without a permit in West Virginia. Firearm mortality was significantly higher (29%) in the years after the enactment of the law; handgun mortality was also higher (48% increase), whereas long gun deaths and firearm sales were unaffected. This may suggest that HB 4145 increased rates of firearm-related mortality in West Virginia without affecting firearm sales in the state. (*Am J Public Health.* 2023;113(11):1163–1166. https://doi.org/10.2105/AJPH.2023.307382)

Several US states have recently enacted permitless concealed firearm carry laws, which do not require an individual to apply for a permit to legally carry a concealed firearm in public.[1] Other systems are more restrictive, with "may-issue" schemes giving states substantial discretion in deciding when to issue a permit and "shall-issue" systems requiring authorities to issue permits to any individual meeting basic requirements.[2] Gun owners in permitless carry states report significantly higher rates of past-30-day loaded handgun carrying than those in permit-issuing states,[3] indicating that such laws have a measurable effect on carrying behavior.

INTERVENTION AND IMPLEMENTATION

In May 2016, the West Virginia legislature enacted HB 4145, a permitless concealed carry law; before enactment of HB 4145, West Virginia was a shall-issue state.[1]

PLACE, TIME, AND PERSONS

HB 4145 was enacted on May 24, 2016, and applied to all legal residents of West Virginia.[4]

PURPOSE

HB 4145 repealed West Virginia's previous shall-issue permit-issuing system, which was established in 1989 and allowed "any United States citizen or legal resident thereof at least twenty-one years of age and not otherwise prohibited from possessing a firearm [to] carry a concealed deadly weapon without a license."[4]

EVALUATION AND ADVERSE EFFECTS

We used both descriptive and inferential statistical approaches to assess the impact of HB 4145 on firearm mortality in West Virginia. We extracted West Virginia firearm fatality data from CDC WONDER (Centers for Disease Control and Prevention Wide-ranging ONline Data for Epidemiologic Research), which reports mortality data collected through state death certificate registries.[5] Mean annual age-adjusted fatality rates per 100 000 population for 1999 through 2015 and 2016 through 2020 were extracted for demographics of interest, including gender, race, and urbanization, as well as by injury intent and gun type involvement. Although annual 2021 data were available at the time of our analysis, age-adjusted rates for a 2016 through 2021 postintervention period could not be obtained as CDC WONDER can be queried only for 1999 through 2020 or only for 2018 through 2021 as a result of a race categorization series break occurring in 2018.

We calculated monthly crude firearm death rates, available for 1999 through 2021, using total monthly firearm mortality counts from CDC WONDER and annual population estimates; CDC WONDER does not provide monthly age-adjusted mortality rates.

AJPH November 2023, Vol 113, No. 11

Monthly firearm sales data for 2000 through 2022 were extracted from The Trace, which estimates state-level firearm sales using Federal Bureau of Investigation background check data.[6]

We used interrupted time series analysis (ITSA) to assess the impact of HB 4145 on monthly firearm mortality and sales in West Virginia. ITSA quantifies temporal effects of interventions for which no control population exists, making it useful for assessing the effects of public health events.[7] The preintervention period was defined as January 1999 to April 2016 and the postintervention period as May 2016 (the month HB 4145 was enacted) to December 2021. Using monthly data, we assessed the intervention effect as a step change, representing an overall increase or decrease in the rate of fatalities. We controlled serial correlation in monthly data using autoregressive integrated moving average modeling[7] (Table A, available as a supplement to the online version of this article at http://www.ajph.org). To allow comparisons with national trends, we conducted an ITSA of monthly US firearm mortality per 100 000 population.

Mean annual firearm mortality rates in West Virginia during 2016 through 2020 were significantly higher (29%) than in 1999 through 2015, both overall and for each of the strata examined except for large fringe metro urbanization, unintentional and undetermined injury intents, and deaths associated with long gun use (Table 1). Homicides and suicides increased by 48% and 22%, respectively. Stratified by urbanization, the largest significant increases were seen in noncore (most rural) areas (34%). Although more than half of firearm types were unspecified, the percentage identified as handguns increased significantly (45%), whereas the percentage identified as long guns did not. Temporally, annual firearm mortality increased after the enactment of HB 4145; homicides showed a steadier increase than suicides (Figure A, available as a supplement to the online version of this article at http://www.ajph.org).

An ITSA of monthly firearm fatalities per 100 000 population showed that rates increased by 26.2% (95% confidence interval [CI] = 19.8, 31.7). US firearm fatality rates exhibited nonsignificant increases after passage of HB 4145 (−0.9%; 95% CI = −6.2, 4.4; Table 2; detailed modeling results are available in Table A). Stratified analyses of monthly West Virginia firearm mortality data were not possible because of data suppression by CDC WONDER. An ITSA of monthly firearm sales in West Virginia did not reveal any impact associated with HB 4145. There was a small spike in sales after HB 4145 was enacted, but the

TABLE 1— Age-Adjusted Firearm Mortality Rates: West Virginia, 1999–2015 Versus 2016–2020

Demographic Category	1999–2015 Rate (95% CI)	2016–2020 Rate (95% CI)	Percentage Increase
Total	13.8 (13.4, 14.2)	17.8 (16.9, 18.7)	29
Gender			
Male	24.1 (23.3, 24.9)	29.6 (27.9, 31.2)	23
Female	4.4 (4.1, 4.8)	6.3 (5.5, 7.1)	43
Race			
African American	17.3 (14.9, 19.8)	27.2 (21.8, 32.5)	57
White	13.8 (13.3, 14.2)	17.3 (16.4, 18.2)	25
Urbanization[a]			
Large fringe metro	8.6 (6.7, 10.9)	12.0 (8.4, 16.7)	40
Medium metro	12.0 (11.1, 12.9)	15.8 (13.8, 17.7)	32
Small metro	13.0 (12.3, 13.6)	16.1 (14.8, 17.5)	24
Micropolitan	15.4 (14.3, 16.5)	19.9 (17.6, 22.3)	29
Noncore (most rural)	16.4 (15.5, 17.4)	21.9 (19.7, 24.1)	34
Injury intent			
Unintentional	0.5 (0.4, 0.6)	0.4 (0.3, 0.6)	−20
Suicide	9.9 (9.6, 10.2)	12.1 (11.4, 12.9)	22
Homicide	3.1 (2.9, 3.3)	4.6 (4.1, 5.1)	48
Undetermined	0.2 (0.1, 0.2)	0.2 (0.1, 0.4)	0
Gun type[b]			
Handgun	3.1 (2.9, 3.3)	4.5 (4.1, 4.9)	45
Long gun	2.5 (2.4, 2.7)	2.6 (2.2, 2.9)	4
Unspecified	8.0 (7.7, 8.3)	10.4 (9.7, 11.1)	30

Note. CI = confidence interval.
Source. Data were derived from CDC WONDER (Centers for Disease Control and Prevention Wide-ranging ONline Data for Epidemiologic Research).

[a]West Virginia has no areas designated "large central metro," the most urban code in the urban–rural classification scheme used in CDC WONDER.
[b]Gun involvement strata were identified via *International Classification of Diseases, 10th Revision* underlying cause of death codes for handgun (W32, X72, X93, and Y22), long gun (W33, X73, X94, and Y23), and undetermined (W34, X74, X95, and Y24) gun involvement.

TABLE 2— Results of Interrupted Time Series Analyses of Mean Monthly Firearm Mortality per 100 000 Population Before and After Implementation of HB 4145: West Virginia and the United States

	Estimated Monthly Firearm Deaths per 100 000 Population		
Region	January 1999–April 2016	May 2016–December 2021	Percentage Increase (95% CI)
West Virginia	1.204	1.519	26.2 (19.8, 31.7)
United States	0.913	0.904	−0.9 (−6.2, 4.4)

Note. CI = confidence interval. Rates were calculated via interrupted time series analyses of monthly firearm mortality per 100 000 population; pre–HB 4145 (January 1999–April 2016) values correspond to the model intercept, whereas post–HB 4145 enactment (May 2016–December 2021) values correspond to the model intercept along with the step change value shown in Table A (available as a supplement to the online version of this article at http://www.ajph.org).

increase was mild relative to historical data (Figure B, available as a supplement to the online version of this article at http://www.ajph.org).

SUSTAINABILITY

Polling research has shown that an estimated 82% of rural US gun owners cite the right to own a firearm as essential to their sense of freedom,[8] emblematic of the strong gun culture in rural areas of the country. As West Virginia is mostly rural, it is unlikely that HB 4145 will be replaced with a more stringent law soon. In fact, future firearm exposure in West Virginia may increase further given that the state legislature recently passed the Campus Self-Defense Act, which allows concealed firearm carrying on college campuses in the state with few exceptions.[9]

PUBLIC HEALTH SIGNIFICANCE

Previous literature has revealed increases in officer-involved shootings in West Virginia after the enactment of HB 4145.[1] To our knowledge, however, this is the first study to assess the impact of HB 4145 on overall firearm mortality in the state. Although suicides were the leading cause of West Virginia firearm deaths throughout the study period, homicides, which are more closely related to concealed firearm carry, showed a greater increase after 2016 (Table 1). Descriptive statistics indicate that the number of handgun deaths was significantly higher after HB 4145 enactment, whereas the number of long gun deaths remained unchanged (Table 1); because long guns are not generally concealable, HB 4145 is unlikely to affect long gun death rates.

Moreover, the number of deaths with no gun specified was significantly higher in 2016 through 2020 than in 1999 through 2015; it is reasonable to assume that these deaths were primarily handgun related given that most US firearm homicides[10] and suicides[11] are associated with handguns, including in rural areas. Evidence-based firearm injury prevention measures may be needed to reduce public exposure to firearms, including safe firearm storage practices and community-driven violence prevention programs.[12] *AJPH*

ABOUT THE AUTHORS

Eric W. Lundstrom and Gordon S. Smith are with the Department of Epidemiology and Biostatistics, West Virginia University, Morgantown. Jacob K. Pence is with the Transitional Year Residency Program, West Virginia University.

CORRESPONDENCE

Correspondence should be sent to Eric W. Lundstrom, PhD, MPH, 64 Medical Center Dr, Morgantown, WV 26506 (e-mail: ewlundstrom@gmail.com). Reprints can be ordered at http://www.ajph.org by clicking the "Reprints" link.

PUBLICATION INFORMATION

Full Citation: Lundstrom EW, Pence JK, Smith GS. Impact of a permitless concealed firearm carry law in West Virginia, 1999–2015 and 2016–2020. *Am J Public Health*. 2023;113(11):1163–1166.

Acceptance Date: June 28, 2023.

DOI: https://doi.org/10.2105/AJPH.2023.307382

CONTRIBUTORS

E. W. Lundstrom drafted the article. E. W. Lundstrom performed the statistical analyses and J. K. Pence performed data extraction. G. S. Smith provided expert opinion on injury epidemiology and prevention. All authors contributed to the conceptualization of the study.

ACKNOWLEDGMENTS

Gordon S. Smith was supported in part by the National Institute of General Medical Sciences (grant 2U54GM104942).

CONFLICTS OF INTEREST

The authors declare no conflicts of interest.

HUMAN PARTICIPANT PROTECTION

The institutional review board of West Virginia University determined that this study did not meet the definition of human participant research.

REFERENCES

1. Doucette ML, Ward JA, McCourt AD, Webster D, Crifasi CK. Officer-involved shootings and concealed carry weapons permitting laws: analysis of gun violence archive data, 2014–2020. *J Urban Health*. 2022;99(3):373–384. https://doi.org/10.1007/s11524-022-00627-5

2. Smart R, Morral AR, Smucker S, et al. Concealed-carry laws. Available at: https://www.rand.org/content/dam/rand/pubs/research_reports/RR2000/RR2088/RAND_RR2088.pdf. Accessed October 19, 2022.
3. Rowhani-Rahbar A, Gallagher A, Azrael D, Miller M. Trend in loaded handgun carrying among adult handgun owners in the United States, 2015–2019. *Am J Public Health.* 2022;112(12):1783–1790. https://doi.org/10.2105/AJPH.2022.307094
4. West Virginia Legislature. House Bill 4145. Available at: https://www.wvlegislature.gov/Bill_Status/bills_text.cfm?billdoc=HB4145%20SUB%20ENG.htm&yr=2016&sesstype=RS&i=4145. Accessed October 19, 2022.
5. Centers for Disease Control and Prevention. Wide-ranging ONline Data for Epidemiologic Research (WONDER). Available at: https://wonder.cdc.gov. Accessed October 19, 2022.
6. Nass D, Barton C. How many guns did Americans buy last month? Available at: https://www.thetrace.org/2020/08/gun-sales-estimates. Accessed January 22, 2023.
7. Schaffer AL, Dobbins TA, Pearson SA. Interrupted time series analysis using autoregressive integrated moving average (ARIMA) models: a guide for evaluating large-scale health interventions. *BMC Med Res Methodol.* 2021;21(1):58. https://doi.org/10.1186/s12874-021-01235-8
8. Kim Parker B, Horowitz J, Igielnik R, et al. America's complex relationship with guns. Available at: https://assets.pewresearch.org/wp-content/uploads/sites/3/2017/06/06151541/Guns-Report-FOR-WEBSITE-PDF-6-21.pdf. Accessed January 22, 2023.
9. Yohe R. West Virginia universities, colleges preparing for campus carry law. Available at: https://wvpublic.org/w-va-universities-colleges-preparing-for-campus-carry-law. Accessed May 25, 2023.
10. Alper M, Glaze L. Source and use of firearms involved in crimes: survey of prison inmates, 2016. Available at: https://bjs.ojp.gov/content/pub/pdf/suficspi16.pdf. Accessed May 25, 2023.
11. Hanlon TJ, Barber C, Azrael D, Miller M. Type of firearm used in suicides: findings from 13 states in the National Violent Death Reporting System, 2005–2015. *J Adolesc Health.* 2019;65(3):366–370. https://doi.org/10.1016/j.jadohealth.2019.03.015
12. Kegler SR, Simon TR, Zwald ML, et al. Vital signs: changes in firearm homicide and suicide rates—United States, 2019–2020. Available at: https://stacks.cdc.gov/view/cdc/116520. Accessed May 25, 2023.

2021 | 300PP | SOFTCOVER
978-087553-3179

APHABOOKSTORE.ORG

Cannabis: Moving Forward, Protecting Health

Edited by: David H. Jernigan, PhD, Rebecca L. Ramirez MPH, Brian C. Castrucci, DrPH, Catherine D. Patterson, MPP, Grace Castillo, MPH

This new book addresses the ongoing debate on cannabis policy and provides guidance on how to regulate its sale and distribution. Instead of taking a stance for or against cannabis use, the book:

- suggests we employ strategies similar to those used in alcohol control to create a solid foundation of policy and best practices;
- focuses on how we can best regulate a complex substance.

APHA PRESS
AN IMPRINT OF AMERICAN PUBLIC HEALTH ASSOCIATION

Impact of the Choose Well Initiative on Contraceptive Access at Federally Qualified Health Centers in South Carolina: A Midline Evaluation

Kate Beatty, PhD, Michael G. Smith, DrPH, Jordan de Jong, MA, Amy Weber, DBH, Rakesh Adelli, MPH, and Amal Khoury, PhD

Choose Well (CW) is a statewide contraceptive access initiative to reduce unintended pregnancy among patients utilizing federally funded family planning services. We examined CW's impact on contraceptive access at South Carolina federally qualified health centers from 2016 to 2019, which reported significantly higher increases in providing the full range of contraceptive methods and training onsite. CW prioritized ensuring change sustainability through obtaining funding and institutionalizing changes. (*Am J Public Health*. 2023;113(11):1167–1172. https://doi.org/10.2105/AJPH.2023.307384)

AJPH November 2023, Vol 113, No. 11

Choose Well (CW), a statewide contraceptive access initiative, aims to reduce unintended pregnancy in South Carolina through enhanced provision of contraception and training for services at federally funded safety net clinics providing family planning services. CW's mission is to promote equitable access to contraception without judgment or coercion.[1]

INTERVENTION AND IMPLEMENTATION

To our knowledge, CW is the only initiative of its kind to be implemented in the US Southeast across multiple clinical sectors. Informed by a statewide needs assessment, CW is founded on collective impact principles and operationalized through four key components (i.e., impact areas): infrastructure and workforce, capacity building and training, integrated marketing and communication, and strategic learning and sustainability.[2] The initiative focused heavily on provider and staff training for contraceptive service provision, method stocking, and recruitment and retention of providers. Additional details about the implementation of CW are available elsewhere.[2]

PLACE, TIME, AND PERSONS

CW is a six-year statewide contraceptive access initiative in South Carolina that operated from 2017 through 2022.[2] This initiative focused primarily on patients seeking care at publicly funded clinics, including federally qualified health centers (FQHCs), health department clinics, and rural health clinics. The initiative prioritized women of reproductive age seeking contraceptive care, in particular those who were uninsured, were underinsured, or had lower incomes. (The term "women" is applied throughout to reflect the terminology used in the cited research. We recognize that gender identities are diverse and that respondents' identities may not have been accurately captured.)

PURPOSE

Unintended pregnancy is a significant public health issue, particularly in the US Southeast. CW aims to reduce unintended pregnancy by providing funding and training to enhance contraceptive provision. Given the important role of FQHCs as safety net providers and that statewide contraceptive access initiatives involving FQHCs are novel,[3–6] we examined the impact of CW on contraceptive access at FQHCs in South Carolina midway through the initiative. Nationally, FQHCs are crucial to the health care safety net, serving 25 million people annually.[7]

Many FQHCs provide essential contraceptive services for free or at a reduced cost to lower-income, underinsured, or uninsured patients, and about 70% of FQHC patients have incomes below the federal poverty level.[8] In South Carolina, FQHCs do not receive Title X funding for family planning services.[9] FQHCs are less likely than are Title X–funded clinics to have onsite availability of all contraceptive methods, particularly intrauterine devices (IUDs) and implants,[10–12] and differences in policies and funding in these systems lead to variability in contraceptive service provision and access.[13] Therefore, assessing the impacts of CW among participating FQHCs is particularly relevant.

EVALUATION AND ADVERSE EFFECTS

As a component of CW's external evaluation, we employed a quasiexperimental design involving CW participating and nonparticipating FQHCs in South Carolina and Alabama. We surveyed clinics in Alabama because the health care–funding mechanisms (nonexpanded Medicaid),[14] policy environment,[15] rates of unintended pregnancy,[16,17] and patient populations are similar to those of South Carolina.[18–22] Our study is unique in that, to our knowledge, an intervention of this level has not been assessed at FQHCs, particularly in the US Southeast. Although FQHC clinics are required to provide family planning services, there is wide variability in their contraceptive care provision at the system level.[13,23]

All FQHCs in Alabama and South Carolina offering any contraceptive service were eligible for the study, and we included the full census of these clinics in the survey. We surveyed FQHCs in 2017 (n = 107) and 2020 (n = 127) to assess contraceptive service provision at baseline (2016) and midline (2019). Surveys examined onsite contraceptive provision and clinical and administrative training. Using a difference-in-differences approach, we assessed changes in outcomes over time between CW and non-CW clinics. We assessed difference-in-differences using binomial regression models with robust SEs to estimate the prevalence of clinics providing contraceptive methods accounting for the repeated measurement of clinics across timepoints. Significant difference-in-differences were indicated by a *P* value of less than .05 for the interaction between the timepoint and CW participation variables.

Although directly assessing the parallel trends assumption for this difference-in-differences analysis was not feasible, as we collected data only to represent the year before the start of the intervention, we conducted extensive research into the similarities between Alabama's and South Carolina's reproductive health and medically underserved landscapes. This indicated that Alabama and South Carolina had similar populations of women of reproductive age,[24] contraceptive utilization patterns among Medicaid-enrolled women in the years leading up to CW,[25,26] and rates of women in need of publicly funded contraceptive services who received those services in the years leading up to CW.[27]

Those FQHCs participating in CW compared with those that did not reported a significantly greater increase in the onsite provision of the full range of contraceptive methods. At baseline, 4.4% of participating FQHCs reported offering all eight contraceptive methods onsite (i.e., IUD, implant, shot, oral contraceptive, patch, ring, condom, diaphragm). At midline, 34.7% of participating FQHCs reported offering all eight contraceptive methods onsite, an increase of 30.3 percentage points. During the same period, FQHCs not participating in CW saw a 5.7 percentage point increase in the proportion of clinics providing all eight contraceptive methods onsite.

The statistically significant difference-in-differences in the proportions of participating and nonparticipating clinics offering all eight methods was 24.7 percentage points (*P* = .009; Figure 1). This finding suggests that CW participation has meaningfully expanded contraceptive provision at participating FQHCs.

Regarding specific methods, the proportion of clinics providing IUDs increased by 48.6 percentage points from baseline to midline among CW participating clinics. Among non-CW clinics, the proportion of clinics providing IUDs increased by 11.8 percentage points from baseline to midline. The resulting 36.8 percentage point difference-in-differences was statistically significant (*P* = .007; Figure 1). Additionally, CW clinics reported a significantly greater increase in offering same-visit IUD placements compared with non-CW clinics (*P* = .001). The proportions of both CW and non-CW clinics reporting onsite provision of contraceptive implants increased at midline relative to baseline, and the difference-in-differences was not significant (Table 1).

More clinics overall reported training in contraceptive counseling and provision at midline than at baseline. The difference-in-differences between participating and nonparticipating clinics was not significant for the clinical training except for training in contraceptive injection. The proportion of participating clinics reporting provider training for contraceptive injection increased by 48.6 percentage points from baseline

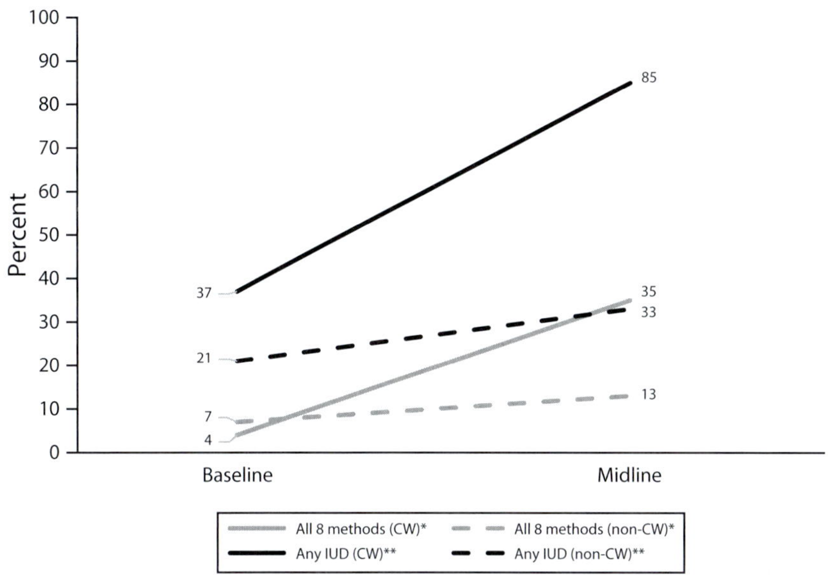

FIGURE 1— Proportion of FQHCs Offering Onsite Contraceptive Methods by Choose Well Participation Status: South Carolina and Alabama, 2016–2019

Note. CW = Choose Well; FQHC = federally qualified health center; IUD = intrauterine device. *$P < .05$; **$P < .01$.

to midline, compared with a 9.9 percentage point increase among non-CW clinics (difference-in-differences = 38.7%; $P = .001$; Table 1).

We noted significant differences between CW and non-CW clinics in their participation in administrative training over time. At baseline, 22.7% of CW clinics reported training for billing and coding for contraceptive services. This proportion increased by 57.8 percentage points at midline. This was statistically significantly greater than the 25.9 percentage point increase observed among non-CW clinics (difference-in-differences = 31.9%; $P = .013$). Additionally, significantly more CW clinics than non-CW clinics reported revenue cycle management training at midline relative to baseline (difference-in-differences = 33.7%; $P = .021$; Table 1). See Table A for clinic and patient demographic information (available as a supplement to the online version of this article at http://www.ajph.org).

SUSTAINABILITY

A primary focus of CW has been ensuring the sustainability of changes. Primary areas in need of sustainability include funding (both for contraceptive supplies and workforce) and continued training. Although, originally, CW's primary metric was a reduction in unintended pregnancy, the organization has acknowledged the shift in the reproductive health field toward a less IUD- and implant-focused goal and has moved into a more access-based operationalized approach. The implementing organization, New Morning (a nonprofit organization located in Columbia, SC), has actively engaged with participating clinics and systems to institutionalize training efforts, enhancements to electronic medical records, and supportive clinic policies and practices. New Morning has secured state agency funding appropriations from the state legislature to support FQHCs and is seeking additional funding from public and private sources.

Additionally, contraceptive care changes appear to have been institutionalized in systems, as evidenced by the increases in the provision of contraceptive methods and enhanced billing, coding, and revenue cycle capacity. In addition, training, webinars, and other opportunities offered through CW will be available on demand online after the conclusion of the intervention. A plan is in place to update the training with the most recent information using in-state partners. Furthermore, we will conduct a final study at the conclusion of the CW funding period to assess the effects of the implementation.

PUBLIC HEALTH SIGNIFICANCE

Our findings indicate a significant positive impact on contraceptive provision at FQHCs participating with CW and have broad implications for safety net systems. Contraceptive access initiatives such as CW have been shown to increase access to contraceptive services by increasing the provision of a full range of methods, including IUDs and implants, and ultimately help decrease unintended pregnancies[3–6]; however, statewide contraceptive access interventions at FQHC clinics are novel, making this study particularly relevant to the field. Because of a lack of Title X and other federal funding specifically for contraceptive services at FQHC clinics in South Carolina and other states, assessing funding mechanisms at FQHC clinics and the improvements they afford is crucial for equitable service delivery among safety net clinics. These results highlight the potential for expanding contraceptive services in FQHC settings, where patients often do

TABLE 1— Contraceptive Provision and Training at Choose Well Participating and Nonparticipating FQHCs at Midline Relative to Baseline: South Carolina and Alabama, 2016–2019

	Baseline No. (%)		Midline No. (%)			
	Nonparticipating FQHC	Participating FQHC	Nonparticipating FQHC	Participating FQHC	Difference	P
Onsite method availability						
Hormonal IUD available onsite**	16 (21.1)	7 (36.8)	24 (32.9)	41 (85.4)	0.368	.007
Nonhormonal IUD available onsite**	9 (12.3)	4 (21.1)	14 (19.7)	35 (76.1)	0.476	.001
Implant available onsite	22 (29.7)	12 (63.2)	26 (34.7)	39 (86.7)	0.186	.19
Same-visit method placement						
Same-visit IUD placement provided**	3 (4.4)	3 (13.5)	2 (3.0)	23 (51.1)	0.388	.001
Same-visit implant placement provided*	4 (5.8)	6 (27.3)	4 (6.1)	24 (53.3)	0.258	.023
Clinical provider training						
Patient-centered contraceptive counseling	26 (36.6)	11 (47.8)	44 (64.7)	42 (97.7)	0.218	.09
IUD placement/removal	12 (16.7)	10 (47.6)	27 (40.9)	43 (91.5)	0.196	.13
Same-visit IUD placement	6 (8.2)	8 (36.4)	21 (31.8)	38 (82.6)	0.227	.07
Implant placement/removal	18 (24.7)	11 (52.4)	26 (40.0)	42 (91.3)	0.236	.08
Same-visit implant placement	9 (12.3)	11 (52.4)	21 (32.8)	38 (84.4)	0.116	.39
Counseling and education on contraceptive implant/IUD placement/removal	17 (23.9)	12 (54.6)	29 (45.3)	44 (95.7)	0.197	.13
Contraceptive injection**	35 (48.6)	8 (38.1)	38 (58.5)	39 (86.7)	0.387	.009
Staff training						
Health center efficiency	53 (72.6)	15 (68.2)	53 (76.8)	37 (86.1)	0.137	.3
Billing and coding for contraceptive services*	25 (34.7)	5 (22.7)	43 (60.6)	33 (80.5)	0.319	.013
Cultural competency/sensitivity	44 (60.3)	14 (63.6)	56 (77.8)	38 (90.5)	0.093	.5
Revenue cycle management*	35 (49.3)	7 (31.8)	41 (59.4)	31 (75.6)	0.337	.021
Stocking/inventory tracking for contraceptive services	35 (48.6)	11 (50.0)	45 (63.4)	31 (73.8)	0.09	.55

Note. FQHC = federally qualified health center; IUD = intrauterine device.
*$P < .05$.
**$P < .01$.

not have access to the full range of contraceptive options and integrating contraceptive care with primary care services.[2,8]

Our findings support the hypothesis that CW's funding for contraceptive methods and training provision has increased the availability of the full range of contraceptive methods at FQHC clinics and demonstrate the feasibility of increased access to contraception at FQHC clinics in general. To our knowledge, CW is the first initiative of its kind to be conducted in the US Southeast's politically conservative environment,[2] thereby making evaluation key in assessing how initiatives such as CW can affect clinics in these settings. The external evaluation of the CW contraceptive access initiative will continue to assess the endline results associated with CW implementation in South Carolina, which will inform ongoing and future initiatives. AJPH

ABOUT THE AUTHORS

All authors are with the College of Public Health, East Tennessee State University, Johnson City.

CORRESPONDENCE

Correspondence should be sent to Kate Beatty, Lamb Hall 168, PO Box 70623, Johnson City, TN 37614 (e-mail: beattyk@etsu.edu). Reprints can be ordered at http://www.ajph.org by clicking the "Reprints" link.

PUBLICATION INFORMATION

Full Citation: Beatty K, Smith MG, de Jong J, Weber A, Adelli R, Khoury A. Impact of the Choose Well initiative on contraceptive access at federally qualified health centers in South Carolina: a midline evaluation. *Am J Public Health*. 2023; 113(11):1167–1172.

Acceptance Date: July 2, 2023.

DOI: https://doi.org/10.2105/AJPH.2023.307384

CONTRIBUTORS

K. Beatty led the project. K. Beatty and M. G. Smith generated the article concept and approved the article. M. G. Smith is the Choose Well evaluation director and developed the analysis plan. J. de Jong managed the research project and collected and analyzed the data. J. de Jong, A. Weber, R. Adelli, and A. Khoury drafted the article. A. Weber edited the article. R. Adelli analyzed the data. A. Khoury is the research center director.

ACKNOWLEDGMENTS

This study was funded by an anonymous philanthropic organization.

CONFLICTS OF INTEREST

The authors have no conflicts of interest to disclose.

HUMAN PARTICIPANT PROTECTION

This study was approved by the East Tennessee State University institutional review board.

REFERENCES

1. New Morning. Our Work—Choose Well SC. 2021. Available at: https://choosewellsc.org/our-work. Accessed December 13, 2021.
2. Smith MG, Hale N, Kelley S, Satterfield K, Beatty KE, Khoury AJ. South Carolina's Choose Well initiative to reduce unintended pregnancy: rationale, implementation design, and evaluation methodology. *Am J Public Health*. 2022;112(suppl 5):S484–S489. https://doi.org/10.2105/AJPH.2022.306889
3. Secura GM, Allsworth JE, Madden T, Mullersman JL, Peipert JF. The Contraceptive CHOICE Project: reducing barriers to long-acting reversible contraception. *Am J Obstet Gynecol*. 2010;203(2):115.e1–115.e7. https://doi.org/10.1016/j.ajog.2010.04.017
4. Bixby Center for Global and Reproductive Health. *Reducing Unintended Pregnancies in Iowa by Investing in Title X Clinics*. Los Angeles, CA; 2012.
5. Colorado Department of Public Health & Environment. Colorado's success with long-acting reversible contraception (LARC). 2021. Available at: https://cdphe.colorado.gov/fpp/about-us/colorados-success-long-acting-reversible-contraception-larc. Accessed December 20, 2021.
6. Skracic I, Lewin AB, Roy KM. Evaluation of the Delaware Contraceptive Access Now (DelCAN) initiative: a qualitative analysis of site leaders' implementation recommendations. *Contraception*. 2021;104(2):211–215. https://doi.org/10.1016/j.contraception.2021.03.015
7. Hasstedt K. Federally qualified health centers: vital sources of care. No substitute for the family planning safety net. *Guttmacher Policy Review*. 2017;20:6. Available at: https://www.guttmacher.org/gpr/2017/05/federally-qualified-health-centers-vital-sources-care-no-substitute-family-planning. Accessed July 31, 2023.
8. Wood S, Beeson T, Bruen B, et al. Scope of family planning services available in federally qualified health centers. *Contraception*. 2014;89(2):85–90. https://doi.org/10.1016/j.contraception.2013.09.015
9. Office of Population Affairs. *Title X Family Planning Directory*. June 2023. Available at: https://opa.hhs.gov/sites/default/files/2023-07/Title_X_Directory_June_2023_508v2.pdf. Accessed July 31, 2023.
10. Beeson T, Wood S, Bruen B, Goldberg DG, Mead H, Rosenbaum S. Accessibility of long-acting reversible contraceptives (LARCs) in federally qualified health centers (FQHCs). *Contraception*. 2014;89(2):91–96. https://doi.org/10.1016/j.contraception.2013.09.014
11. Bornstein M, Carter M, Zapata L, Gavin L, Moskosky S. Access to long-acting reversible contraception among US publicly funded health centers. *Contraception*. 2018;97(5):405–410. https://doi.org/10.1016/j.contraception.2017.12.010
12. de Bocanegra HT, Maguire F, Hulett D, Horsley K, Puffer M, Brindis CD. Enhancing service delivery through Title X funding: findings from California. *Perspect Sex Reprod Health*. 2012;44(4):262–269. https://doi.org/10.1363/4426212
13. White K, Potter JE, Kopkins K, Grossman D. Variation in postpartum contraceptive method use: results from the Pregnancy Risk Assessment Monitoring System (PRAMS). *Contraception*. 2014;89(1):57–62. https://doi.org/10.1016/j.contraception.2013.10.005
14. Kaiser Family Foundation. Status of state Medicaid expansion decisions: interactive map. May 8, 2023. Available at: https://www.kff.org/medicaid/issue-brief/status-of-state-medicaid-expansion-decisions-interactive-map. Accessed May 18, 2023.
15. National Conference of State Legislatures. State legislator demographics. December 1, 2020. Available at: https://www.ncsl.org/about-state-legislatures/state-legislator-demographics. Accessed May 18, 2023.
16. Guttmacher Institute. State facts about unintended pregnancy: South Carolina. 2016. Available at: https://www.guttmacher.org/sites/default/files/factsheet/sc_8_0.pdf. Accessed May 13, 2020.
17. Guttmacher Institute. State facts about unintended pregnancy: Alabama. 2014. Available at: https://www.guttmacher.org/sites/default/files/factsheet/al_15.pdf. Accessed January 10, 2022.
18. County Health Rankings and Roadmaps. % Rural in Alabama. 2021. Available at: https://www.countyhealthrankings.org/app/alabama/2021/measure/factors/58/data. Accessed January 27, 2022.
19. County Health Rankings and Roadmaps. % Rural in South Carolina. 2021. Available at: https://www.countyhealthrankings.org/explore-health-rankings/south-carolina/data-and-resources. Accessed July 27, 2021.
20. DePietro A. US poverty rate by state in 2021. *Forbes Magazine*. November 4, 2021. Available at: https://www.forbes.com/sites/andrewdepietro/2021/11/04/us-poverty-rate-by-state-in-2021/?sh=6326d1061b38. Accessed January 27, 2022.
21. US Census Bureau. QuickFacts: Alabama. Available at: https://www.census.gov/quickfacts/AL. Accessed February 1, 2022.
22. US Census Bureau. QuickFacts: South Carolina. Available at: https://www.census.gov/quickfacts/SC. Accessed February 2, 2022.
23. Frost JJ, Gold RB, Frohwirth LF, Blades N. Variation in service delivery practices among clinics providing publicly funded family planning services in 2010. May 2012. Available at: https://www.guttmacher.org/report/variation-service-

delivery-practices-among-clinics-providing-publicly-funded-family-planning. Accessed July 31, 2023.

24. Hale N, Smith M, Baker K, Khoury A. Contraceptive use patterns among women of reproductive age in two Southeastern states. *Womens Health Issues.* 2020;30(6):436–445. https://doi.org/10.1016/j.whi.2020.08.005
25. Hale N, Manalew WS, Leinaar E, et al. Contraceptive use and pregnancy outcomes among women enrolled in South Carolina Medicaid programs. *Matern Child Health J.* 2021;25(12):1960–1971. https://doi.org/10.1007/s10995-021-03260-x.
26. Sharma P, Sen B, Hale N, Manalew W, Leinaar E, Khoury A. Contraception use and pregnancy outcomes for Alabama Medicaid enrollees: a baseline analysis using 2012–2017 data. *South Med J.* 2022;115(12):899–906. https://doi.org/10.14423/SMJ.0000000000001482
27. Frost JJ, Zolna MR, Frohwirth LF, et al. Publicly supported family planning services in the United States: likely need, availability and impact, 2016. Available at: https://www.guttmacher.org/report/publicly-supported-FP-services-US-2016. Accessed July 31, 2023.

2021, SOFTCOVER, 250 PP
ISBN: 978-0-87553-319-3

APHABOOKSTORE.ORG

Public Health Under Siege: Improving Policy in Turbulent Times

Edited by: Brian C. Castrucci, DrPH, Georges C. Benjamin, MD, Grace Guerrero Ramirez, MSPH, Grace Castillo, MPH

This new book focuses on the importance of health policy through a variety of perspectives, and addresses how policy benefits society, evidently through increased life expectancy and improved health. The book describes how detrimental social determinants can be to the overall population health and emphasizes how the nation is centered on policy change to create equal health care opportunities for all sectors of health.

APHA PRESS
AN IMPRINT OF AMERICAN PUBLIC HEALTH ASSOCIATION

Environmental Injustice and Cumulative Environmental Burdens in Neighborhoods Near Oil and Gas Development: Los Angeles County, California, and Beyond

Nicole C. Deziel, PhD, MHS

ABOUT THE AUTHOR

Nicole C. Deziel is with the Department of Environmental Health Sciences, Yale School of Public Health, New Haven, CT.

See also Oil and Gas: Environmental Justice, pp. 1173–1200.

Residential proximity to oil and gas wells has been increasingly recognized to threaten the health and environmental quality of nearby communities. There are nearly 1 000 000 onshore oil and gas wells in operation and approximately 18 million US residents living within 1600 meters (one mile) of an active oil or gas well, placing them in the path of multiple hazards.[1] Much of the oil and gas activity is occurring in the state of California, where more than one million residents live within one kilometer of an active well.[1]

Living near active oil and gas wells has been associated with a range of health problems, such as increased adverse pregnancy outcomes, childhood cancer incidence, hospitalizations, asthma exacerbations, mental health issues, and mortality in the elderly.[2] Oil and gas development contributes to air pollution, noise, odors, water contamination, and ecological disruption.[2]

Several studies, often focusing on more rural areas, have shown that oil and gas wells and their associated hazards are not distributed equally across communities. This issue of *AJPH* presents a new environmental justice study that took a detailed look at Los Angeles County, the most populous county in the nation, which also has thousands of oil and gas wells. Chan et al. (p. 1182) found that oil and gas wells are disproportionately located in areas already burdened by multiple socio-environmental hazards and that have a higher proportion of Black residents.

The combination of numerous environmental hazards and social stressors has long been understood to contribute to heightened health risks and health disparities.[3] Spatial methods and policy tools for analyzing and visualizing the intersection of these hazards have advanced in recent years, with California leading the way with its California Environmental Justice Screening Tool (CalEnviroScreen). Chan et al. leveraged CalEnviroScreen to evaluate socio-environmental factors related to having an oil or gas well within one kilometer of a census block centroid. The results were striking: census blocks with the highest quintile of pollution burden had four times the odds of having an active or idle oil and gas well within one kilometer compared with the lowest quintile in multivariable models. After adjusting for other factors, a 10% increase in the number of Black residents was associated with a statistically significant 1.17-times-greater odds of having a nearby active or idle oil or gas well. The authors point out that the effect size for race was greater than that of other demographic factors, emphasizing the role of environmental racism.

These new results amplify findings observed in other states. In Texas, oil and gas wastewater disposal wells were more likely to be sited in communities of color,[4] and Hispanic populations were more likely to be exposed to flaring, a practice of burning excess gas yielding light at night, noise, and noxious odors.[5] In Ohio, oil and gas waste wells were disproportionately sited in areas of lower income.[6] Communities with high proportions of lower-income and elderly individuals in rural areas were found to be more vulnerable to groundwater pollution from unconventional oil and gas drilling in the Appalachian Basin.[7] A statewide analysis in California from 2005 to 2019 found that the proportion of Black, Hispanic and Latinx, and low-income people living within one kilometer of oil and gas wells was substantially higher compared with their representation statewide.[8]

AJPH November 2023, Vol 113, No. 11

The Chan et al. study shows that in addition to these distributive injustices with respect to the location of oil and gas wells, communities near oil and gas wells are also facing concurrent exposure to other environmental hazards.

ENHANCING SPATIAL TOOLS FOR DISPARITIES

One notable feature of this study was that it illustrated how screening tools like CalEnviroScreen can and should be adapted to capture additional hazards critical to local communities. The authors emphasized that their analysis required acquisition of additional oil and gas well data from the California Geologic Energy Management Division because petroleum extraction sites are not yet included in the CalEnviroScreen tool. Consideration of oil and gas emissions wells in the tool or other neighborhood-level cumulative burden indices would enable spatial analyses that could help policymakers and community groups visualize or understand the impact of adding new wells or closing or phasing out existing wells.

CONSIDERATIONS REGARDING BOTH ACTIVE AND IDLE WELLS

Another important aspect of the study is the inclusion of idle wells—wells that have not been used for 24 consecutive months but are not properly sealed and therefore can be reactivated. Most health studies have focused on active wells. However, idle wells can release fugitive methane emissions, emit hazardous or odorous air pollutants such as volatile organic compounds and hydrogen sulfide, and contaminate groundwater.[9] Although they are required to be properly sealed when they are no longer intended for use, many oil and gas wells remain idle for years because of the high costs and low operator incentives for plugging. As such, the United States has more than two million orphaned, idle, or abandoned wells.[10,11]

POLICY NEEDS

While the Chan et al. study and other studies help illuminate environmental injustices, they must be followed up with action to reduce disparities and protect public health. Two types of major policy protections are already being enacted in California: (1) setbacks, the allowable distance between an oil and gas well and a sensitive receptor such as homes, schools, and other places where people live, work, and play, and (2) restrictions or phaseouts, eliminating new or existing wells. In August 2022, California passed a landmark bill, Senate Bill 1137, which mandates a one-kilometer (3200-foot) setback between oil and gas wells and sensitive receptors, informed by the body of scientific evidence (https://bit.ly/47TGJY5). Los Angeles County also passed a motion to phase out oil drilling (https://bit.ly/47RHS2m). While setbacks offer critical public health protections to nearby communities, many states have not updated them to reflect the current science. In addition, setbacks are often considered for each industrial source separately and do not necessarily consider cumulative burden. Despite offering critical protections to overburdened communities, attempts to thwart these actions are underway. For example, Senate Bill 1137 has been suspended pending a statewide vote on a referendum supported by the oil and gas industry (https://bit.ly/3sBsyXO).

In their latest *AJPH* article, Chan et al. contribute further evidence of the environmental injustices and cumulative burdens facing fenceline communities in Los Angeles County. The results from this study, in conjunction with other epidemiological and environmental justice literature, provide strong support for policy actions such as setbacks and drilling restrictions, and efforts to delay public health protections place marginalized communities at risk. AJPH

CORRESPONDENCE

Correspondence should be sent to Nicole C. Deziel, Yale School of Public Health, One Church St, Room 628, New Haven, CT 06512 (e-mail: nicole.deziel@yale.edu). Reprints can be ordered at https://ajph.org by clicking the "Reprints" link.

PUBLICATION INFORMATION

Full Citation: Deziel NC. Environmental injustice and cumulative environmental burdens in neighborhoods near oil and gas development: Los Angeles County, California, and beyond. *Am J Public Health*. 2023;113(11):1173–1175.

Acceptance Date: August 15, 2023.

DOI: https://doi.org/10.2105/AJPH.2023.307422

CONFLICTS OF INTEREST

The author reports no conflicts of interest.

REFERENCES

1. Czolowski ED, Santoro RL, Srebotnjak T, Shonkoff SBC. Toward consistent methodology to quantify populations in proximity to oil and gas development: a national spatial analysis and review. *Environ Health Perspect*. 2017;125(8):086004. https://doi.org/10.1289/EHP1535
2. Deziel NC, Clark CJ, Casey JA, Bell ML, Plata DL, Saiers JE. Assessing exposure to unconventional oil and gas development: strengths, challenges, and implications for epidemiologic research. *Curr Environ Health Rep*. 2022;9(3):436–450. https://doi.org/10.1007/s40572-022-00358-4
3. Morello-Frosch R, Zuk M, Jerrett M, Shamasunder B, Kyle AD. Understanding the cumulative impacts of inequalities in environmental health: implications for policy. *Health Aff (Millwood)*. 2011;30(5):879–887. https://doi.org/10.1377/hlthaff.2011.0153
4. Johnston JE, Werder E, Sebastian D. Wastewater disposal wells, fracking, and environmental injustice in Southern Texas. *Am J Public Health*. 2016;106(3):550–556. https://doi.org/10.2105/AJPH.2015.303000

5. Franklin M, Chau K, Cushing LJ, Johnston JE. Characterizing flaring from unconventional oil and gas operations in south Texas using satellite observations. *Environ Sci Technol.* 2019;53(4):2220–2228. https://doi.org/10.1021/acs.est.8b05355
6. Silva GS, Warren JL, Deziel NC. Spatial modeling to identify sociodemographic predictors of hydraulic fracturing wastewater injection wells in Ohio census block groups. *Environ Health Perspect.* 2018;126(6):067008. https://doi.org/10.1289/EHP2663
7. Soriano MA, Jr., Warren JL, Clark CJ, et al. Social vulnerability and groundwater vulnerability to contamination from unconventional hydrocarbon extraction in the Appalachian Basin. *GeoHealth.* 2023;7(4):e2022GH000758. https://doi.org/10.1029/2022GH000758
8. González DJX, Morton CM, Hill LAL, et al. Temporal trends of racial and socioeconomic disparities in population exposures to upstream oil and gas development in California. *GeoHealth.* 2023;7(3):e2022GH000690. https://doi.org/10.1029/2022GH000690
9. El Hachem K, Kang M. Methane and hydrogen sulfide emissions from abandoned, active, and marginally producing oil and gas wells in Ontario, Canada. *Sci Total Environ.* 2022;823:153491. https://doi.org/10.1016/j.scitotenv.2022.153491
10. Saint-Vincent PMB, Sams JI III, Hammack RW, Veloski GA, Pekney NJ. Identifying abandoned well sites using database records and aeromagnetic surveys. *Environ Sci Technol.* 2020;54(13):8300–8309. https://doi.org/10.1021/acs.est.0c00044
11. Boutot J, Peltz AS, McVay R, Kang M. Documented orphaned oil and gas wells across the United States. *Environ Sci Technol.* 2022;56(20):14228–14236. https://doi.org/10.1021/acs.est.2c03268

2021, SOFTCOVER
230 PAGES, 9780875533117

Gun Violence Prevention: A Public Health Approach

Edited By: Linda C. Degutis, DrPH, MSN, and Howard R. Spivak, MD

Gun Violence Prevention: A Public Health Approach acknowledges that guns are a part of the environment and culture. This book focuses on how to make society safer, not how to eliminate guns. Using the conceptual model for injury prevention, the book explores the factors contributing to gun violence and considers risk and protective factors in developing strategies to prevent gun violence and decrease its toll. It guides you with science and policy that make communities safer.

APHABOOKSTORE.ORG

APHA PRESS
AN IMPRINT OF AMERICAN PUBLIC HEALTH ASSOCIATION

Fossil Fuel Racism: The Ongoing Burden of Oil and Gas Development in the Shadows of Regulatory Inaction

Mary D. Willis, PhD, MPH, and Jonathan J. Buonocore, ScD, MS

ABOUT THE AUTHORS

Mary D. Willis is with the Department of Epidemiology and Jonathan J. Buonocore is with the Department of Environmental Health, Boston University School of Public Health, Boston, MA.

See also Oil and Gas: Environmental Justice, pp. 1173–1200.

AJPH November 2023, Vol 113, No. 11

With the slow pace of protective regulatory measures, low-income, racially segregated, or otherwise disadvantaged areas (i.e., persistently marginalized populations) continue to bear the brunt of exposures to oil and gas development and associated infrastructure, a phenomenon often called fossil fuel racism.[1] Two articles in this issue of *AJPH* reveal that, unsurprisingly, the reality of California's Los Angeles County is no different. Berberian et al. (p. 1191) and Chan et al. (p. 1182) conducted environmental justice analyses that show how California's oil and gas development excessively exposes persistently marginalized populations to preventable health-relevant hazards.

Berberian et al. demonstrate higher potential for community water supply contamination from oil and gas development in areas that were historically redlined or are currently racially segregated. This finding is particularly important given the relative research and regulatory focus on air pollution as opposed to water-related pathways. Chan et al. elucidate how neighborhoods with oil and gas development are often colocated with environmental hazards beyond the resource extraction itself (e.g., cleanup sites, hazardous waste facilities, groundwater threats). This demonstrates an inherent issue with regulating environmental hazards "one by one" because many persistently marginalized communities are experiencing a toxic combination of polluting industries, each of which may affect health.

Both studies also find clear evidence that Black communities are particularly affected, reflecting decades of racist land-use policies. This scenario is a prime example of the "double jeopardy" of environmental hazards and structural racism, creating conditions that can exacerbate existing health disparities among different racial/ethnic and socioeconomic groups.[2] Importantly, the recent analyses focus on one component (extraction) of the massive oil and gas supply chain and infrastructure across the United States,[3] therefore likely underestimating the true burden of fossil fuels on persistently marginalized communities.

Time[4] and time[5] and time[6] and time[3] again, scientists have called for stronger public health protective regulation on oil and gas development. Researchers have summarized and synthesized evidence of the health harms from oil and gas development, discussed how oil and gas production is disproportionately sited in persistently marginalized communities, and highlighted shortcomings and inadequacies of existing regulations to protect against health harms from oil and gas development.[3–6] Despite these calls and ongoing community concerns, limited regulation exists and the United States continues its heavy dependence on oil and gas; in fact, the US Energy Information Administration projects that production of both oil and natural gas will continue at its present level through at least the year 2050.[7]

California has recently made admirable, albeit incremental, progress on regulating where oil and gas development is sited (Figure 1).[8] In 2019, the state convened a health-oriented expert panel of epidemiologists, exposure scientists, and toxicologists who were tasked with creating evidence-based policy recommendations related to setback distances (i.e., the distance between an extraction site and a residence, school, nursing home, etc.).[9]

Although the panel determined that a 3200-foot setback distance would be health protective,[9] their final report has not yet come to light. California also plans to stop issuing fracking permits (a subtype of oil and gas development that is relatively uncommon in the state) in 2024 and phase out oil extraction by 2045.[8] However, this regulatory work functionally began in late 2019, almost a decade after the publication of the first peer-reviewed evidence of human health hazards related to modern oil and gas development.[4]

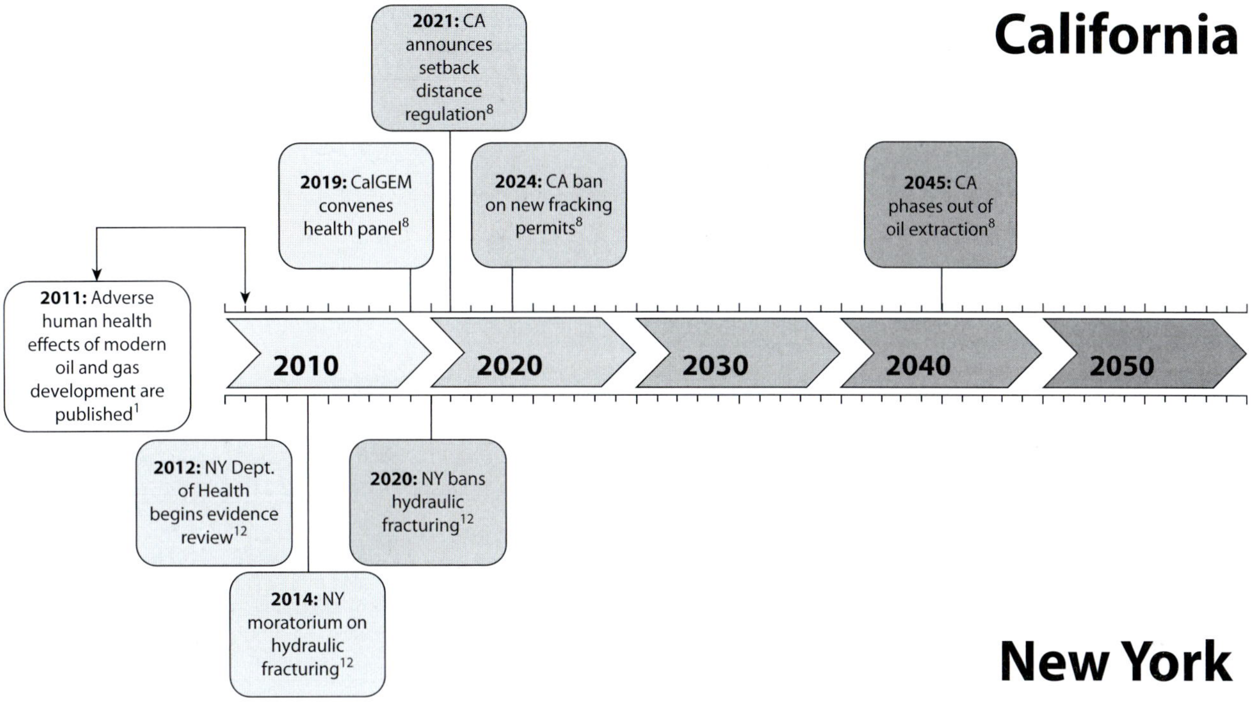

FIGURE 1— A Comparative Timeline of Health-Protective Policy for Oil and Gas Development in California and New York

Note. CalGEM = California Geologic Energy Management Division.

Regulatory implementation will lag even further behind the initial scientific alarm bell.[8] Even more importantly, all of these regulations will likely be delayed even further because of ongoing legal challenges—even California, a liberal state leading on climate change, cannot successfully create health-protective regulations around oil and gas activity.

Meanwhile, as the clock ticks, fossil fuel racism will continue to run rampant.[1] California's regulatory measures offer greater health protection potential than almost any other state, yet the residents are still going to be burdened by two additional decades of fossil fuel hazards before these protections are fully in place. As highlighted by Berberian et al. and Chan et al., these ongoing hazards from fossil fuels will disproportionately affect persistently marginalized populations, particularly Black communities, especially hard.

Although we do not know what exact component of oil and gas development is most toxic (e.g., drilling, frac fluid, flaring, truck traffic), the literature is remarkably consistent across states—oil and gas development harms population health and unduly affects persistently marginalized communities.[3–6,9,10] Although weaker interventions exist,[10] stopping the construction of fossil fuel facilities and retiring existing infrastructure are the most protective measures for public health. Rather than waiting until harms are overwhelmingly apparent, regulatory action could (and should) have been taken at the first evidence of harm.[11] Now, the only remaining opportunity is to prevent further harm.

Outside of California, there are examples of where a precautionary health-protective policy for oil and gas development was implemented, the most notable of which is New York State (Figure 1).[12] A mere two years after the first evidence of potential harm of hydraulic fracturing appeared in the scientific literature in 2012, the New York Department of Health began reviewing the literature on the harms of hydraulic fracturing. Two years after their review commenced, the state of New York announced a moratorium on hydraulic fracturing via an executive order in 2014.[12] This executive order was codified into law in 2020, although other types of extraction remain legal and active. New York's ban was based on evidence of the potential harms to public health. It went in place despite uncertainty and gaps in the evidence, and only four years after the first indications of potential harm from hydraulic fracturing. Most importantly, the executive order explicitly cites the spirit and intent of the precautionary principle in making this decision.[12]

California has codified in regulation the ability to use the precautionary principle in response to evidence of potential public health harms in other domains (e.g., the state's Safer Consumer Products program). In the case of oil and gas production, there exists not just ample evidence of potential health harms, but rigorous, empirical evidence of current health harms. Here, Berberian et al. and Chan et al. provide further evidence of fossil fuel racism running rampant in the case of oil and gas development.[1] Even if this industry was banned tomorrow, a plan would still be needed to dismantle the epic quantity of oil and gas infrastructure across the country, including both the supply and demand sides, to protect communities from the harms of abandoned and legacy infrastructure.[3,6]

What will it take for California to act on these early indications of harm and take action to protect public health from the long-term effects of oil and gas activity? More importantly, what bar of evidence is needed for the Biden administration (or subsequent executives) to act at the federal level, or for state governors to act at the state level? Although we do not know what it will take to pass and implement health-protective regulations, we do know that "lack of evidence" is no longer a legitimate argument against policy action for oil and gas development. AJPH

CORRESPONDENCE

Correspondence should be sent to Mary D. Willis, 715 Albany St, Boston, MA 02118 (e-mail: mwillis1@bu.edu). Reprints can be ordered at http://www.ajph.org by clicking the "Reprints" link.

PUBLICATION INFORMATION

Full Citation: Willis MD, Buonocore JJ. Fossil fuel racism: the ongoing burden of oil and gas development in the shadows of regulatory inaction. *Am J Public Health*. 2023;113(11):1176–1178.

Acceptance Date: July 24, 2023.

DOI: https://doi.org/10.2105/AJPH.2023.307403

CONTRIBUTORS

M. D. Willis and J. J. Buonocore jointly developed the concept and drafted the manuscript.

ACKNOWLEDGMENTS

We would like to express gratitude for excellent research assistance from Erin J. Campbell, BA, BS (Boston University) and Erin N. Polka, MPH (Boston University). We also thank Joan A. Casey, PhD, MA (University of Washington), M. Patricia Fabian, ScD, MS (Boston University), and Patrick Kinney, ScD, MS (Boston University) for insightful comments on an earlier draft.

CONFLICTS OF INTEREST

The authors declare no conflicts of interest related to this article.

REFERENCES

1. Donaghy TQ, Healy N, Jiang CY, Battle CP. Fossil fuel racism in the United States: how phasing out coal, oil, and gas can protect communities. *Energy Res Soc Sci.* 2023;100:103104. https://doi.org/10.1016/j.erss.2023.103104
2. Morello-Frosch R, Shenassa ED. The environmental "riskscape" and social inequality: implications for explaining maternal and child health disparities. *Environ Health Perspect.* 2006; 114(8):1150–1153. https://doi.org/10.1289/ehp.8930
3. Willis MD, Cushing LJ, Buonocore JJ, Deziel NC, Casey JA. It's electric! An environmental equity perspective on the lifecycle of our energy sources. *Environ Epidemiol.* 2023;7(2):e246. https://doi.org/10.1097/EE9.0000000000000246
4. Colborn T, Kwiatkowski CF, Schultz K, Bachran M. Natural gas operations from a public health perspective. *Hum Ecol Risk Assess.* 2011;17(5): 1039–1056. https://doi.org/10.1080/10807039.2011.605662
5. Korfmacher KS, Jones WA, Malone SL, Vinci LF. Public health and high volume hydraulic fracturing. *New Solut.* 2013;23(1):13–31. https://doi.org/10.2190/NS.23.1.c
6. Landrigan PJ, Frumkin H, Lundberg BE. The false promise of natural gas. *N Engl J Med.* 2020; 382(2):104–107. https://doi.org/10.1056/NEJMp1913663
7. US Energy Information Administration. Annual Energy Outlook 2023. Available at: https://www.eia.gov/outlooks/aeo/pdf/AEO2023_Narrative.pdf. Accessed July 5, 2023.
8. Office of Governor, California. California moves to prevent new oil drilling near communities, expand health protections. 2021. Available at: https://www.gov.ca.gov/2021/10/21/california-moves-to-prevent-new-oil-drilling-near-communities-expand-health-protections-2. Accessed July 5, 2023.
9. Shonkoff SBC, Morello-Frosch R, Casey JA, et al. Response to CalGEM questions for the California Oil and Gas Public Health Rulemaking Scientific Advisory Panel. October 1, 2021. Available at: https://www.gov.ca.gov/wp-content/uploads/2021/10/Public-Health-Panel-Memo.pdf. Accessed November 14, 2022.
10. Deziel NC, McKenzie LM, Casey JA, et al. Applying the hierarchy of controls to oil and gas development. *Environ Res Lett.* 2022;17(7):071003. https://doi.org/10.1088/1748-9326/ac7967
11. Woodruff TJ, Rayasam SDG, Axelrad DA, et al. A science-based agenda for health-protective chemical assessments and decisions: overview and consensus statement. *Environ Health.* 2023; 21(suppl 1):132. https://doi.org/10.1186/s12940-022-00930-3
12. New York State Dept of Environmental Conservation. High-volume hydraulic fracturing in NYS. Available at: https://www.dec.ny.gov/energy/75370.html. Accessed July 5, 2023.

A Practical, Balanced Guide to Understanding Health Insurance

APHA PRESS
AN IMPRINT OF AMERICAN PUBLIC HEALTH ASSOCIATION

Written from the perspective of the consumer, this new text is a comprehensive yet accessible examination of health insurance in the United States.

Instructor exam copies available at **go.jblearning.com/Pozen**

JONES & BARTLETT LEARNING
An Ascend Learning Company

The Imperative of Equitable Protection: Structural Racism and Oil Drilling in Los Angeles

Bhavna Shamasunder, PhD, MES, and Jill E. Johnston, PhD, MS

ABOUT THE AUTHORS

Bhavna Shamasunder is with the Urban & Environmental Policy Department and the Public Health Program, Occidental College, Los Angeles, CA. Jill E. Johnston is with the Department of Population & Public Health Sciences, University of Southern California Keck School of Medicine, Los Angeles.

See also Oil and Gas: Environmental Justice, pp. 1173–1200.

Oil extraction has been ongoing in the Los Angeles basin for more than a century. Starting in the 1890s and reaching a peak in the 1930s, Los Angeles made up nearly half of California's oil output and nearly one quarter of the world's oil at the time. Today, thousands of active oil wells continue to operate in Los Angeles County, and nearly 10 million residents live alongside wells that are interspersed in close proximity to homes, schools, playgrounds, parks, and hospitals.[1] Idle wells (that have not produced oil recently), plugged wells, and buried wells also remain scattered across southern California's geography and can pose concerns if not properly abandoned.[2] Oil extraction in Los Angeles can adversely affect groundwater as wells operate, are plugged, or are remediated, an issue that has not been at the forefront of regulation, policy, or research.

The oil extraction process produces gaseous emissions of multiple health-hazardous pollutants and can affect soil, water, and air.[3] Chemicals used during the extraction process can be known endocrine disruptors, carcinogens, mutagens, and reproductive and developmental toxins, and a growing public health literature has linked proximity to oil and gas extraction to increased cancer, adverse birth outcomes, neurological harm, and asthma.[4,5] Little to no research has considered how this extensive network of oil extraction in Los Angeles plays a role in drinking water contamination, a central contribution of the article by Berberian et al. (p. 1191), which assesses the vulnerability of groundwater in Los Angeles County from nearby oil wells. Here we situate Berberian et al.'s analysis of drinking water within ongoing considerations of environmental justice and oil drilling in Los Angeles.

STRUCTURAL RACISM AND GROUNDWATER VULNERABILITY

Oil wells in low-income communities of color in Los Angeles often operate much closer to residents than in wealthier neighborhoods, have uncovered as opposed to enclosed fields, lack noise protections, and maintain outdated emissions equipment.[6] In South Los Angeles, a neighborhood that faces cumulative environmental and social burdens, we found lung function to be diminished among residents living close to active or recently idled well sites, even after adjustment for other risk factors such as smoking, asthma, and proximity to a freeway.[7] Despite southern California's considerable reliance on groundwater, effects on community water systems (CWSs) from extensive nearby oil drilling have been underconsidered.

Berberian et al. provide a screening-level assessment of the potential contamination of drinking water systems from oil operations near active and former oil sites in Los Angeles County, including whether historic redlining practices and current-day residential segregation may be predictors of vulnerability (defined by the authors as living within one kilometer of an active or idle oil well). Groundwater contamination from oil and gas development has been a concern around the country including in Ohio, Pennsylvania, Colorado, Texas, and Wyoming, where studies have shown evidence of volatile organic compounds, trace elements, and other organic compounds, some of which are known endocrine disruptors, carcinogens, neurotoxins, or developmental toxins. Factors such as well failures, poor maintenance, and failure to properly plug idle wells can cause contaminants to migrate to underground drinking water sources.

Berberian et al. found that almost a quarter of Los Angeles County's CWSs serving more than seven million residents have drinking water supply wells located within one kilometer of an active or idle well, a proximity that increases the possibility of contamination. CWSs that have a greater reliance

AJPH November 2023, Vol 113, No. 11

on groundwater than purchased water are considered more vulnerable. Racial/ethnic composition, residential segregation, and historic redlining were significant predictors of drinking water risk from oil development. CWSs with higher proportions of Hispanic, Black, and Asian/Pacific Islander residents; a higher proportion of their service area redlined in the 1930s; or a higher degree of present-day racialized economic segregation were more likely to have oil wells within one kilometer of their drinking water supply wells.

Berberian et al.'s work draws attention to the importance of a focus on groundwater-dependent water systems in Los Angeles County as they operate near active and idle oil wells. The study raises concern over potential contamination of these drinking water resources, particularly those that are proximate to oil wells and located in communities that have been vulnerable to structural racism. The Berberian et al. screening-level analysis suggests that additional investigation into CWSs nearby active and idle wells is warranted.

Thus, to facilitate community engagement and prioritization given that these wells are dispersed across a vast county, it would be useful to have a detailed list of examined CWSs and their locations. This type of assessment can also help prioritize which CWSs may be most vulnerable and should thus be monitored and undergo testing for relevant contaminants. Communities that contend with historic or present-day racism or segregation and rely on CWSs using groundwater resources should be a priority in ongoing efforts to ensure that idle wells are properly abandoned and that health protections from active wells are enforced.

TOWARD ENVIRONMENTAL JUSTICE NEARBY OIL EXTRACTION

Low-income communities of color in Los Angeles bear a disproportionate burden of hazardous facility siting, including active oil extraction nearby homes, schools, hospitals, and playgrounds (Chan et al., p. 1182).[1] Redlining and related discriminatory lending practices have structured residential housing since the 1930s,[8] and today Los Angeles remains highly segregated. Oil extraction has shaped the Los Angeles landscape and has persisted through early worker and resident protests[9] and decades of racialized policies that reshaped land use and residential land access.[10] Data suggest that historically redlined areas contend with a greater density of oil wells[11] and suffer from higher rates of health burdens such as asthma.[12]

Over the past decade, a coalition of frontline environmental justice communities have sought remedy from active oil drilling in their neighborhoods.[6] Their sustained efforts have led to victories, including recent ordinances by the county board of supervisors and the Los Angeles city council to phase out oil drilling over the next two decades. Increased attention and state resources have been directed to properly capping and remediating orphaned wells that have been improperly abandoned and are now wards of the state. Berberian et al. add drinking water to existing and ongoing concerns over oil development in Los Angeles.

Protecting the quality and usability of scarce water resources in the American West has become ever more pressing. The challenges posed by oil extraction nearby CWSs raises the importance of gathering data on how CWS groundwater may be affected by proximate active and idle wells. Drinking water should be included in efforts to reduce public health harm from neighborhood oil extraction as a means of ensuring equitable access to healthy neighborhoods and the right to clean water. AJPH

CORRESPONDENCE

Correspondence should be sent to Bhavna Shamasunder, 1600 Campus Rd, MS-M1, Occidental College, Los Angeles, CA 90041 (e-mail: bhavna@oxy.edu). Reprints can be ordered at http://www.ajph.org by clicking the "Reprints" link.

PUBLICATION INFORMATION

Full Citation: Shamasunder B, Johnston JE. The imperative of equitable protection: structural racism and oil drilling in Los Angeles. *Am J Public Health*. 2023;113(11):1179–1181.

Acceptance Date: July 26, 2023.

DOI: https://doi.org/10.2105/AJPH.2023.307405

CONTRIBUTORS

B. Shamasunder conceptualized the editorial. The authors jointly wrote the editorial.

ACKNOWLEDGMENTS

Our work has been supported in part by a grant from the National Institute of Environmental Health Sciences (ES033478).

Thanks to Emma Silber for her helpful edits.

REFERENCES

1. Sadd J, Shamasunder B. Oil extraction in Los Angeles: health, land use, and environmental justice consequence. In: *Drilling Down: The Community Consequences of Expanded Oil Development in Los Angeles.* Los Angeles, CA: Liberty Hill Foundation; 2015:7–14.
2. Townsend-Small A, Hoschouer J. Direct measurements from shut-in and other abandoned wells in the Permian Basin of Texas indicate some wells are a major source of methane emissions and produced water. *Environ Res Lett.* 2021;16(5):054081. https://doi.org/10.1088/1748-9326/abf06f
3. Garcia-Gonzales DA, Shonkoff SBC, Hays J, Jerrett M. Hazardous air pollutants associated with upstream oil and natural gas development: a critical synthesis of current peer-reviewed literature. *Annu Rev Public Health.* 2019;40:283–304. https://doi.org/10.1146/annurev-publhealth-040218-043715
4. Johnston JE, Lim E, Roh H. Impact of upstream oil extraction and environmental public health: a review of the evidence. *Sci Total Environ.* 2019;657:187–199. https://doi.org/10.1016/j.scitotenv.2018.11.483
5. Deziel NC, Brokovich E, Grotto I, et al. Unconventional oil and gas development and health

outcomes: a scoping review of the epidemiological research. *Environ Res.* 2020;182:109124. https://doi.org/10.1016/j.envres.2020.109124

6. Liberty Hill Foundation. The power of persistence: the fight to end neighborhood oil drilling in Los Angeles. Available at: https://libertyhill-assets-2.s3-us-west-2.amazonaws.com/media/documents/STAND_LA_2022_Drilling_Down_Report_LR_online.pdf. Accessed June 20, 2023.
7. Johnston JE, Enebish T, Eckel SP, Navarro S, Shamasunder B. Respiratory health, pulmonary function and local engagement in urban communities near oil development. *Environ Res.* 2021;197:111088. https://doi.org/10.1016/j.envres.2021.111088
8. Lipsitz G. *How Racism Takes Place.* Philadelphia, PA: Temple University Press; 2011.
9. Quam-Wickham N. "Cities sacrificed on the altar of oil": popular opposition to oil development in 1920s Los Angeles. *Environ Hist.* 1998;3(2):189–209. https://doi.org/10.2307/3985379
10. Logan JR, Molotch H. *Urban Fortunes: The Political Economy of Place, 20th Anniversary Edition, With a New Preface.* Berkeley, CA: University of California Press; 2007.
11. Gonzalez DJX, Nardone A, Nguyen AV, Morello-Frosch R, Casey JA. Historic redlining and the siting of oil and gas wells in the United States. *J Expo Sci Environ Epidemiol.* 2023;33(1):76–83. https://doi.org/10.1038/s41370-022-00434-9
12. Nardone A, Casey JA, Morello-Frosch R, Mujahid M, Balmes JR, Thakur N. Associations between historical residential redlining and current age-adjusted rates of emergency department visits due to asthma across eight cities in California: an ecological study. *Lancet Planet Health.* 2020;4(1):e24–e31. https://doi.org/10.1016/S2542-5196(19)30241-4

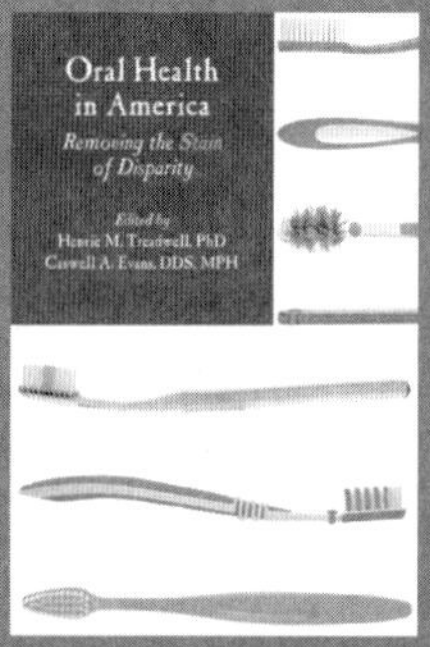

Oral Health in America: Removing the Stain of Disparity

Edited by: Henrie M. Treadwell, PhD and Caswell A. Evans, DDS, MPH

Oral Health in America details inequities to an oral health care system that disproportionately affects the poor, those without insurance, underrepresented and underserved communities, the disabled, and senior citizens. This book addresses issues in workforce development including the use of dental therapists, the rationale for the development of racially/ethnically diverse providers, and the lack of public support through Medicaid, which would guarantee access and also provide a rationale for building a system, one that takes into account the impact of a lack of visionary and inclusive leadership on the nation's ability to insure health justice for all.

Place orders at **aphabookstore.org**. Email **bookstoreservices@apha.org** to request exam copy for classroom use.

ISBN: 978-087553-3056 2019, Softcover List Price: $30 APHA Member Price: $21

APHA PRESS
AN IMPRINT OF AMERICAN PUBLIC HEALTH ASSOCIATION

Social and Environmental Stressors of Urban Oil and Gas Facilities in Los Angeles County, California, 2020

Marissa Chan, SM, Bhavna Shamasunder, PhD, MES, and Jill E. Johnston, PhD, SM

See also Oil and Gas: Environmental Justice, pp. 1173–1200.

Objectives. To examine patterns of cumulative environmental injustice with respect to operations of urban oil and gas development in Los Angeles County, California.

Methods. Using CalEnviroScreen (CES) 4.0, oil and gas data permit records, and US census data, we examined the association between CES score (grouped into equal quintiles, with the lowest representing low cumulative burden) and oil and gas development (presence or absence of an oil and gas production well) within 1 kilometer of a census block centroid.

Results. Among census blocks in the highest quintile of CES score, we observed 94% increased odds of being within 1 kilometer of a well compared with census blocks in the lowest quintile of CES score (odds ratio = 1.94; 95% confidence interval = 1.83, 2.10). In our multivariable model, the proportion of Black residents and higher quintiles of CES score were also associated with increased odds of a nearby oil and gas well.

Conclusions. These findings suggest that oil and gas facilities are operating in neighborhoods already cumulatively burdened and with higher proportions of Black residents. (*Am J Public Health*. 2023;113(11): 1182–1190. https://doi.org/10.2105/AJPH.2023.307360)

AJPH November 2023, Vol 113, No. 11

Social inequalities and discriminatory policies related to race, ethnicity, and socioeconomic status have led to spatial patterning in health risk factors. Certain groups, including Hispanic and Black populations, are disproportionately exposed to environmental hazards such as air pollutants and industrial facilities, and to place-based social stressors such as poverty, substandard housing quality (e.g., lead paint), and neighborhood deprivation.[1] These cumulative environmental exposures and social stressors can be experienced at the neighborhood level and contribute to health inequities.[2] In response to evidence that environmental pollutants and population vulnerabilities may jointly contribute to adverse health outcomes, methods have been developed to assess cumulative burden at a neighborhood scale.[3]

In the past decades, the United States experienced rapid growth in domestic oil and gas (OG) production, extracting from more than 1 million active onshore OG wells.[4] OG development produces a range of environmental hazards including noise and chemicals that can be distributed across and persist in neighborhood-level air, water, and soil.[5,6] These pollutants include known irritants, carcinogens, and endocrine disruptors and can be volatilized or aerosolized via active evaporating pits, flares, surface spills, acidization, processing, and transportation.[5] Studies in communities living near petroleum activity have observed adverse health impacts associated with OG extraction such as worse birth outcomes,[7] adverse respiratory impacts,[8] and a range of acute health symptoms.[9] Previous research, predominantly based in rural communities facing new hydraulic fracturing, suggests distributive injustices in populations living near OG development.[10–12] However, there is limited research examining the existing cumulative burdens facing urban neighborhoods near OG facilities.

Los Angeles (LA) County, California, has one of the highest concentrations of petroleum extraction facilities in the world with thousands of OG wells spanning 70 communities.[13] The oil industry in LA County has operated for longer than a century. By the mid-1920s,

LA County was the largest oil-exporting region in the world.[14] As government and industry negotiated to continue oil drilling within residential zones, oil extraction in LA County became increasingly hidden from public view, often by utilizing tall walls or hedges, and consolidating operations into fewer neighborhoods.[15] LA County currently requires no buffers or setbacks between oil extraction and homes. Recent research in LA County has documented unparalleled proximity and density of urban OG drilling and potential impacts on community health.[8,16]

LA County has a distinct residential and industrial landscape that has resulted in residential neighborhoods adjacent to multiple environmental hazards.[17] These neighborhood-level hazards may contribute to the disparities in health outcomes experienced by certain communities in LA County.[18] While growing evidence demonstrates the health impacts of living proximate to OG development, OG emissions are not yet considered a part of the environmental hazards that may burden low-income communities of color in cumulative burden metrics. Thus, we examined whether OG development was more likely to occur in environmentally burdened and socially vulnerable neighborhoods in LA County.

METHODS

We examined the location of onshore OG production wells in LA County with respect to the cumulative environmental hazard and social vulnerability score of the neighborhood.

Oil and Gas Data

The location and information about all OG wells were retrieved from California Geologic Energy Management Division.[19] We extracted the well location, American Petroleum Institute identification number, well status (active, idle, closed), and well production type. We included both active (drilled and completed wells) and idle wells (wells that have not been used for 24 consecutive months but have also not been properly plugged and abandoned, so they can be reactivated[19]) in our analysis. We included OG wells classified as active or idle as of May 30, 2020, in the analysis (Figure A, available as a supplement to the online version of this article at https://ajph.org). We extracted monthly OG production volumes from 2010 through 2019 from Enverus.[20]

Cumulative Vulnerability Score

Our primary analysis examined the presence of OG wells in relation to CalEnviroScreen (CES) 4.0 score. CES is a tool to identify and map the combined environmental hazards and social burden of communities.[3] The racial/ethnic composition of the census tract is not considered in the development of CES. CES ranks every populated census tract in California based on 13 indicators of pollution burden and 8 indicators of population characteristics, which are described in detail elsewhere.[3] While OG hazards are not explicitly included in the CES pollution burden indicators (other than production ponds from well stimulation activity in the groundwater threats indicator), OG production contributes to neighborhood-level hazards and emissions.[21,22] We extracted CES 4.0 data from the CA Office of Environmental Health Hazard Assessment in December 2021. We assigned tract-level CES scores to each census block in the study area.

Study Area and Exposure

We abstracted census block (referred to as "blocks" from here on) demographic and population data from the IPUMS National Historical Geographic Information System based on the 2010 US Census.[23] We included all populated blocks in LA County. No wells were identified on Santa Catalina and San Clemente islands, and, thus, they were excluded. We considered a block to be near a well if the centroid of the block was located within a 1-kilometer circular buffer of an active or idle OG well. One kilometer was selected as the primary buffer distance based on the growing body of evidence in California suggesting adverse health impacts at a minimum of 1 kilometer from extraction sites.[7,8] In addition, we calculated the total well count and the combined production of OG for wells within a 1-kilometer buffer of each block centroid. We calculated production volumes for active OG wells by converting the gas production into barrels of oil equivalent (BOE) and then summing it with the oil production.[7]

Statistical Analysis

We examined the association between CES score and race/ethnicity (10% increase in the proportion of Hispanic, Black, and Asian residents in a block) with the presence or absence of an OG production well within 1 kilometer of a block centroid separately, using univariable logistic regression models. We included race/ethnicity based on its absence in CES. We included communities of color that comprised at least 5% of the total population in LA County. We also examined a multivariable model that included CES score and race/ethnicity. We grouped CES scores into equal quintiles with the lowest indicating the lowest environmental and social burden.

We further disaggregated CES score into the 2 main components and considered the association between pollution burden, population characteristics, and race/ethnicity with the presence or absence of a well within 1 kilometer. In addition, we examined the change in the number of OG production wells using a negative binomial model. We assessed the average annual OG production (annualized BOE volume 2010–2019) with respect to CES score through a linear regression model. We replicated the methods at 500 meters and 1.5 kilometers as sensitivity analyses. Lastly, as a sensitivity analysis, we used a generalized linear mixed model with a logit link to examine the association between quintiles of CES score and the presence of an OG well within 1 kilometer. This model included a random intercept for census tract and addressed spatial autocorrelation using a spherical correlation structure. All models employed robust standard errors when possible. We conducted the statistical analyses using Stata IC version 16 (StataCorp LP, College Station, TX) and R version 4.1.1 (R Foundation for Statistical Computing, Vienna, Austria).

RESULTS

There were 109 115 total blocks in LA County, with 75 048 (68.8%) containing 1 or more residents. For populated blocks, the median number of residents per block was 85 (interquartile range = 115). We identified 5576 active and idle OG wells in the study area. Of those wells, a total of 124 million BOE were produced between 2010 and 2019. In total, 947 blocks contained at least 1 well, and 108 168 blocks had no wells. In addition, 2962 blocks, 7614 blocks, and 13 318 blocks were located within 500 meters, 1 kilometer, and 1.5 kilometers of an active or idle OG well, respectively. Among the blocks near an active or idle well (within 1 kilometer), the median number of wells was 2 with a range from 1 to 621 (1st percentile = 1 well; 25th = 1; 50th = 2; 75th = 15; and 99th = 313). Approximately 500 000 residents lived in blocks scoring in the highest quintile of CES score in LA County (among the most cumulatively burdened in California; 90th–100th percentile) and were located within 1 kilometer of an active or idle OG well (Table 1). Of the Black residents, Hispanic residents, and Asian residents living in the most cumulatively burdened neighborhoods (highest CES score quintile), 32.0% of the Black residents, 21.5% of the Hispanic residents, and 29.6% of the Asian residents lived within 1 kilometer of an active or idle OG well, respectively.

We observed a 94% increased odds of being within 1 kilometer of an active or idle well among blocks in the highest CES quintile as compared with blocks in the lowest CES quintile (odds ratio [OR] = 1.94; 95% confidence interval [CI] = 1.83, 2.05; Table 2). The ORs were higher among all blocks with scores in the second through fifth quintiles compared with the lowest quintile. In the univariable race/ethnicity model, each 10% increase in the proportion of Black residents was associated with 16% increased odds of an active or idle well within 1 kilometer (OR = 1.16; 95% CI = 1.15, 1.17). Positive but smaller ORs were reported for each 10% increase in Asian (OR = 1.05; 95% CI = 1.04, 1.06) and Hispanic (OR = 1.02; 95% CI = 1.02, 1.03) residents. Furthermore, the multivariable results followed a similar pattern with both 10% increases in the proportion of Black and Asian populations and higher quintiles of CES score associated with an increased odds of an OG well nearby. For example, we observed a 112% increase in the odds of a nearby active or idle well among the highest quintile of CES score compared with the lowest quintile (OR = 2.12; 95% CI = 1.97, 2.28). However, a small decreased odds of a nearby active or idle well was observed for each 10% increase in the proportion of Hispanic residents (OR = 0.97; 95% CI = 0.96, 0.97).

Secondary Analysis

Table 3 presents the ORs for the presence of an OG well within 1 kilometer from the multivariable model incorporating both quintiles of pollution burden and population characteristics, and racial/ethnic composition. Blocks in the highest quintile of pollution burden had a 315% increased odds of a nearby active or idle OG well compared with blocks in the lowest quintile (OR = 4.15; 95% CI = 3.86, 4.47). We did not observe notable associations based on population characteristics for almost all the CES quintiles—yet the highest quintile of population characteristics had a lower odds of a nearby well (OR = 0.56; 95% CI = 0.51, 0.60). In comparison, each 10% increase in Black residents was associated with significantly increased odds of a nearby active or idle well (OR = 1.17; 95% CI = 1.16, 1.19).

Table 4 presents the rate ratios (RRs) for the change in the number of active and idle OG wells within 1 kilometer from the multivariable model incorporating CES quintiles and racial/ethnic composition. Blocks with CES scores in the highest quintile had an average of 5.91 (95% CI = 5.01, 6.98) more wells compared with blocks with CES scores in the lowest quintile. Similarly, each

AJPH November 2023, Vol 113, No. 11

TABLE 1— Population 500 Meters, 1 Kilometer, and 1.5 Kilometers From an Active or Idle Oil and Gas Well and Total Black, Hispanic, and Asian Residents Within 1 Kilometer of an Active or Idle Oil and Gas Well by CalEnviroScreen (CES) Score Quintile: Los Angeles County, CA

CES Score Quintile (Statewide Percentile Range)	Total Population,[a] No.	Population in Blocks, No.			Total Residents Within 1 km of a Well, No. (%)[b]		
		Within 500 m of a Well	Within 1 km of a Well	Within 1.5 km of a Well	Black	Hispanic	Asian
First (0.29th–34.8th)[c]	1 483 694	74 689	222 250	387 373	5 808 (13.0)	28 811 (13.0)	31 026 (12.9)
Second (34.82nd–55.21st)	1 667 011	149 719	361 942	567 018	23 528 (25.5)	62 988 (14.6)	79 422 (24.9)
Third (55.23rd–74.1st)	1 957 865	137 286	365 247	605 121	49 654 (27.7)	156 827 (18.1)	67 304 (20.6)
Fourth (74.17th–89.7th)	2 353 846	238 018	559 509	935 076	63 313 (27.3)	345 668 (23.9)	75 435 (26.7)
Fifth (89.71st–99.97th)[d]	2 311 566	199 380	532 557	902 109	83 559 (32.0)	368 490 (21.5)	43 917 (29.6)
Total population	9 773 982	799 092	2 041 505	3 396 697	225 862	962 784	297 104

Source. Data from the 2010 US Census,[23] 2021 CalEnviroScreen 4.0,[3] and 2020 California Geologic Energy Management Division.[19]
[a]Total population among census blocks with CES scores.
[b]The percentage of residents of a racial/ethnic group (Black, Hispanic, Asian) within 1 kilometer from an active or idle well in each quintile of CES score. For example, of the Black residents living in the fifth CES score quintile, 32% of them lived within 1 km from an active or idle oil and gas well.
[c]Lowest burden.
[d]Highest burden.

10% increase in the proportion of Black and Asian residents was associated with a slight, but not extremely notable, increase in the number of proximate wells (RR Black = 1.08 wells [95% CI = 1.05, 1.10]; RR Asian = 1.08 wells [95% CI = 1.10, 1.11]). By contrast, we did not observe a notable positive association for Hispanic populations.

The association between CES quintiles and OG production per year was nonmonotonic. Blocks with CES scores in the second, third, fourth, and fifth quintiles were near wells that produced, on average, 7072 (95% CI = 6418, 9525), 3282 (95% CI = 1922, 4642), 5923 (95% CI = 4459, 7286), and 3709 (95% CI = 2246, 5172) more BOE per year, respectively, compared with blocks with CES scores in the lowest quintile.

Sensitivity Analyses

The documented pattern of an increased burden from OG development in blocks already burdened by cumulative neighborhood stressors held when using a 500-meter and 1.5-kilometer buffer. In general, at 500 meters, many of the associations previously reported at 1 kilometer were strengthened (Table A, available as a supplement to the online version of this article at https://ajph.org). At 1.5 kilometers, both higher and lower ORs were observed compared with 1 kilometer (Table B, available as a supplement to the online version of this article at https://ajph.org). Notably, the ORs for higher quintiles of CES in the univariable model and race/ethnicity in both the univariable and multivariable models were slightly higher at 1.5 kilometers compared with 1 kilometer. Finally, the mixed effects model including a random intercept for census tract

TABLE 2— Comparison of the Presence or Absence of an Active or Idle Oil and Gas Well Within 1 Kilometer by CalEnviroScreen (CES) Quintile, by CES and Race/Ethnicity, and by Race/Ethnicity Only: Los Angeles County, CA

	OR (95% CI)
CES quintile	
First (Ref)	1
Second	1.38 (1.30, 1.47)
Third	1.34 (1.27, 1.43)
Fourth	1.82 (1.71, 1.92)
Fifth	1.94 (1.83, 2.05)
CES and race/ethnicity	
First CES quintile (Ref)	1
Second CES quintile	1.39 (1.30, 1.47)
Third CES quintile	1.35 (1.27, 1.44)
Fourth CES quintile	1.93 (1.81, 2.07)
Fifth CES quintile	2.12 (1.97, 2.28)
Proportion Black (10% increase)[a]	1.10 (1.09, 1.12)
Proportion Hispanic (10% increase)[a]	0.97 (0.96, 0.97)
Proportion Asian (10% increase)[a]	1.03 (1.02, 1.04)
Race/ethnicity only (10% increase)[a]	
Proportion Black	1.16 (1.15, 1.17)
Proportion Hispanic	1.02 (1.02, 1.03)
Proportion Asian	1.05 (1.04, 1.06)

Note. CI = confidence interval; OR = odds ratio.
Source. Data from the 2010 US Census,[23] 2021 CalEnviroScreen 4.0,[3] and 2020 California Geologic Energy Management Division.[19]
[a]A 10% increase in the proportion of Hispanic, Black, or Asian residents in a census block.

and accounting for spatial autocorrelation reported slightly higher associations compared with the main models, which supported our findings of an increased odds of the presence of OG activity among higher quintiles of CES score (Table C, available as a supplement to the online version of this article at https://ajph.org). Of note, the 95% CIs between the main and sensitivity analyses overlapped.

DISCUSSION

OG development has an extensive footprint in LA County with wells operating in densely populated urban neighborhoods near homes, schools, playgrounds, and health care facilities.[15] As research has identified higher levels of environmental pollutants near OG extraction sites,[21,24] there has been increasing attention toward identifying the populations at risk and the role proximity to these facilities may play in contributing to adverse health outcomes.[4] Residents in these neighborhoods may be facing exposure to environmental hazards from OG development including poor air quality and noise, in addition to other exposures from other nearby polluting sources.[1] Our analysis observed that higher quintiles of the overall CES score and pollution burden score and higher proportions of Black residents were associated with increased presence of OG operations.

Research in LA County has demonstrated neighborhood-level exposure to these pollutants and environmental toxics near OG operations.[16,21,22] Yet, aside from the consideration of production ponds from well stimulation activities as part of the groundwater threats indicator, the distribution of OG hazards with existing environmental and social stressors has not been considered in statewide metrics for assessing neighborhood-level burden. Statewide air pollution indicators capture regional air pollutants (e.g., ozone and particulate matter that is 2.5 micrometers or smaller in diameter [$PM_{2.5}$]) and have not incorporated neighborhood-level air pollutants (e.g., volatile organic compounds and other hazardous air pollutants) produced by OG operations. Furthermore, the air pollutants incorporated in CES that may be produced by OG operations (diesel PM, $PM_{2.5}$) do not directly correlate with OG development, because these pollutants are produced by other sources (including combustion of gasoline), and they are estimated at a larger scale (e.g., diesel PM at a 1 kilometer × 1 kilometer grid) that may not adequately reflect local, neighborhood-level exposures experienced by communities living, working, or playing near these facilities. Therefore, while OG development contributes to a variety of environmental hazards that are reported to burden certain communities in LA County,[16,21,22] it is not adequately captured in current neighborhood-level exposure metrics.

Environmental justice dimensions of OG development have been less studied, particularly in urban contexts. Previous research has considered questions around neighborhood sociodemographic characteristics, largely in rural communities, with differing

TABLE 3— Multivariable Model of the Presence or Absence of an Active or Idle Oil and Gas Well Within 1 Kilometer by Quintiles of Pollution Burden, Quintiles of Population Characteristics, and 10% Increase in the Proportion of Each Racial/Ethnic Group: Los Angeles County, CA

	OR (95% CI)
Pollution burden	
First quintile (Ref)	1
Second quintile	2.14 (2.00, 2.29)
Third quintile	2.61 (2.44, 2.79)
Fourth quintile	3.32 (3.13, 3.59)
Fifth quintile	4.15 (3.86, 4.47)
Population characteristics	
First quintile (Ref)	1
Second quintile	1.03 (0.97, 1.09)
Third quintile	0.91 (0.86, 0.97)
Fourth quintile	1.00 (0.93, 1.07)
Fifth quintile	0.56 (0.51, 0.60)
Race/ethnicity (10% increase)[a]	
Proportion Black	1.17 (1.16, 1.19)
Proportion Hispanic	1.00 (0.99, 1.00)
Proportion Asian	1.01 (1.00, 1.02)

Note. CI = confidence interval; OR = odds ratio.
Source. Data from the 2010 US Census,[23] 2021 CalEnviroScreen 4.0,[3] and 2020 California Geologic Energy Management Division.[19]
[a]A 10% increase in the proportion of Hispanic, Black, or Asian residents in a census block.

TABLE 4— Multivariable Model of the Change in the Number of Active and Idle Oil and Gas Wells by CalEnviroScreen (CES) Score Quintiles and 10% Increase in the Proportion of Each Racial/Ethnic Group: Los Angeles County, CA

	RR (95% CI)
CES score quintiles	
First (Ref)	1
Second	2.06 (1.85, 2.29)
Third	2.35 (2.05, 2.69)
Fourth	5.14 (4.44, 5.95)
Fifth	5.91 (5.01, 6.98)
Race/ethnicity (10% increase)[a]	
Proportion Black	1.08 (1.05, 1.10)
Proportion Hispanic	0.92 (0.90, 0.94)
Proportion Asian	1.08 (1.06, 1.11)

Note. CI = confidence interval; RR = rate ratio.
Source. Data from the 2010 US Census,[23] 2021 CalEnviroScreen 4.0,[3] and 2020 California Geologic Energy Management Division.[19]
[a]A 10% increase in the proportion of Hispanic, Black, or Asian residents in a census block.

results. A study in Ohio presented evidence that the odds of a block group containing an injection well decreased as median income increased.[11] Similar findings from the Marcellus Shale reported that census tracts near unconventional gas wells had a significantly higher percentage of people below the poverty line compared with census tracts farther away.[25] Researchers examining housing costs and the location of active wells reported lower home values within 500 feet of OG wells in 2 basins that have a history of substantial OG development.[10] An analysis in South Texas reported that neighborhoods with high Hispanic populations were less likely to live within 5 kilometers of active OG development, yet more likely to be near active gas flaring and wastewater wells.[12]

LA County is one of the few regions in the United States where OG extraction occurs in densely populated communities. More than 500 000 residents live in blocks within 1 kilometer of an active or idle well that are also among the most cumulatively burdened in the state (CES score > 90th percentile). Furthermore, we found that blocks with higher quintiles of CES scores had an increased odds of being near OG facilities. Our sensitivity analysis adjusting for spatial autocorrelation presented stronger associations but generally aligned with our main analysis. Past research examining neighborhood-scale environmental injustices suggests that accounting for spatial autocorrelation may produce similar findings.[26]

We observed an increased odds of a nearby (1 kilometer) OG production well with an increase in the proportion of Black residents. These findings support previous research (based on CES 1.1) demonstrating that non-Hispanic Black, Hispanic, Native American,

Asian/Pacific Islander, and multiracial populations were more likely to live in the top 10% of burdened zip codes compared with non-Hispanic White populations.[27] Furthermore, another study that examined disparities in methane super-emitters in California (including dairy, manure, and OG production) reported that increases in the percentage of non-Hispanic Black, Hispanic, and Native American residents was observed to be associated with an increased odds of exposure.[28] By contrast with previous research, we did not find strong associations for the odds of a nearby well with increasing proportions of Hispanic and Asian residents. As Hispanic populations are the largest growing ethnic group in LA County (47.7% of the population in this study), other factors may influence where they live. Future research on OG development in LA County should examine more specific ethnic groups that are predominant in the county instead of using broad racial/ethnic classifications.

Our findings of inequities in the location of OG development based on the proportion of Black residents and CES score (notably pollution burden score) may be attributable to racial, political, and social disenfranchisement where low-income communities and communities of color frequently host undesirable industrial operations and facilities because of a perceived lack of political clout or following the "path of least resistance" because of limited resources.[29] We observed stronger effects based on the racial/ethnic composition of the block rather than the CES population characteristics indicator, pointing to the role of environmental racism as an important factor to consider in the historical locations of OG facilities.

In multiple models, the odds of a nearby OG well were positively associated with the proportion of Black residents, suggesting racial patterning. While some previous research has identified that measures of socioeconomic status are positively associated with OG production,[25] others presented evidence that even after adjusting for poverty, racial disparities in the presence of disposal wells persist—which could indicate that race/ethnicity may be more of a driving factor in the presence of OG development compared with socioeconomic status.[30] Furthermore, higher quintiles of pollution burden were associated with an increased odds of the presence of an OG well. This finding adds to the evidence of LA County being an environmental "riskscape" where multiple polluting facilities and hazardous pollutants are clustered in low-income communities of color.[17]

Limitations

Our analysis focused on available data from the 2010 Census and does not capture changes in population over time. From 2010 to 2020, the population of LA County increased by almost 200 000, which may indicate a larger population at risk depending on migration and housing patterns within the county.[23] We also used blocks for this analysis (the smallest spatial unit) but, without residential parcel data, we do not know the location of residents within blocks. In addition, assigning the tract-level CES score to each block limits our ability to identify block-level disparities. However, CES scores are only available at the census tract level, and we did conduct a sensitivity analysis including a random effect for census tract, which presented slightly stronger results. As with many geospatial analyses using discrete boundaries as the spatial unit, our findings may be limited by the "modifiable areal unit problem." There may also be misclassification of blocks as unexposed based on our categorization of blocks as within 1 kilometer based on the block centroid.

Public Health Implications

Our findings suggest greater proximity to OG development among cumulatively burdened communities, which may result in higher exposures to a range of environmental hazards[5,6] and amplify existing health disparities.[7] Additional research should further explore the associations between cumulatively burdened communities in California and other threats from OG development. Furthermore, future efforts should focus on ensuring that OG operations are included in neighborhood-level cumulative burden indexes because these environmental hazards are not currently adequately captured.

While these actions will help elucidate the environmental hazards found in neighborhoods across California, they will not directly reduce OG-related exposures.[31] Recently, LA County voted to phase out OG production in unincorporated areas, which would reduce exposure burdens from these operations if enacted.[32] The city of Los Angeles also passed a motion to phase out oil drilling in city boundaries over the next 20 years.[33] However, other incorporated cities within the county, such as Carson, would require their own policy response to ongoing oil operations. Policies that aim to reduce exposure at the neighborhood level, such as setbacks and phase-outs, and address existing environmental injustices attributable to OG extraction are central to reduce overall exposures and support the creation of healthier environments for burdened communities. Our findings suggest that OG facilities are operating in neighborhoods already cumulatively burdened and with higher proportions of Black residents and may guide the development of future policies and neighborhood-level indexes aiming to identify communities at risk and reduce cumulative exposures. AJPH

ABOUT THE AUTHORS

Marissa Chan is with the Harvard T. H. Chan School of Public Health, Boston, MA. Bhavna Shamasunder is with Occidental College, Los Angeles, CA. Jill E. Johnston is with the University of Southern California, Los Angeles.

CORRESPONDENCE

Correspondence should be sent to Marissa Chan, SM, Department of Environmental Health, 665 Huntington Ave, Bldg 1, 13th floor, Room 1303, Boston, MA 02115 (e-mail: marissachan@hsph.harvard.edu). Reprints can be ordered at https://ajph.org by clicking the "Reprints" link.

PUBLICATION INFORMATION

Full Citation: Chan M, Shamasunder B, Johnston JE. Social and environmental stressors of urban oil and gas facilities in Los Angeles County, California, 2020. *Am J Public Health*. 2023;113(11):1182–1190.

Acceptance Date: May 25, 2023.

DOI: https://doi.org/10.2105/AJPH.2023.307360

CONTRIBUTORS

M. Chan abstracted the data, conducted data analysis, and prepared the article. B. Shamasunder conceptualized the research question and oversaw the interpretation of the results and article preparation. J. E. Johnston conceptualized the research question and oversaw the abstraction of data, data analysis, interpretation of the results, and article preparation.

ACKNOWLEDGMENTS

This work was supported in part by a grant from the National Institute of Environmental Health Sciences (ES027695).

We thank Khang Chau for the compilation of oil and gas production data and Benjamin MacCormack-Gelles for recommending a statistical model used in our analysis.

CONFLICTS OF INTEREST

The authors have no potential or actual conflicts of interest to report.

HUMAN PARTICIPANT PROTECTION

No human participants were involved.

REFERENCES

1. Morello-Frosch R, Lopez R. The riskscape and the color line: examining the role of segregation in environmental health disparities. *Environ Res*. 2006;102(2):181–196. https://doi.org/10.1016/j.envres.2006.05.007
2. Morello-Frosch R, Zuk M, Jerrett M, Shamasunder B, Kyle AD. Understanding the cumulative impacts of inequalities in environmental health: implications for policy. *Health Aff (Millwood)*. 2011;30(5):879–887. https://doi.org/10.1377/hlthaff.2011.0153
3. Office of Environmental Health Hazard Assessment. CalEnviroScreen 4.0. September 20, 2021. Available at: https://oehha.ca.gov/calenviroscreen/report/calenviroscreen-40. Accessed January 12, 2022.
4. Czolowski ED, Santoro RL, Srebotnjak T, Shonkoff SBC. Toward consistent methodology to quantify populations in proximity to oil and gas development: a national spatial analysis and review. *Environ Health Perspect*. 2017;125(8):086004. https://doi.org/10.1289/EHP1535
5. Garcia-Gonzales DA, Shonkoff SBC, Hays J, Jerrett M. Hazardous air pollutants associated with upstream oil and natural gas development: a critical synthesis of current peer-reviewed literature. *Annu Rev Public Health*. 2019;40(1):283–304. https://doi.org/10.1146/annurev-publhealth-040218-043715
6. Allshouse WB, McKenzie LM, Barton K, Brindley S, Adgate JL. Community noise and air pollution exposure during the development of a multi-well oil and gas pad. *Environ Sci Technol*. 2019;53(12):7126–7135. https://doi.org/10.1021/acs.est.9b00052
7. Tran KV, Casey JA, Cushing LJ, Morello-Frosch R. Residential proximity to oil and gas development and birth outcomes in California: a retrospective cohort study of 2006–2015 births. *Environ Health Perspect*. 2020;128(6):067001. https://doi.org/10.1289/EHP5842
8. Johnston JE, Enebish T, Eckel SP, Navarro S, Shamasunder B. Respiratory health, pulmonary function and local engagement in urban communities near oil development. *Environ Res*. 2021;197:111088. https://doi.org/10.1016/j.envres.2021.111088
9. Rabinowitz PM, Slizovskiy IB, Lamers V, et al. Proximity to natural gas wells and reported health status: results of a household survey in Washington County, Pennsylvania. *Environ Health Perspect*. 2015;123(1):21–26. https://doi.org/10.1289/ehp.1307732
10. McKenzie LM, Allshouse WB, Burke T, Blair BD, Adgate JL. Population size, growth, and environmental justice near oil and gas wells in Colorado. *Environ Sci Technol*. 2016;50(21)11471–11480. https://doi.org/10.1021/acs.est.6b04391
11. Silva GS, Warren JL, Deziel NC. Spatial modeling to identify sociodemographic predictors of hydraulic fracturing wastewater injection wells in Ohio census block groups. *Environ Health Perspect*. 2018;126(6):067008. https://doi.org/10.1289/EHP2663
12. Johnston JE, Chau K, Franklin M, Cushing L. Environmental justice dimensions of oil and gas flaring in South Texas: disproportionate exposure among Hispanic communities. *Environ Sci Technol*. 2020;54(10):6289–6298. https://doi.org/10.1021/acs.est.0c00410
13. Gamache MT, Frost PL. Urban development of oil fields in the LA Basin area, 1983 to 2001. Paper presented at: Society of Petroleum Engineers Western Regional Meeting; May 19–24, 2003; Long Beach, CA. https://doi.org/10.2118/83482-MS
14. Quam-Wickham N. "Cities sacrificed on the altar of oil": popular opposition to oil development in 1920s Los Angeles. *Environ Hist*. 1998;3(2):189–209. https://doi.org/10.2307/3985379
15. Shamasunder B, Blickley J, Chan M, et al. Crude justice: community-based research amid oil development in South Los Angeles. In: Davies T, Mah A, eds. *Toxic Truths: Environmental Justice and Citizen Science in a Post-Truth Age*. Manchester, England: Manchester University Press; 2020:82–98.
16. Shamasunder B, Collier-Oxandale A, Blickley J, et al. Community-based health and exposure study around urban oil developments in South Los Angeles. *Int J Environ Res Public Health*. 2018;15(1):138. https://doi.org/10.3390/ijerph15010138
17. Morello-Frosch R, Pastor M, Sadd J. Environmental justice and Southern California's "riskscape": the distribution of air toxics exposures and health risks among diverse communities. *Urban Aff Rev*. 2016;36(4):551–578. https://doi.org/10.1177/10780870122184993
18. LA County Department of Public Health. Key indicators of health by service planning area. 2017. Available at: http://publichealth.lacounty.gov/ha/docs/2015LACHS/KeyIndicator/PH-KIH_2017-sec%20UPDATED.pdf. Accessed January 24, 2021.
19. California Department of Conservation. Geologic Energy Management Division. Available at: https://www.conservation.ca.gov/calgem. Accessed August 28, 2020.
20. Enverus. Drillinginfo Web App. October 18, 2017. Available at: https://www.enverus.com. Accessed August 28, 2020.
21. Okorn K, Jimenez A, Collier-Oxandale A, Johnston J, Hannigan M. Characterizing methane and total non-methane hydrocarbon levels in Los Angeles communities with oil and gas facilities using air quality monitors. *Sci Total Environ*. 2021;777:146194. https://doi.org/10.1016/j.scitotenv.2021.146194
22. Collier-Oxandale A, Wong N, Navarro S, Johnston J, Hannigan M. Using gas-phase air quality sensors to disentangle potential sources in a Los Angeles neighborhood. *Atmos Environ (1994)*. 2020;233:117519. https://doi.org/10.1016/j.atmosenv.2020.117519
23. National Historical Geographic Information System. IPUMS. Available at: https://www.nhgis.org. Accessed August 30, 2020.
24. Gonzalez DJX, Francis CK, Shaw GM, Cullen MR, Baiocchi M, Burke M. Upstream oil and gas production and ambient air pollution in California. *Sci Total Environ*. 2022;806:150298. https://doi.org/10.1016/j.scitotenv.2021.150298
25. Ogneva-Himmelberger Y, Huang L. Spatial distribution of unconventional gas wells and human populations in the Marcellus Shale in the United States: vulnerability analysis. *Appl Geogr*. 2015;60:165–174. https://doi.org/10.1016/j.apgeog.2015.03.011
26. Chen S, Sleipness OR, Christensen KM, Feldon D, Xu Y. Environmental justice and park quality in an intermountain west gateway community: assessing the spatial autocorrelation. *Landsc Ecol*. 2019;34(10):2323–2335. https://doi.org/10.1007/s10980-019-00891-y

27. Cushing L, Faust J, August LM, Cendak R, Wieland W, Alexeeff G. Racial/ethnic disparities in cumulative environmental health impacts in California: evidence from a statewide environmental justice screening tool (CalEnviroScreen 1.1). *Am J Public Health.* 2015;105(11):2341–2348. https://doi.org/10.2105/AJPH.2015.302643
28. Casey JA, Cushing L, Depsky N, Morello-Frosch R. Climate justice and California's methane superemitters: environmental equity assessment of community proximity and exposure intensity. *Environ Sci Technol.* 2021;55(21):14746–14757. https://doi.org/10.1021/acs.est.1c04328
29. Mohai P, Saha R. Which came first, people or pollution? Assessing the disparate siting and post-siting demographic change hypotheses of environmental injustice. *Environ Res Lett.* 2015;10(11):115008. https://doi.org/10.1088/1748-9326/10/11/115008
30. Johnston JE, Werder E, Sebastian D. Wastewater disposal wells, fracking, and environmental injustice in Southern Texas. *Am J Public Health.* 2016;106(3):550–556. https://doi.org/10.2105/AJPH.2015.303000
31. Department of Conservation Geologic Energy Management Division. Draft rule for protection of communities and workers from health and safety impacts from oil and gas production operations pre-rulemaking release for public review and consultation. Available at: https://www.conservation.ca.gov/calgem/Documents/public-health/PHRM%20Draft%20Rule.pdf. Accessed January 22, 2022.
32. Mitchell HJ, Hahn J. Developing a comprehensive strategy for a just transition away from fossil fuels in Los Angeles County. 2021. Available at: http://file.lacounty.gov/SDSInter/bos/supdocs/161699.pdf. Accessed January 14, 2022.
33. Holly J. Mitchell, Los Angeles County Supervisor, 2nd District. LA County set to launch community air monitoring program and new policies aligned with the state to protect residents during phase out of oil drilling. September 28, 2022. Available at: https://mitchell.lacounty.gov/community-air-monitoring-program. Accessed October 5, 2022.

Our Communities Our Sexual Health

Awareness and Prevention for African Americans

Edited By: Madeline Sutton, MD, MPH;
Jo A. Valentine, MSW; and
William C. Jenkins, PhD, MS, MPH

This groundbreaking book provides a comprehensive historical prospective of the disproportionate burden of HIV and other sexually transmitted infections (STIs) among African Americans.Chapters that follow explore the context of HIV and STIs in African American communities and include discussions of sexuality and the roles of faith and spirituality in HIV and STI prevention efforts. Additional chapters provide insight into strategies, e.g., HIV testing, condom distribution and marketing campaigns, parent-child communication, effective clinical care and support, and partnerships, for addressing HIV and other STI-related health disparities within these communities. The book is a valuable resource for practitioners, scholars, clinicians, educators, providers, policy makers and students.

2016, 283 pp., soft cover
ISBN: 978-0-87553-275-2
Order Online at
www.aphabookstore.org

APHA PRESS
AN IMPRINT OF AMERICAN PUBLIC HEALTH ASSOCIATION

Race, Racism, and Drinking Water Contamination Risk From Oil and Gas Wells in Los Angeles County, 2020

Alique G. Berberian, MPH, MIA, Jenny Rempel, MA, Nicholas Depsky, MS, Komal Bangia, MPH, Sophia Wang, and Lara J. Cushing, PhD, MPH

See also Oil and Gas: Environmental Justice, pp. 1173–1200.

Objectives. To evaluate the potential for drinking water contamination in Los Angeles (LA) County, California, based on the proximity of supply wells to oil and gas wells, and characterize risk with respect to race/ethnicity and measures of structural racism.

Methods. We identified at-risk community water systems (CWSs) as those with supply wells within 1 kilometer of an oil or gas well. We characterized sociodemographics of the populations served by each CWS by using the 2013–2017 American Community Survey. We estimated the degree of redlining in each CWS service area by using 1930s Home Owners' Loan Corporation security maps, and characterized segregation by using the Index of Concentration at the Extremes. Multivariable regression models estimated associations between these variables and CWS contamination risk.

Results. A quarter of LA County CWSs serving more than 7 million residents have supply wells within 1 kilometer of an oil or gas well. Higher percentages of Hispanic, Black, and Asian/Pacific Islander residents and a greater degree of redlining and residential segregation were associated with higher contamination risk.

Conclusions. Redlining and segregation predict drinking water contamination risks from oil development in LA County, with people of color at greater risk. (*Am J Public Health*. 2023;113(11): 1191–1200. https://doi.org/10.2105/AJPH.2023.307374)

AJPH November 2023, Vol 113, No. 11

Oil production in the United States has nearly doubled over the past decade,[1] with more than 17 million people now living within 1 mile of an active oil or gas well.[2] Studies have found evidence of groundwater contamination near oil and gas development from volatile organic compounds (e.g., benzene, toluene, ethylbenzene, and xylenes), trace elements (e.g., arsenic, lead), and other organic compounds (e.g., methane), some of which are known endocrine disruptors, carcinogens, neurotoxins, or developmental toxins.[3–5] Groundwater contamination can result from well and wellbore failures, deterioration, and poor maintenance, or via contamination pathways formed during well stimulation (e.g., acidization, hydraulic fracturing or "fracking"). Idle wells can be conduits for contaminants from active wells to migrate to underground drinking water sources,[6] and deteriorating cement and steel casings in high-pressure storage wells can cause leaks.[7]

Fossil fuel development in California is concentrated in neighborhoods with higher proportions of people of color and lower socioeconomic status.[8,9] Historical redlining has also been associated with the present-day distribution of oil and gas wells.[10] Nationwide, neighborhoods that received the poorest investment risk grade in redlining maps published by the federal Home Owners' Loan Corporation (HOLC) in the 1930s have nearly twice the density of oil and gas wells as neighborhoods that received the best grade.[10]

The unusual proximity of oil and gas wells to a population of 10 million people makes Los Angeles (LA) County, California, an important setting for examining drinking water contamination risks from oil and gas development. LA County has more than 20 000 active and inactive oil and gas wells and produces almost 14 million barrels of oil annually.[11] Approximately 500 000 residents live within half a mile of an active well.[12] LA County is also unique with respect to its number of drinking water providers. While most major US metropolitan areas are served by a few providers, LA County residents are served by approximately 200 community water systems (CWSs)—systems that serve at least 25 year-round residents or have at least 15 service connections. CWSs serve drinking water that may come from a single or variety of groundwater wells, surface water, and purchased water sources that are often blended before distribution. Nearly 30% of the county's total water supply is sourced from groundwater, and almost half of its CWSs rely entirely on groundwater.[13]

We sought to determine how racism in the housing market relates to the risk of drinking water contamination from oil and gas development in LA County. We used information about the location of oil and gas and groundwater supply wells to estimate the potential for contamination based on proximity. We then examined whether the racial/ethnic makeup, degree of historical redlining, and present-day racial residential segregation of a CWS's service area were associated with the likelihood that 1 or more of its supply wells are located near an oil or gas well. We examined race/ethnicity to describe disparities in risk and considered redlining and segregation as measures of structural racism in the housing market that may have contributed to present-day racialized disparities.[14]

METHODS

We considered all CWSs in LA County, with systems as the unit of analysis. We first combined data on the location of (1) oil and gas wells from the California Department of Conservation Geologic Energy Management Division (CalGEM) and (2) drinking water supply wells from the California State Water Resources Control Board to define CWSs at risk for oil and gas–related contamination based on spatial proximity of supply wells to oil or gas wells. We then used CWS service area boundaries from the Tracking California Drinking Water Systems Geographic Reporting Tool and data from the American Community Survey (ACS) to characterize the sociodemographic characteristics and degree of residential segregation of the population served by each CWS. Redlining measures were derived by overlaying CWS service area boundaries with 1930s HOLC investment risk maps. We used multivariable regression models to test the associations between race/ethnicity, redlining, and segregation and drinking water contamination risk.

Oil and Gas Wells

We downloaded oil and gas well coordinates, status (e.g., active, idle), and type (e.g., oil and gas, storage, injection) from the CalGEM database of permits on July 18, 2021.[15] Because it is unclear how frequently well status is updated in the CalGEM database, we used monthly production data from the California Department of Conservation to identify active versus inactive or idle extraction wells.[11] Extraction wells were considered active if any oil or gas production was reported from 2018 to 2020 and inactive if no production was reported or production data were missing during this period, resulting in a change in status for about 3% of production wells relative to their CalGEM designation. We then grouped oil and gas wells based on type and production status: active extraction wells (n = 2700), inactive extraction wells (n = 16 616), and storage and disposal wells (n = 804). We excluded offshore facilities and canceled wells (i.e., permit canceled before drilling; Figure A, available as a supplement to the online version of this article at https://ajph.org).

Drinking Water Supply Wells

We obtained coordinates and unique CWS identifiers for active public drinking water supply wells (n = 1064) from the Division of Drinking Water at the California State Water Resources Control Board. We restricted our analysis to wells that supply groundwater to CWSs in LA County with complete location information, leaving a final subset of 901 wells (Figure A).

Supply wells were considered at risk of potential contamination if they were located within 1 kilometer of at least 1 active extraction, inactive extraction, storage, or disposal well (Figure B, available as a supplement to the online version of this article at https://ajph.org). We selected this 1-kilometer buffer in accordance with a state law banning new oil and gas development within 3200 feet (~1 km) of homes, schools, and health care facilities. We also conducted a sensitivity analysis using a 2-kilometer buffer.

Community Water Systems

We obtained service area boundaries for 196 CWSs that directly served residential populations (i.e., excluding wholesale systems) and were listed as "active" in California's Safe Drinking Water Information System as of 2018 from the Tracking California Drinking

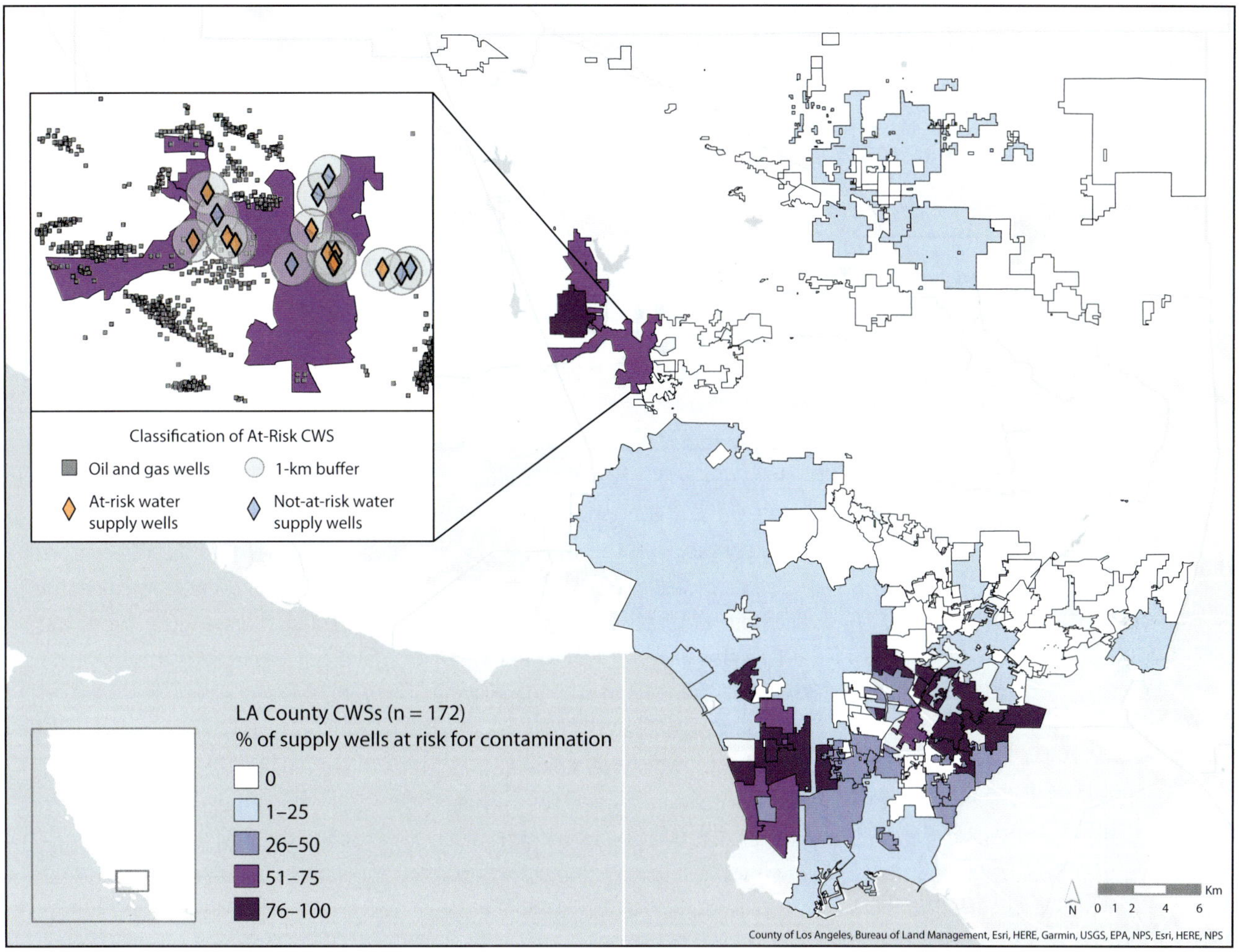

FIGURE 1— Percentage of Drinking Water Supply Wells at Risk for Oil and Gas Contamination per Community Water System (CWS): Los Angeles County, CA, 2020

Note. A CWS was considered at risk if 1 or more of its drinking water supply wells was within 1 km of an oil or gas well. At-risk systems are shaded, whereas ones not at risk are white.

Water Systems Geographic Reporting Tool.[16,17] We obtained system size (number of service connections) from the Division of Drinking Water's Electronic Data Transfer Library, and we obtained data on systems' primary water source from California's Safe Drinking Water Information System. We excluded CWSs that served incarcerated populations for which facility-specific sociodemographic data were unavailable (n = 2), relied exclusively on surface or purchased water (n = 21), or were located on the Channel Islands (n = 1), leaving 172 CWSs. We resolved service area boundary overlaps by following the approach used by Pace et al.[18] We calculated the fraction of at-risk supply wells for each CWS, and we classified those with at least 1 supply well within the 1-kilometer buffer area of any oil or gas well as at-risk (Figure 1).

Sociodemographic Characteristics

We characterized the population served by each CWS by using block group–level sociodemographic estimates from the 2013–2017 5-year ACS downscaled via dasymetric mapping, following the approach described in Pace et al.[18] For each CWS, we calculated the percentage of residents identifying as Hispanic/Latino, non-Hispanic White, non-Hispanic Black, non-Hispanic Asian/Pacific Islander, non-Hispanic Native American, and non-Hispanic other races (including multiracial), as well as the proportion of renters and population with income below twice the federal poverty level as determined by the US Census. Household metrics included median annual household income and the percentage of linguistically isolated households (where no one aged older than 14 years speaks English "very well").

Redlining Measures

Redlining measures were assigned using digitized 1939 HOLC-graded neighborhood boundaries obtained from the Mapping Inequality Project (n = 416 HOLC neighborhood polygons).[19] Because HOLC neighborhood boundaries did not overlap perfectly with CWS service area boundaries, we used areal apportionment to assign redlining measures. We first calculated the area of the CWS that overlapped any HOLC polygon to find the percentage area that was graded versus ungraded. For CWSs whose service areas overlapped with HOLC polygons (n = 85), we calculated the percentage of the graded area within the CWS that was graded A ("best"), B ("still desirable"), C ("definitely declining"), or D ("hazardous"; i.e., redlined). We additionally constructed a weighted redlining score ranging from 0 to 100 by weighting each graded portion of the CWS as follows:

$$\frac{\sum (p_i \times w_i)}{\sum p_i} \quad (1)$$

where p is the percentage of the CWS area given grade i, and w is the weight, with grade A weight = 25; B = 50; C = 75; and D = 100. For example, if a CWS boundary was intersected by 2 HOLC polygons such that 30% of its area overlapped with a "B"-graded HOLC polygon, 50% with a "C"-graded polygon, and 20% was not covered by HOLC polygons (i.e., ungraded), the score would be [(30 × 50) + (50 × 75)]/(30 + 50) = 66. Weighted redlining scores closer to 100 indicate that a greater proportion of the CWS's service area received poorer HOLC grades.

Segregation Metrics

We used 2013–2017 ACS data to compute the Index of Concentration at the Extremes (ICE), an area-based measure of concentrated racialized economic segregation, based on household income and race/ethnicity by census tract,[20] following the method described in Krieger et al.[21] We assigned census tracts to CWSs if their centroid intersected with CWS boundaries. For CWSs that did not intersect with any centroids, we assigned them the tracts with which they overlapped.

ICE ranges from −1 to 1, with the lowest values indicating the highest concentration of marginalized populations—which we defined as people of color in households earning less than $25 000 per year—and values closer to 1 indicating higher concentrations of privilege—which we defined as non-Hispanic White people in households earning more than $100 000 per year. We then categorized this measure by quartiles, with Q1 representing the most marginalized and Q4 the most privileged. We also calculated a weighted ICE score ranging from 0 to 100 using a formula analogous to the weighted redlining score, where p is the percentage of tracts in each CWS in quartile i, and w is the weight, with Q4 weight = 25; Q3 = 50; Q2 = 75; and Q1 = 100. The numerator was divided by 100.

Statistical Analysis

We calculated descriptive statistics and correlation coefficients to examine the distribution and bivariate associations between all variables of interest. We then used multivariable regression to estimate associations between the race/ethnicity, redlining, and ICE variables, and 2 outcomes: (1) at-risk status (yes or no, Poisson with robust standard errors) and (2) the percentage of CWS supply wells at risk (linear, ordinary least-squares with robust standard errors). We estimated prevalence ratios (PRs) by using a modified Poisson model rather than odds ratios because the outcome was not rare and to increase the interpretability of the effect estimates.[22] We used robust standard errors with a "sandwich" estimator because Poisson regression overestimates error for relative risk measures and to help address likely issues with spatial autocorrelation attributable to the clustering of oil and gas wells.[23] Poisson models estimating associations with the binary outcome included all CWSs in our sample (n = 172). We restricted linear models estimating associations with the continuous outcome to at-risk CWSs (n = 47 systems with at least 1 at-risk drinking water supply well). We scaled continuous predictor variables in all 5 models to facilitate comparison of model coefficients by subtracting the mean from each variable and dividing by the standard deviation (SD). We exponentiated coefficients from the Poisson models to obtain PRs.

We assessed unadjusted associations between our outcomes and CWS racial/ethnic makeup in models including the following variables, with percentage non-Hispanic White as the reference group: percentage Hispanic, percentage non-Hispanic Black, percentage non-Hispanic Asian/Pacific Islander, percentage non-Hispanic Native American, and percentage non-Hispanic other race including multiracial. Non-Hispanic Asian and Pacific

Islander were collapsed despite the considerable diversity across and within these groups because of limitations of sample size. Adjusted models additionally controlled for CWS size as a precision variable (< 10 000 service connections [small or medium] vs ≥ 10 000 [large]), and measures of socioeconomic status chosen a priori: housing tenure (% renters), linguistic isolation, and poverty. In the case of the linear model estimating the association between racial/ethnic makeup and the proportion of CWS supply wells at risk, we omitted percentage of linguistic isolation because of multicollinearity. We omitted median household income from both sets of models given collinearity with poverty.

We assessed unadjusted associations between our outcomes and CWS redlining in separate models that considered percentage graded C or D or the weighted redlining score as the exposure metric. We combined the 2 least-desirable grades of C and D because of multicollinearity. Adjusted redlining models considering percentage graded C or D additionally controlled for percentage graded B (with percentage graded A as the reference group), percentage ungraded, and CWS size. Adjusted redlining models considering the weighted redlining score additionally controlled for percentage ungraded and CWS size. Percentage ungraded was included in both models as a precision variable.

We assessed unadjusted associations between our outcomes and ICE in separate models that considered the percentage ICE Q1 (most marginalized) or the weighted ICE score. Adjusted models with percentage ICE Q1 additionally controlled for percentage ICE in Q2 and Q3 (with ICE Q4 as the reference group) and system size as a precision variable. Adjusted models with the weighted ICE score additionally controlled for system size.

RESULTS

The final sample included 172 CWSs and 901 groundwater supply wells across LA County. We estimated that 47 medium and large (i.e., > 200 service connections) CWSs were at risk for oil and gas–related contamination, leaving 125 CWSs not at risk (Table 1). At-risk CWSs had higher average proportions of people of color, renters, linguistically isolated households, poverty rates, and lower median household income compared with CWSs not at risk (Table 1). On average, at-risk CWSs had a lower proportion of their service area graded "A" ("desirable"), a higher proportion graded "D" ("hazardous"), and a higher mean weighted redlining score compared with CWSs not at risk. Similarly, when compared with not-at-risk systems, at-risk systems had a higher proportion of their census tracts in ICE Q1 (marginalized) and a higher mean weighted ICE score. Among at-risk CWSs, almost one third had more than three quarters of their supply wells located within 1 kilometer of an oil or gas well (Figure 1, Figure B).

Sociodemographic variables were moderately correlated with redlining variables (Pearson's correlation coefficients [ρ] between −0.39 and 0.38) and strongly correlated with ICE variables (ρ between −0.85 and 0.81). Redlining and ICE variables were weakly correlated (ρ between −0.30 and 0.29), and the percentage of at-risk supply wells was weakly correlated with sociodemographic, redlining, and ICE variables (ρ between −0.27 and 0.30; Figure C, available as a supplement to the online version of this article at https://ajph.org).

Unadjusted and adjusted Poisson models suggested that higher percentages of Hispanic, non-Hispanic Black, and non-Hispanic Asian/Pacific Islander residents were associated with a higher likelihood of being served by an at-risk CWS (Figure 2; Table A, available as a supplement to the online version of this article at https://ajph.org). A 1-unit-SD increase in percentage Hispanic, percentage non-Hispanic Black, and percentage non-Hispanic Asian/Pacific Islander was associated with a 181%, 33%, and 24% higher likelihood of being served by an at-risk system in adjusted models, respectively, holding other variables constant (percentage Hispanic: PR = 2.81; 95% confidence interval [CI] = 1.84, 4.30; percentage non-Hispanic Black: PR = 1.33; 95% CI = 1.10, 1.61; and percentage non-Hispanic Asian/Pacific Islander: PR = 1.24; 95% CI = 0.87, 1.78).

Redlining and racialized economic marginalization were associated with a higher likelihood of being served by an at-risk CWS in unadjusted and adjusted Poisson models (Figure 3; Tables B and C, available as supplements to the online version of this article at https://ajph.org). A 1-unit-SD increase in percentage graded C or D was associated with a 126% higher likelihood of being served by an at-risk system, controlling for percentage graded B, percentage ungraded, and system size (PR = 2.26; 95% CI = 1.13, 4.50). A 1-unit-SD increase in weighted redlining score was associated with a 27% higher likelihood of being served by an at-risk system, holding percentage ungraded and system size constant (PR = 1.27; 95% CI = 1.03, 1.56). A 1-unit-SD increase in percentage of CWS census tracts in Q1 of ICE was associated with 49% higher likelihood of being served by an at-risk system, controlling for

TABLE 1— Characteristics of At-Risk and Not-At-Risk Community Water Systems Based on Drinking Water Supply Well Proximity to Oil and Gas Wells: Los Angeles County, CA, 2020

	At-Risk CWS (n = 47)	Not-at-Risk CWS (n = 125)
Total population served, no.	7 180 196	2 204 316
CWS size, no.		
Small (< 200 connections)	0	47
Medium (200–9999 connections)	24	61
Large (≥ 10 000 connections)	23	17
Sociodemographics, mean %		
Hispanic	59.8	40.2
Non-Hispanic White	19.3	39.2
Non-Hispanic Asian/Pacific Islander	11.0	10.9
Non-Hispanic Black	7.5	6.5
Non-Hispanic other race including multiracial	2.0	2.8
Non-Hispanic Native American	0.2	0.3
Linguistically isolated	13.4	9.4
Renters	48.8	35.5
Poverty[a]	37.9	36.0
Median household income, mean $	66 214	66 810
HOLC redlining grade,[b] mean %		
A	2.6	9.1
B	13.6	17.6
C	55.8	55.4
D	28.0	17.9
Ungraded	65.8	52.2
Weighted redlining score (0–100),[c] mean	77.3	70.5
ICE quartile[d], mean %		
1	29.5	11.5
2	29.9	21.0
3	19.8	32.8
4	19.7	34.0
Weighted ICE score (0–100),[e] mean	66.8	52.2
Amount of supply wells within 1 km of an oil or gas well, no. (%)		
Low (≤ 25%)	10 (21)	0
Medium (26%–50%)	16 (34)	0
High (51%–75%)	6 (13)	0
Very high (76%–100%)	15 (32)	0
Primary water source, no. (%)		
Groundwater	14 (29.8)	76 (60.8)
Surface water	33 (70.2)	49 (39.2)

Note. CWS = community water system; HOLC = Home Owners' Loan Corporation; ICE = Index of Concentration at the Extremes. Descriptive statistics are provided for at-risk and not-at-risk CWSs based on their service area. An at-risk CWS was defined as having at least 1 water supply well within 1 km of an active, inactive, or storage or disposal well. Eleven systems had at least 1 supply well within 1 km of an active oil or gas well.

[a]Poverty was defined as below twice the federal poverty level based on the US Census.
[b]Only 85 out of 172 CWSs intersected with neighborhoods assigned a grade of A ("best"), B ("still desirable"), C ("definitely declining"), or D ("hazardous"; i.e., redlined) for investment by HOLC.
[c]Weighted redlining scores closer to 100 indicate that a greater proportion of the CWS's HOLC-graded area received lower HOLC grades (e.g., more D-graded areas).
[d]We categorized ICE (−1 to 1) into quartiles, with Q1 representing the highest concentration of racialized economic marginalization and Q4 the highest concentration of racialized economic privilege.
[e]Weighted ICE scores closer to 100 indicate that a greater proportion of the CWS's census tracts are marginalized.

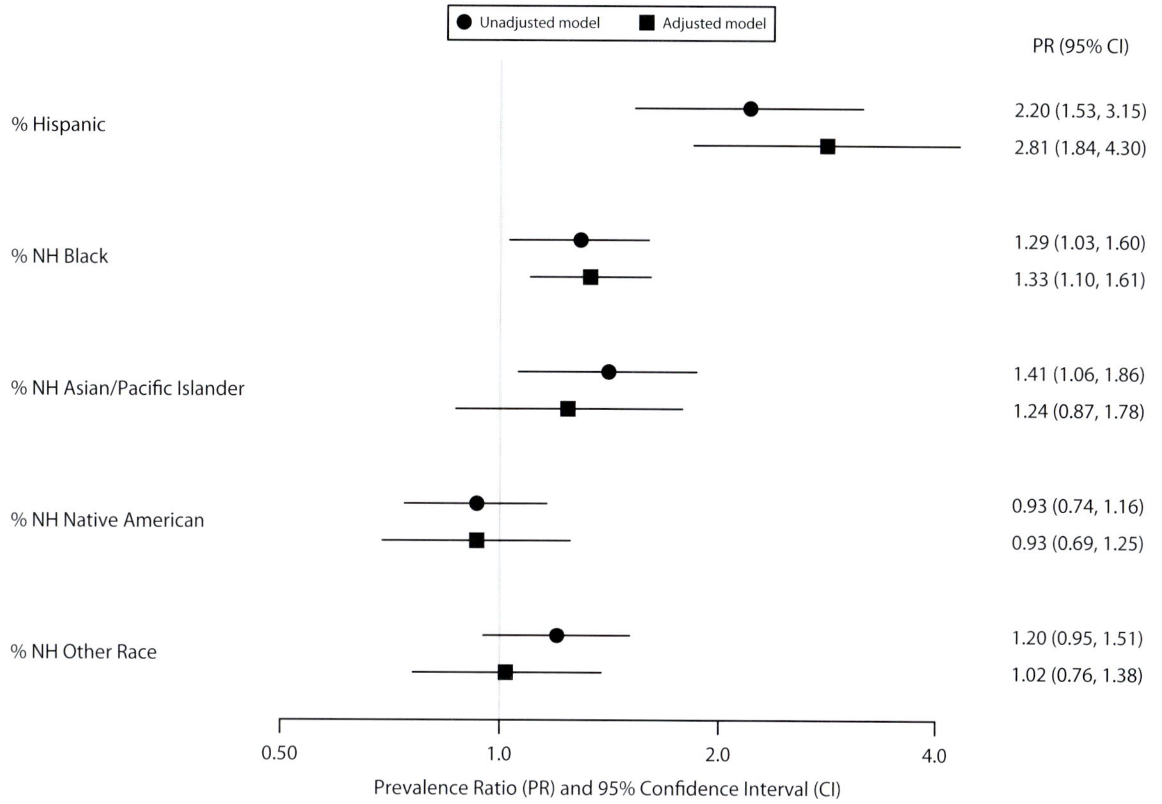

FIGURE 2— **Likelihood of Being Served by an At-Risk Community Water System (CWS) Associated With Racial/Ethnic Make-Up: Los Angeles County, CA, 2020**

Note. NH = non-Hispanic. The sample size was n = 172. The adjusted model for race/ethnicity (model 1) controlled for CWS size, percentage linguistically isolated, percentage renters, and percentage poverty. Explanatory variables have been scaled in units of SD.

percentage ICE Q2, percentage ICE Q3, and system size (PR = 1.49; 95% CI = 1.18, 1.88). A 1-unit-SD increase in weighted ICE score was associated with 62% higher likelihood of being served by an at-risk system, controlling for system size (PR = 1.62; 95% CI = 1.24, 2.13).

Linear models similarly suggested that among at-risk systems, higher percentages of Hispanic and non-Hispanic Black residents were associated with a greater percentage of at-risk drinking water supply wells, particularly when controlling for socioeconomic variables, although estimates were less precise (Table D, available as a supplement to the online version of this article at https://ajph.org). A 1-unit-SD increase in percentage Hispanic and percentage non-Hispanic Black was associated with a 38% and 8% increase, respectively, in the percentage of at-risk supply wells per CWS (percentage Hispanic: mean difference = 38.47; 95% CI = 9.90, 67.03; percentage non-Hispanic Black: mean difference = 7.62; 95% CI = −0.57, 15.81). Redlining was also weakly associated with an increase in percentage of at-risk supply wells, while ICE Q1 was associated with a slight decrease; however, in both cases, CIs were wide and crossed the null (Tables E and F, available as supplements to the online version of this article at https://ajph.org).

Effect estimates were consistent in direction in our sensitivity analysis using a 2-kilometer buffer distance to define at-risk drinking water supply wells (Tables A–F).

DISCUSSION

We found that almost a quarter of LA County CWSs serving more than 7 million residents have drinking water supply wells located within 1 kilometer of an oil or gas well, increasing the possibility of contamination. Five systems serving more than 162 000 residents source their water entirely from at-risk groundwater wells; one of these systems serves the Pitchess Detention Facility and was excluded from our analysis because sociodemographic data were unavailable. Seven additional systems serving more than 189 000

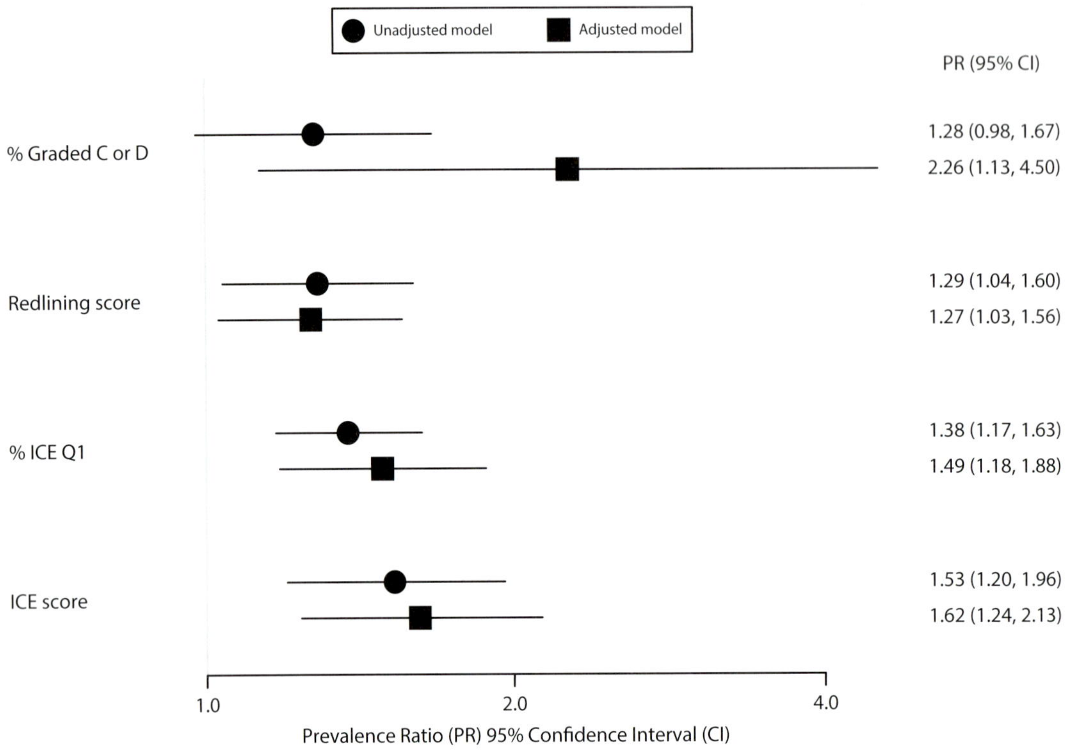

FIGURE 3— Likelihood of Being Served by an At-Risk Community Water System Associated With Historical Redlining (HOLC Grade) and Segregation (ICE): Los Angeles County, CA, 2020

Note. HOLC = Home Owners' Loan Corporation; ICE = Index of Concentration at the Extremes. The adjusted model for percentage graded C or D (model 2; n = 85) controlled for percentage graded B, percentage ungraded, and CWS size. The adjusted model for redlining score (model 3; n = 85) controlled for percentage ungraded and CWS size. The adjusted model for percentage ICE Q1 (model 4; n = 172) controlled for percentage ICE Q2, percentage ICE Q3, and CWS size. The adjusted model for ICE score (model 5; n = 172) controlled for CWS size. Explanatory variables have been scaled in units of SD.

residents also source their groundwater entirely from at-risk supply wells but additionally purchase surface water, making their water supply less vulnerable to possible oil and gas development–related groundwater contamination.

Several studies document associations between oil and gas development and elevated drinking water contamination risk in regions where fracking is common. A Wyoming study identified well-stimulation chemicals like naphthalene in groundwater and benzene, toluene, ethylbenzene, and xylenes in a drinking water well in an area of oil and gas production.[4] A study of more than a dozen US states found that almost half of all fracking wells stimulated in 2014 were located within 2 to 3 kilometers of at least 1 domestic groundwater well.[24] In the LA Basin, fracking has been used in close vertical proximity to protected aquifers.[25] Acidization using hydrochloric and hydrofluoric acids, methanol, naphthalene, ethylbenzene, and xylene is a more frequently used well-stimulative technique in LA County and can contaminate groundwater through improper wastewater management or disposal (e.g., injection into protected aquifers).[26] Many chemicals used in oil and gas development are not currently regulated in drinking water, including per- and polyfluoroalkyl substances, which means little monitoring data exist to assess potential impacts.

Racial/ethnic composition, residential segregation, and historical redlining were significant predictors of drinking water contamination risks from oil and gas development in LA County in our study. CWSs with higher proportions of Hispanic, non-Hispanic Black, and non-Hispanic Asian/Pacific Islander residents, a higher proportion of their service area redlined in the 1930s, and a higher degree of present-day racialized economic segregation were all more likely to have oil or gas wells within 1 kilometer of their drinking water supply wells. Although we did not perform a formal mediation analysis, this suggests racism in the housing market contributed to present-day racial disparities in oil and gas contamination risk. Our analysis adds to a growing body of literature on the likely disproportionate impact of oil and gas development on communities of color[27,28] and the influence of past redlining on contemporary residential proximity to environmental hazards.[29]

Interestingly, in models assessing the influence of racial/ethnic composition on drinking water contamination risk, higher CWS poverty levels were associated with a reduced risk. This is in contrast with an Ohio study that found lower-income block groups were associated with the presence of oil and gas wastewater injection wells[30] and a study in Southern Texas that found disproportionate siting of disposal wells in high-poverty block groups.[31] Our contrasting findings may relate to the fact that our study area included suburban and urban areas with wide variation in the cost of living that was not factored into our measure of poverty.

Within at-risk systems, we also found that higher concentrations of marginalized populations (ICE Q1) were associated with a reduced proportion of at-risk supply wells, counter to our hypothesis. This suggests that segregation is more reflective of the likelihood of contamination risk but not necessarily the severity.

We were limited by a small sample size of at-risk CWSs in our linear models (n = 47), which reduced the precision of our results. Because of limited data, we were not able to account for the extent, chemistry, and depth of drinking water aquifers, or the age, depth, or condition of oil and gas wells. We were also not able to consider blending of different water sources by CWSs before drinking water distribution. Our outcome measure of an at-risk CWS should therefore be interpreted as an indication of potential contamination risk and not a measure of exposure.

Some of the oil and gas wells in our analysis were likely drilled before the creation of LA County redlining maps in the late 1930s; therefore, part of the associations we observed between historical redlining and drinking water contamination risk may be the result of differences in the distribution of oil and gas wells that predated the maps. The presence of nearby oil and gas wells was treated inconsistently during HOLC neighborhood appraisals, with majority-White neighborhoods with racially restrictive covenants not being penalized for the presence of oil and gas wells, while neighborhoods with a majority of people of color were downgraded.[32]

The 2 measures of structural racism that we considered do not capture all forms of structural racism in the housing market, including block busting, restrictive covenants, urban renewal programs, or predatory lending. Nor do they capture other relevant dimensions of structural racism. For example, patterns of municipal annexation, including processes of "underbounding," have often systematically excluded racially marginalized populations in unincorporated areas from public services, including drinking water provision.[33]

As water scarcity increases across the western United States, reliance on groundwater is projected to increase, and safeguarding groundwater quality will become even more critical to achieving California's goal to ensure access to safe and affordable water as a human right.[34] The County and City of LA have recently passed ordinances to phase out existing oil and gas operations because of health concerns.[35] Study findings highlight the need to consider drinking water threats and possibly prioritize wells for closure and remediation in communities of color disproportionately impacted by fossil fuel extraction. AJPH

ABOUT THE AUTHORS

Alique G. Berberian and Lara J. Cushing are with the Department of Environmental Health Sciences, Fielding School of Public Health, University of California, Los Angeles (UCLA). Jenny Rempel and Nicholas Depsky are with the Energy and Resources Group, Rausser College of Natural Resources, University of California, Berkeley. Komal Bangia is with the Office of Environmental Health Hazard Assessment, California Environmental Protection Agency, Oakland. Sophia Wang is with the Institute of the Environment and Sustainability, UCLA.

CORRESPONDENCE

Correspondence should be sent to Lara J. Cushing, 650 Charles E Young Dr S, 71-259 CHS, Los Angeles, CA 90095 (e-mail: lcushing@ucla.edu). Reprints can be ordered at https://ajph.org by clicking the "Reprints" link.

PUBLICATION INFORMATION

Full Citation: Berberian AG, Rempel J, Depsky N, Bangia K, Wang S, Cushing LJ. Race, racism, and drinking water contamination risk from oil and gas wells in Los Angeles County, 2020. *Am J Public Health*. 2023;113(11):1191–1200.

Acceptance Date: June 23, 2023.

DOI: https://doi.org/10.2105/AJPH.2023.307374

CONTRIBUTORS

A. G. Berberian curated the data, conducted the analysis, prepared figures and tables, and wrote the original draft. J. Rempel provided redlining data and reviewed and edited the article. N. Depsky created the population sociodemographic estimates for community water systems and reviewed and edited the article. K. Bangia cleaned community water system boundaries and reviewed and edited the article. S. Wang assisted in data cleaning and analysis and reviewed and edited the article. L. J. Cushing originated the study, supervised the analysis, and reviewed and edited the article.

ACKNOWLEDGMENTS

This work was supported by the National Institute of Environmental Health Sciences (award P42ES004705), California Proposition 1 Sustainable Groundwater Planning Grant (award 4600012684), the UCLA Sustainable LA Grand Challenge, the Anthony and Jeanne Pritkzer Family Foundation, the JPB Environmental Health Fellowship, and the UCLA Fielding Presidential Chair in Health Equity.

We thank Clare Pace, Katherine Wolf, and Rachel Morello-Frosch (University of California Berkeley) for assistance in the curation of community water system data. We thank Felicia Federico (UCLA Institute of the Environment and

Sustainability) and Rita Kampalath (Los Angeles County Chief Sustainability Office) for helpful discussions on the methodology.

CONFLICTS OF INTEREST

All authors declare that they have no competing interests.

HUMAN PARTICIPANT PROTECTION

The study did not involve human participants.

REFERENCES

1. US Energy Information Administration. US Field Production of Crude Oil. 2022. Available at: https://www.eia.gov/dnav/pet/hist/LeafHandler.ashx?n=PET&s=MCRFPUS2&f=M. Accessed July 3, 2022.
2. Czolowski ED, Santoro RL, Srebotnjak T, Shonkoff SBC. Toward consistent methodology to quantify populations in proximity to oil and gas development: a national spatial analysis and review. *Environ Health Perspect.* 2017;125(8):086004. https://doi.org/10.1289/EHP1535
3. McMahon PB, Barlow JRB, Engle MA, et al. Methane and benzene in drinking-water wells overlying the Eagle Ford, Fayetteville, and Haynesville shale hydrocarbon production areas. *Environ Sci Technol.* 2017;51(12):6727–6734. https://doi.org/10.1021/acs.est.7b00746
4. Kassotis CD, Vu DC, Vo PH, et al. Endocrine-disrupting activities and organic contaminants associated with oil and gas operations in Wyoming groundwater. *Arch Environ Contam Toxicol.* 2018;75(2):247–258. https://doi.org/10.1007/s00244-018-0521-2
5. Clark CJ, Xiong B, Soriano Jr MA, et al. Assessing unconventional oil and gas exposure in the Appalachian basin: comparison of exposure surrogates and residential drinking water measurements. *Environ Sci Technol.* 2022;56(2):1091–1103. https://doi.org/10.1021/acs.est.1c05081
6. California Department of Conservation. Idle well program. 2019. Available at: https://www.conservation.ca.gov/calgem/idle_well. Accessed July 4, 2022.
7. Chilingar GV, Endres B. Environmental hazards posed by the Los Angeles Basin urban oilfields: an historical perspective of lessons learned. *Env Geol.* 2005;47(2):302–317. https://doi.org/10.1007/s00254-004-1159-0
8. González DJX, Morton CM, Hill LAL, et al. Temporal trends of racial and socioeconomic disparities in population exposures to upstream oil and gas development in California. *GeoHealth.* 2023;7(3):e2022GH000690. https://doi.org/10.1029/2022GH000690
9. Sadd J, Shamasunder B. Oil extraction in Los Angeles: health, land use, and environmental justice consequences. In: Liberty Hill Foundation. Drilling down: the community consequences of expanded oil development in Los Angeles. 2015: 7–14. Available at: https://libertyhill-assets.s3-us-west-2.amazonaws.com/media/documents/Drilling_Down_Report_-_Full.pdf. Accessed July 3, 2022.
10. Gonzalez DJX, Nardone A, Nguyen AV, Morello-Frosch R, Casey JA. Historic redlining and the siting of oil and gas wells in the United States. *J Expo Sci Environ Epidemiol.* 2023;33(1):76–83. https://doi.org/10.1038/s41370-022-00434-9
11. California Department of Conservation. Monthly production data. Available at: https://filerequest.conservation.ca.gov. Accessed April 17, 2022.
12. Environmental Defense Fund. Filling the void: the value of new technology to reduce air pollution and improve information at oil and gas sites in California. 2017. Available at: https://www.edf.org/sites/default/files/california-monitoring_filling-the-void.pdf. Accessed July 5, 2022.
13. Pierce G, McCann H. Los Angeles County Community Water Systems: Atlas and Policy Guide. 2015. Available at: https://www.collinslaw.com/files/water_atlas_0.pdf. Accessed April 28, 2022.
14. Adkins-Jackson PB, Chantarat T, Bailey ZD, Ponce NA. Measuring structural racism: a guide for epidemiologists and other health researchers. *Am J Epidemiol.* 2022;191(4):539–547. https://doi.org/10.1093/aje/kwab239
15. California Department of Conservation, Geologic Energy Management Division. Oil and gas wells table, California. Available at: https://gis.conservation.ca.gov/portal/home/item.html?id=0d30c4d9ac8f4f84a53a145e7d68eb6b. Accessed April 17, 2022.
16. California State Water Resources Control Board. Drinking water—public water system information—California Open Data. Available at: https://data.ca.gov/dataset/drinking-water-public-water-system-information. Accessed April 17, 2022.
17. Tracking California. Water system service areas. Available at: https://trackingcalifornia.org/water-systems/water-systems-landing. Accessed April 17, 2022.
18. Pace C, Balazs C, Bangia K, et al. Inequities in drinking water quality among domestic well communities and community water systems, California, 2011–2019. *Am J Public Health.* 2022;112(1):88–97. https://doi.org/10.2105/AJPH.2021.306561
19. Nelson RK, Winling L, Marciano R, Connolly N. Mapping Inequality. *American Panorama.* Available at: https://dsl.richmond.edu/panorama/redlining. Accessed June 3, 2022.
20. Massey DS. The age of extremes: concentrated affluence and poverty in the twenty-first century. *Demography.* 1996;33(4):395–412, discussion 413–416. https://doi.org/10.2307/2061773
21. Krieger N, Waterman PD, Spasojevic J, Li W, Maduro G, Van Wye G. Public health monitoring of privilege and deprivation with the Index of Concentration at the Extremes. *Am J Public Health.* 2016;106(2):256–263. https://doi.org/10.2105/AJPH.2015.302955
22. Deddens JA, Petersen MR. Approaches for estimating prevalence ratios. *Occup Environ Med.* 2008;65(7):481, 501–506. https://doi.org/10.1136/oem.2007.034777
23. Zou G. A modified Poisson regression approach to prospective studies with binary data. *Am J Epidemiol.* 2004;159(7):702–706. https://doi.org/10.1093/aje/kwh090
24. Jasechko S, Perrone D. Hydraulic fracturing near domestic groundwater wells. *Proc Natl Acad Sci USA.* 2017;114(50):13138–13143. https://doi.org/10.1073/pnas.1701682114
25. Shonkoff SBC, Gautier D. A case study of the petroleum geological potential and potential public health risks associated with hydraulic fracturing and oil and gas development in the Los Angeles Basin. In: An Independent Scientific Assessment of Well Stimulation in California. Vol. III. Sacramento, CA: California Council on Science & Technology. 2015. Available at: http://ccst.us/publications/2015/vol-III-chapter-4.pdf. Accessed August 3, 2023.
26. Abdullah K, Malloy TF, Stenstrom MK, Suffet IH. Toxicity of acidization fluids used in California oil exploration. *Toxicol Environ Chem.* 2017;99(1):78–94. https://doi.org/10.1080/02772248.2016.1160285
27. Johnston JE, Chau K, Franklin M, Cushing L. Environmental justice dimensions of oil and gas flaring in South Texas: disproportionate exposure among Hispanic communities. *Environ Sci Technol.* 2020;54(10):6289–6298. https://doi.org/10.1021/acs.est.0c00410
28. Cushing LJ, Chau K, Franklin M, Johnston JE. Up in smoke: characterizing the population exposed to flaring from unconventional oil and gas development in the contiguous US. *Environ Res Lett.* 2021;16(3):034032. https://doi.org/10.1088/1748-9326/abd3d4
29. Swope CB, Hernandez D, Cushing LJ. The relationship of historical redlining with present-day neighborhood environmental and health outcomes: a scoping review and conceptual model. *J Urban Health.* 2022;99(6):959–983. https://doi.org/10.1007/s11524-022-00665-z
30. Silva GS, Warren JL, Deziel NC. Spatial modeling to identify sociodemographic predictors of hydraulic fracturing wastewater injection wells in Ohio census block groups. *Environ Health Perspect.* 2018;126(6):067008. https://doi.org/10.1289/EHP2663
31. Johnston JE, Werder E, Sebastian D. Wastewater disposal wells, fracking, and environmental injustice in southern Texas. *Am J Public Health.* 2016;106(3):550–556. https://doi.org/10.2105/AJPH.2015.303000
32. Cumming DG. Black gold, White power: mapping oil, real estate, and racial segregation in the Los Angeles Basin, 1900–1939. *Engag Sci Technol Soc.* 2018;4:85–110. https://doi.org/10.17351/ests2018.212
33. Balazs CL, Ray I. The drinking water disparities framework: on the origins and persistence of inequities in exposure. *Am J Public Health.* 2014;104(4):603–611. https://doi.org/10.2105/AJPH.2013.301664
34. Eng M. Assembly Bill No. 685 (2012). Available at: http://www.leginfo.ca.gov/pub/11-12/bill/asm/ab_0651-0700/ab_685_bill_20120925_chaptered.pdf. Accessed April 25, 2023.
35. Shamasunder B, Johnston J. LA's long, troubled history with urban oil drilling is nearing an end after years of health concerns. *The Conversation.* January 27, 2023. Available at: http://theconversation.com/las-long-troubled-history-with-urban-oil-drilling-is-nearing-an-end-after-years-of-health-concerns-198650. Accessed April 24, 2023.

Design and Implementation of a National Program to Monitor the Prevalence of SARS-CoV-2 IgG Antibodies in England Using Self-Testing: The REACT-2 Study

Helen Ward, PhD, Christina Atchison, PhD, Matthew Whitaker, PhD, Bethan Davies, PhD, Deborah Ashby, PhD, Ara Darzi, MD, Marc Chadeau-Hyam, PhD, Steven Riley, DPhil, Christl A. Donnelly, ScD, Wendy Barclay, PhD, Graham S. Cooke, PhD, and Paul Elliott, PhD

See also Tancredi and Chiolero, p. 1143.

Data System. The UK Department of Health and Social Care funded the REal-time Assessment of Community Transmission-2 (REACT-2) study to estimate community prevalence of SARS-CoV-2 IgG (immunoglobulin G) antibodies in England.

Data Collection/Processing. We obtained random cross-sectional samples of adults from the National Health Service (NHS) patient list (near-universal coverage). We sent participants a lateral flow immunoassay (LFIA) self-test, and they reported the result online. Overall, 905 991 tests were performed (28.9% response) over 6 rounds of data collection (June 2020–May 2021).

Data Analysis/Dissemination. We produced weighted estimates of LFIA test positivity (validated against neutralizing antibodies), adjusted for test performance, at local, regional, and national levels and by age, sex, and ethnic group and area-level deprivation score. In each round, fieldwork occurred over 2 weeks, with results reported to policymakers the following week. We disseminated results as preprints and peer-reviewed journal publications.

Public Health Implications. REACT-2 estimated the scale and variation in antibody prevalence over time. Community self-testing and -reporting produced rapid insights into the changing course of the pandemic and the impact of vaccine rollout, with implications for future surveillance. (*Am J Public Health*. 2023;113(11):1201–1209. https://doi.org/10.2105/AJPH.2023.307381)

AJPH November 2023, Vol 113, No. 11

The REal-time Assessment of Community Transmission-2 (REACT-2) study sought to provide reliable and timely estimates of the prevalence of antibodies to severe acute respiratory syndrome coronavirus 2 (SARS-CoV-2) infection from random samples of England's adult population.

DATA SYSTEM

This study involved 6 rounds of data collection: from June 20, 2020, to May 25, 2021 (Figure 1).

Name and Sponsor

The REACT-2 study was funded by the Department of Health and Social Care in England and sponsored by Imperial College London.

Purpose

We aimed to estimate the number and distribution of SARS-CoV-2 infections during the first and second waves of the COVID-19 pandemic in England by place and person, identify trends in antibody positivity, and subsequently measure the impact of vaccine rollout on population antibody prevalence.

Public Health Significance

REACT-2 was established following the first wave of the COVID-19 pandemic in England when little was known about the extent of SARS-CoV-2 transmission in the community because of limited access to diagnostic testing outside

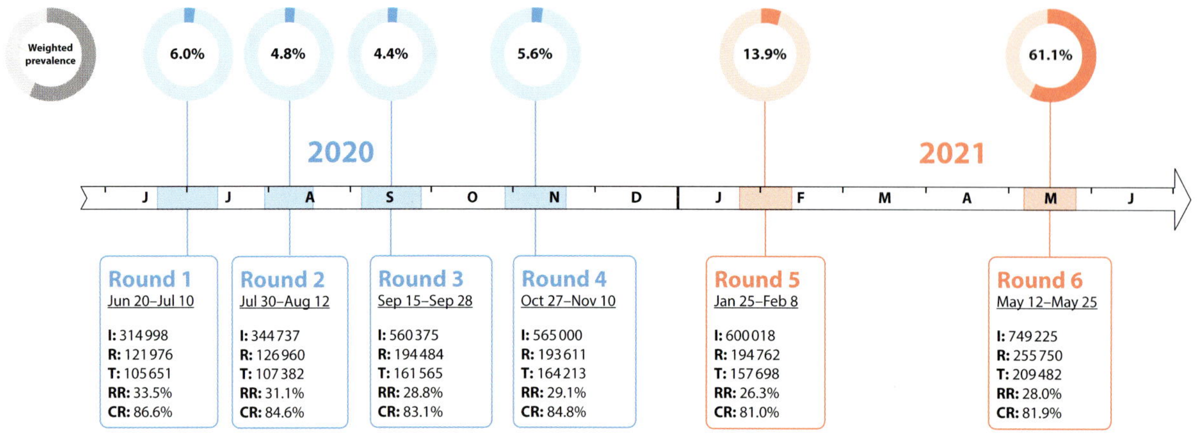

FIGURE 1— REACT-2 Study Timeline From June 20, 2020, to May 25, 2021, Over 6 Rounds of Data Collection: England

Note. CR = completion rate (tests/registrations); I = invitations sent; R = registrations; RR = response rate (tests/invitations); T = lateral flow immunoassay tests completed. CR is defined by the number of completed tests over the number of kits sent out and the prevalence of antibody positivity, adjusted for test characteristics and weighted to England's adult population. Note the reported response rates are conservative because (1) not all invitations would have been received (or opened) by the potential participants, and (2) recruitment was stopped once the required sample size had been reached.

hospital settings. We provided estimates of cumulative community prevalence of SARS-CoV-2 IgG (immunoglobulin G) antibody test positivity with a rapid test and identified groups at highest risk of infection. In addition, we estimated the total number of individuals in England who had been infected and the infection fatality ratio overall and by age, sex, and ethnic group. REACT-2 was designed to provide repeated snapshots of the cumulative prevalence of test positivity for antibodies above the threshold of the rapid test initially from infection and later from vaccination. These data fed directly into the government through written and verbal reports to a weekly data debrief group of the UK Health Security Agency (previously Public Health England) to inform the public health response.

DATA COLLECTION/ PROCESSING

We invited random samples of adults in the community to use at-home testing with a finger prick lateral flow immunoassay (LFIA) device and to report the results along with demographic, behavioral, and clinical details in an online or telephone survey.

Data Sources and Collection Mode

Source population. We invited random cross-sectional samples of individuals aged 18 years and older in England to participate. Our sample frame was individuals on the National Health Service (NHS) patient list, which includes name, address, age, and sex of everyone registered with a general practitioner in England (almost the entire population).

Survey instruments. We collected data through a Web-based survey instrument designed and piloted with public input and hosted by our logistics partner, Ipsos (Paris, France). We mailed an invitation letter to named individuals, who were directed to an online or telephone registration site where they could consent to the study. The registration form confirmed date of birth and gathered additional information on household size and composition, occupation, education, and ethnic group (see the Appendix, available as a supplement to the online version of this article at http://www.ajph.org). We asked eligible people (which was everyone except those with possible bleeding risk from use of a lancet) for their e-mail address and mobile telephone number. Following registration, we sent participants a self-test LFIA kit, an instruction booklet linked to an online video, and a link to a Web site (or telephone option) to complete a further user survey once they had completed the test. The survey instruments are available on the study Web site (https://bit.ly/44eyByr).

Finger prick antibody test. We selected the LFIA (Fortress Diagnostics, Antrim, Northern Ireland) after we evaluated its performance characteristics (sensitivity and specificity) against predefined criteria for detection of SARS-CoV-2 IgG.[1,2] The LFIA uses the structural spike (*S*) protein of the virus as the target antigen for antibody-based detection. We initially evaluated it for (1) sensitivity in an NHS health care worker cohort known to have been infected with SARS-CoV-2, as confirmed by RT-PCR (reverse transcription–polymerase chain reaction), at least 21 days earlier and who were not hospitalized; and (2) specificity using 500 prepandemic sera. Compared with results from at least 1 of 2 in-house ELISAs (enzyme-linked immunosorbent assay), sensitivity and specificity of finger prick blood self-test were 84.4% (95% confidence interval [CI] = 70.5%, 93.5%) and 98.6% (95% CI = 97.1%, 99.4%), respectively.[1]

The in-house ELISAs used were the spike protein ELISA (S-ELISA) and a hybrid spike protein receptor–binding domain double antigen–bridging assay.[3] Further validation of the LFIA showed equivalent performance in an occupational cohort of people who were not health care workers[4] and a cohort consisting of health care workers and renal transplant patients, all of whom self-tested after they were vaccinated.[5] We also compared the self-test LFIA to a commercially available quantitative assay in 3758 participants, a majority of whom had been vaccinated or reported previous infection. The LFIA was less sensitive than the laboratory assay, being positive in 73.9% compared with 96.4% of participants; however, in a subset of 250 samples, the LFIA correlated better with live virus neutralization.[6]

Testing and reporting. Graphic designers specializing in health care designed the testing kit, instruction booklet, and video, with input from 300 public volunteers in a pilot study, which identified the need for improvements in elements of the kit, instructions, and interpretation of results. This was followed by a larger pilot study of more than 14 000 randomly selected members of the public, which showed high levels of acceptability and usability.[7] Using the instructions provided, participants carried out the LFIA using a finger prick capillary blood sample, read the results, and reported them in the survey along with additional sociodemographic, behavioral, and clinical details (see the Appendix, available as a supplement to the online version of this article at http://www.ajph.org). We asked participants to upload a photograph of the completed test.

Ethical Procedures

Ethics. Participants gave individual consent to participate either online or by telephone. We obtained approval for use of the test kit from the Medicines and Healthcare Products Regulatory Agency (https://bit.ly/3qu6Lk9), with the caveat that the test was to be clearly labeled as for research purposes only and that participants were given advice not to change their behavior because of the result.

Public involvement. A public advisory panel provided input on the design, conduct, and dissemination of the study, and lay members sit on a data access committee governing further access to the data.

Population and Geographic Coverage

Population. The target population was England's adult population aged 18 years and older. We aimed to provide data at the lower-tier local authority area (LTLA) level in England to aid local administrative and public health response to the pandemic. We included data for 316 of the 317 LTLAs in England (excluding Isles of Scilly), and by combining the 2 smallest with neighboring areas we report on 315 areas. We also provide national and regional estimates of antibody positivity and prevalence estimates for key demographic subgroups, including by age, ethnic group, socioeconomic status (as determined by an area-level deprivation score), and occupation. Estimates of weighted prevalence over the 6 rounds of the study are shown in Figure 1.

Sampling frame. The sampling frame was all adults 18 years and older who were registered with an NHS general practitioner in England. The NHS England holds this information, which provides near-complete coverage of the resident population.

Sampling strategy. We obtained random samples from the NHS patient list and mailed individual invitations. We stratified the sample by LTLA to achieve similar numbers of participants in each local area. For round 6 (May 2021), we adjusted the sampling to achieve a boost of 70 000 people in age groups 55 to 64 and 65 to 74 years to include additional numbers after their first and second vaccinations, because vaccines were rolled out in order of decreasing age starting in December 2020.[8]

Unit of Data Collection and Sample Size

Unit of data collection. We collected data at the individual level. The samples were nonoverlapping until the final boosted round, when some overlap with earlier rounds occurred, with 4950 people taking part twice over the 6 rounds.

Sample size and response rates. Over the 6 rounds of data collection from June 20, 2020, to May 25, 2021, 905 991 completed tests were included from 3 134 353 invitations, giving an overall response rate (number of completed tests/number of invitations sent out) of 28.9%. The response rate varied by round (range = 26.3%–33.5%), with completed tests ranging from 105 651 to 209 482 per round (Figure 1). The response rate also varied by sex, age, region, and deprivation score (Table A, available as a supplement to the online version of this article at http://www.ajph.org).

Sample size determination. In rounds 1 to 5, we aimed for 100 000 completed tests per round to provide meaningful information on England's 315 LTLAs. The highest levels of uncertainty were in populations with low prevalence, where the point antibody positivity could be so low that there were no positive tests in that area. With a total of 100 000 completed tests, we were able to exclude (95% confidence) a prevalence of more than 1.7% in each LTLA recording zero positive tests. In round 6, we aimed for a total sample size of 240 000 test results, including, as noted, a boost of 70 000 people in age groups 55 to 64 and 65 to 74 years powered to detect a clinically important difference in outcome (relative risk = 0.5 for hospitalization) between individuals who tested positive and those who tested negative.

Completeness. By design, we aimed for approximately equal numbers of participants in England's 315 LTLAs. The achieved samples at the LTLA level ranged from 200 to 598 in rounds 1 to 5 and 517 to 802 in round 6 with the boosted sample. We achieved sufficient data by round to estimate prevalence by age, region, and other key demographic groups, including ethnic group, deprivation index, and occupation.

Generalizability. Our study had a lower response among men, the youngest and oldest groups, people from minority ethnic groups, and those in more deprived areas (Table A). Unequal participation is observed in almost all population surveys. To account for the differential response, we weighted the data at each round to represent England as a whole, although this may not fully correct estimates.

Surveillance Design

This was a serial cross-sectional design, randomly selected, with largely nonoverlapping samples across 6 rounds of the study. The key was our use of at-home self-testing and results reporting from a point-of-care rapid test, which enabled us to obtain results at scale and disseminate them quickly. Most data collected were reported by participants, including history of COVID-19, comorbidities, and vaccination. However, where we had specific consent for data linkage, we were able to link to routine health data to confirm vaccination status and obtain outcome data (i.e., hospitalizations, deaths).

Frequency of Data Collection

The study was initially commissioned to estimate the total number of people who had been infected with SARS-CoV-2 in the first wave in England, which peaked in March 2020 and decreased rapidly after the introduction of a strict lockdown on March 23.[9] The first round took place at the end of June 2020, followed by 3 more rounds[2–4] at 6-week intervals in July and August as well as September and October 2020 (Figure 1). There was a 2-week reporting window for participants to upload their results, and the overwhelming majority performed the test and reported the results in the first few days of those periods. The final 2 rounds took place after a gap of 3 and 4 months (January and May 2021). We timed the rounds to capture the prevalence and trends in population antibody positivity: (1) after the first wave (rounds 1 and 2), (2) during the emergence of the second wave (rounds 3 and 4), and (3) to assess the impact of vaccination (rounds 5 and 6). We did not commission any further rounds.

Key Data Elements and Data Quality/Editing

Prevalence estimates. We calculated prevalence as the proportion of individuals with a positive IgG test result on the LFIA, adjusted for test performance using

$$p = (q + \text{specificity} - 1)/(\text{sensitivity} + \text{specificity} - 1), \quad (1)$$

where p is the adjusted proportion positive and q is the observed proportion positive.[10]

We weighted prevalence estimates (and 95% CIs) to account for the geographic sample design and for variation in response rates to be representative of the population (aged ≥ 18 years) of England (Table A). In our approach we used random iterative method weighting[11] to adjust to population estimates for age, sex, index of multiple deprivation decile,[12] LTLA, and ethnic group. We based the weighting approach on that described in Elliott et al.[13] but for 7 rather than 9 age categories.

We used logistic regression to identify sociodemographic variation in antibody positivity by estimating the odds ratio (OR). An OR greater than 1 indicated that the group was more likely to have higher prevalence of antibody test positivity relative to the reference group per sociodemographic variable. We adjusted models for age, sex, and region as well as for ethnic group, deprivation score, household size, and occupation.

We estimated the infection fatality ratio from the total number of COVID-19 deaths among adults in England[14] divided by our estimate of the total number of SARS-CoV-2 infections since the start of the pandemic until mid-July 2020. We estimated this by multiplying the weighted and adjusted antibody prevalence by the midyear population size at aged 18 years and older in England. We obtained an overall infection fatality ratio estimate of 0.90% (95% CI = 0.86, 0.94) as well as estimates stratified by age, sex, and ethnic group.[15]

LFIA self-testing procedure. The LFIA requires a blood sample from a finger prick and produces a test result after 10 to 15 minutes. The test kits sent to participants included 1 LFIA device, 1 bottle of buffer solution, 2 pressure-activated 23-gauge lancets, 1 alcohol wipe, and a 1-milliliter plastic pipette, alongside an instruction booklet with a link to an online video.

The key visual features of the Fortress SARS-CoV-2 LFIA device include the test result window and blood sample well (Figure 2). The result window has an initially blue control line, which will remain if the test is unsuccessful (i.e., invalid). In a successful test, the control line turns red, and if IgG antibodies are present in the blood sample above a threshold, a secondary line will appear below the control. There is also a line indicating IgM (immunoglobulin M), but this performed poorly in our initial laboratory evaluation and was not analyzed. We provided participants with detailed instructions on how to record the result in the questionnaire response as either negative, Ig M positive, Ig G positive, IgG and IgM positive, or invalid. We informed participants that results were not reliable at an individual level.

Data security. We transferred data securely from Ipsos to Imperial College London and held them on secure servers in an ISO27001 environment managed by the School of Public Health. We assigned study participants a study ID and stripped data of identifying information for the statistical analyses; only a few named and designated individuals have access to identifying information, in line with a published privacy policy (see Privacy Notice Imperial College London: https://bit.ly/3YDT1Qp and Department of Health and Social Care: https://bit.ly/3skKHJf) and compliant with the UK Data Protection Act 2018, which is the UK implementation of the General Data Protection Regulation (https://www.gov.uk/data-protection).

Managing disclosure risks. To protect confidentiality, we do not release individual data, and we suppress tabular data if there are fewer than 5 entries in a cell where 1 or more person is positive for SARS-CoV-2 IgG on LFIA.

DATA ANALYSIS/ DISSEMINATION

We fed the results of the REACT-2 study each round through written and verbal reports to a weekly data debrief group of the UK Health Security Agency (previously Public Health England) to provide situational awareness and inform public health policy. In addition, we placed REACT-2 data and results in the public domain in near real time (through preprints and media press releases), thus informing both the public and the international scientific community of emerging data on the prevalence of SARS-CoV-2 antibody test positivity.

Interpretation Issues

During the study period, we observed a gradual fall in response rates: from a high of 33.5% in round 1 (June 2020),

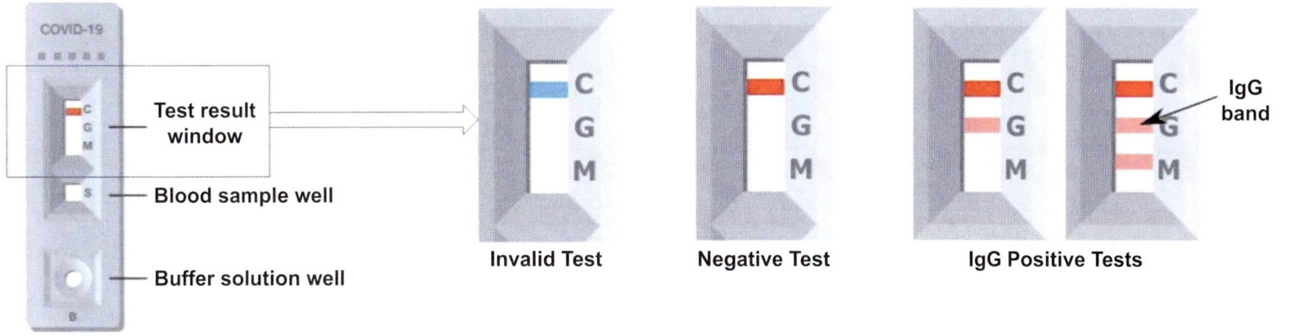

FIGURE 2— Diagram of Lateral Flow Immunoassay (LFIA) Kit With Guide to Reading and Reporting the Result: England, June 20, 2020–May 25, 2021

Note. IgG = immunoglobin G. The detail of the test result window indicates what invalid, negative, and positive results look like.

which was carried out following the first wave in England, to 26.3% in round 5 (January 2021), which was conducted in the early stages of vaccine rollout. In round 6, the response rate rose to 28.0%, reflecting the boosted sample of individuals aged 55 to 74 years, who generally had high response rates to our surveys. Our surveys also had a lower response rate among people from minority ethnic groups and those in more deprived areas. We reweighted the sample in each round to account for differential variation in response to be representative of England's population (≥ 18 years) as a whole, although this may not have overcome unknown participation biases.

We used a qualitative (yes/no) at-home self-administered LFIA on a finger prick capillary blood sample instead of more resource-intensive gold standard quantitative laboratory tests performed on venous blood samples. To demonstrate the validity of this approach, we conducted extensive evaluation of the selected LFIA, which showed it to have acceptable performance (sensitivity and specificity) compared with confirmatory laboratory tests.[1] We took steps to measure and improve usability, including ability to perform and read an LFIA test at home.[4,7] By adjusting our survey results for known LFIA performance, we demonstrated that, despite not meeting regulatory standards for clinical use in individuals, self-testing and -reporting using LFIAs provide a valid tool for obtaining reliable community-wide prevalence estimates in a cost-effective manner, rapidly, and at scale.

For those with a self-reported clinical history of confirmed or suspected

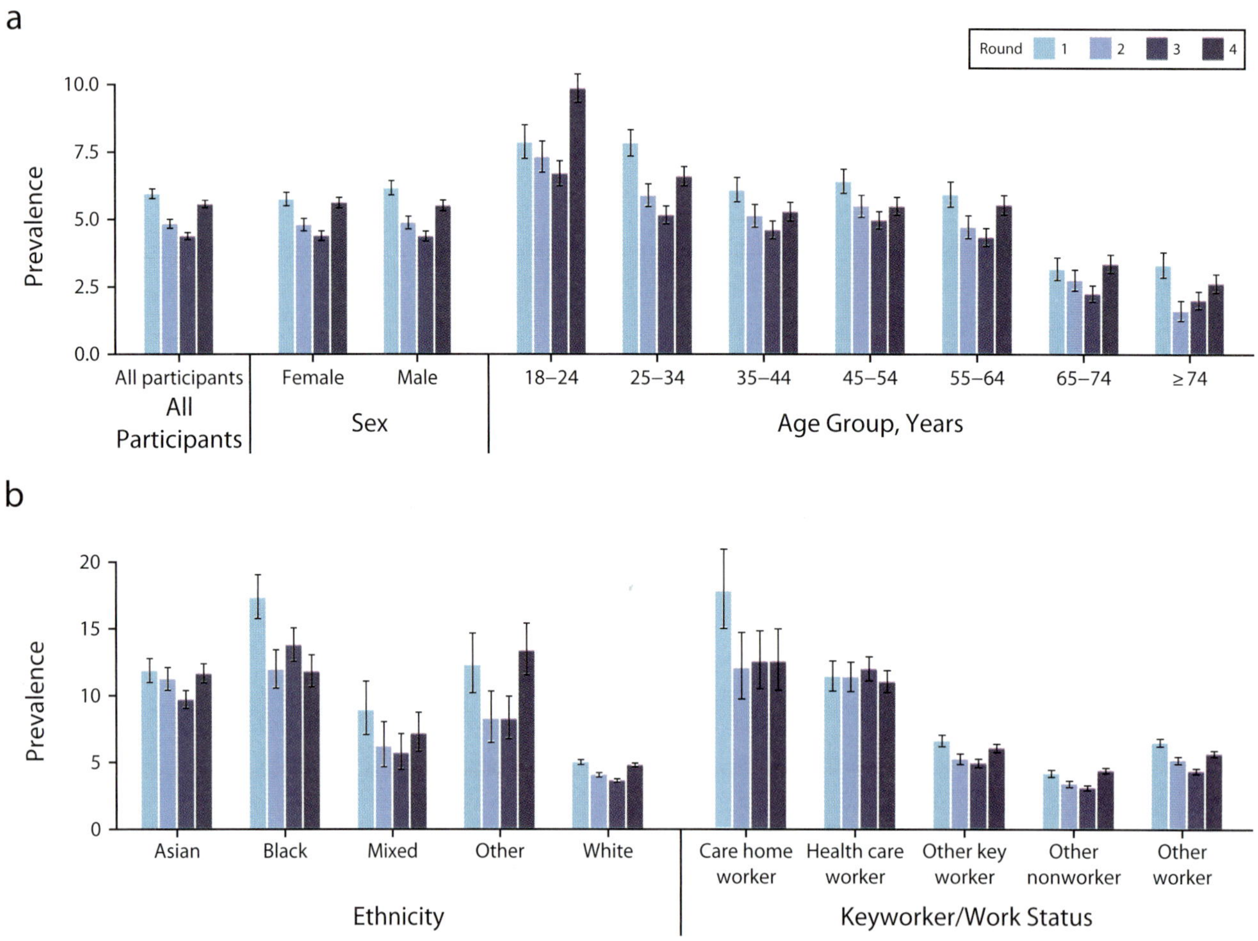

FIGURE 3— **Antibody Prevalence With Confidence Intervals by Round for Rounds 1–4 (before vaccination), in the Sample (a) Overall and Stratified by Sex and Age, and (b) Stratified by Ethnic Group and Employment: England, June 20, 2020–May 25, 2021**

Note. Estimates were adjusted and weighted except for employment where data were not available for weighting.

COVID-19, there was a potential for reporting bias because respondents were not blinded to their test results; however, there was high concordance of self-test with clinician-read results. To support ongoing quality assurance for the self-tests, we designed an automated lateral flow analysis computerized pipeline using machine learning, computer vision techniques, and signal-processing algorithms to analyze the uploaded images of the test[16]; we found high concordance with reported self-test results.

Our study demonstrated a substantial decrease (26.5%) in population antibody test positivity over 3 months between rounds 1 and 3 (June 20–September 28, 2020), indicating antibody waning 3 and 6 months after the first wave of infections (Figure 3).[17] To exclude the possibility that that this could be attributable to differences in LFIA batch, we compared the laboratory performance of the LFIAs used in rounds 1 and 2 (where we had seen the strongest decrease in positive tests) and found no difference between the 2 rounds.

Linkage Ability

Data linkage (based on unique NHS number) to vaccination status (i.e., vaccine type and date) and outcome data (i.e., hospitalizations, deaths) is available for participants who consented to linkage to their health records.

Data Release/Accessibility

Access to REACT-2 individual-level data is restricted to protect participants' anonymity. Summary statistics, descriptive tables, and code from REACT-2 are available on Github (https://bit.ly/3EC15be), and study materials for each round are on the study Web site (https://bit.ly/3sgrybg).

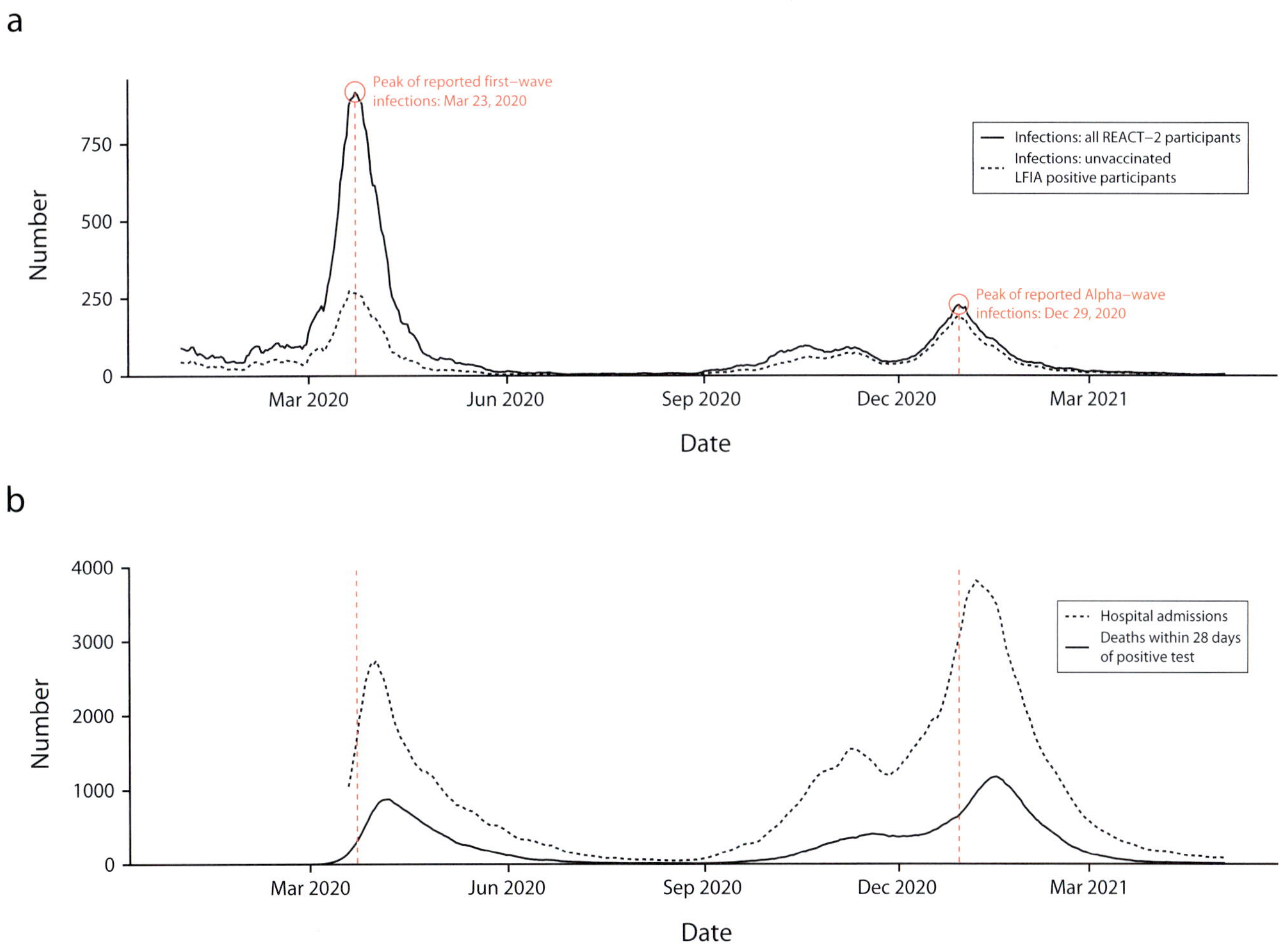

FIGURE 4— Reconstruction of COVID-19 Pandemic Curve by (a) Week of Symptom Onset Reported by REACT-2 Participants, Alongside (b) National Data on Admissions and Deaths From COVID-19: England, June 20, 2020–May 25, 2021

Note. LFIA = lateral flow immunoassay; REACT-2 = REal-time Assessment of Community Transmission-2. In part a, the solid line includes date of onset for all cases of COVID-19 reported by participants, and the dashed line is limited to those who had a positive LFIA test result in the REACT-2 study.

Key References and Other Information

We published our initial protocol[18] and our key findings during the 11 months of fieldwork,[15,17,19–21] including clinical and laboratory evaluation of antibody tests and feasibility studies of at-home self-testing and -reporting using LFIAs[2,5–7,16] in preprints and peer-reviewed journal publications. Links to all our publications are given on the study Web site (https://bit.ly/3KPg8l4) and included for reference in the appendix.

PUBLIC HEALTH IMPLICATIONS

REACT-2 provided reliable and robust estimates of population prevalence of SARS-CoV-2 IgG antibody test positivity during the first 2 waves of the COVID-19 pandemic and the initial stages of vaccine rollout in England. It demonstrated high feasibility and acceptability of using at-home self-administered LFIA tests (self-reported and uploaded photo for verification) as a means of providing reliable, cost-effective, community-wide prevalence estimates rapidly and at scale. This contrasts with the use of quantitative laboratory assays, which require blood to be collected, transported, and processed in a laboratory.

REACT-2 confirmed early reports that SARS-CoV-2 disproportionately affected people from disadvantaged and minority ethnic groups in England, as well as health and care workers (Figure 3), suggesting that the higher hospitalization and mortality from COVID-19 in these population groups reflected higher rates of infection. We found no difference in the estimated infection fatality ratio between people of broad ethnic categories (Black, Asian, White) when stratified by age and sex.[15] Based on participant responses to questions about onset of previous COVID-19 symptoms, we were able to reconstruct a pandemic curve for infection in early 2020 that closely matched but slightly predated the curves of hospitalizations and deaths.[15] This gives context validity and provides an indication of the size and shape of the first and second waves (Figure 4). The pandemic curve was replicated in each round, providing further validation of the approach.[15,17,19,20]

We also provided timely information on changes in the prevalence of antibody positivity over time as a result of both natural infection and vaccination (Figure 1). The observed decrease in population antibody positivity following the first wave (Figure 3) supported emerging data on SARS-CoV-2 that indicated a decrease over time in antibody levels (i.e., waning) in a proportion of individuals followed in longitudinal studies.[22] Before vaccination, we observed waning of 26.5% over 3 months, with the biggest decrease in older people.[17] In the later rounds, by tracking antibody test positivity to COVID-19 following vaccination and showing differential waning, our study provided key data underpinning vaccination policy and contributed to recommendations regarding groups who might benefit from additional vaccine doses.[20,21]

Finally, the success of REACT-2 was strengthened by rapid public involvement at every stage. Public volunteers and a diverse advisory panel provided input into the design and conduct of the study. Their desire to support the national response shows that public involvement is both possible and necessary during periods of emergency response.

Antibody self-testing at home is feasible and acceptable and can provide essential data to policymakers within days. To roll this out quickly in future pandemics, it is important to invest in the necessary technologies and infrastructure,[23] including test production, implementation logistics, and study design and data analysis. AJPH

ABOUT THE AUTHORS

Helen Ward, Christina Atchison, Matthew Whitaker, Bethan Davies, Deborah Ashby, Marc Chadeau-Hyam, Steven Riley, and Paul Elliott are with the School of Public Health, Imperial College London, UK. Ara Darzi is with the Institute of Global Health Innovation, Imperial College London. Christl A. Donnelly is with the Department of Statistics, University of Oxford, Oxford, UK. Wendy Barclay and Graham S. Cooke are with the Department of Infectious Disease, Imperial College London.

CORRESPONDENCE

Correspondence should be sent to Professor Helen Ward or Professor Paul Elliott, School of Public Health, Imperial College London, St Mary's Campus, London W2 1PG, UK (e-mail: h.ward@imperial.ac.uk; p.elliott@imperial.ac.uk). Reprints can be ordered at http://www.ajph.org by clicking the "Reprints" link.

PUBLICATION INFORMATION

Full Citation: Ward H, Atchison C, Whitaker M, et al. Design and implementation of a national program to monitor the prevalence of SARS-CoV-2 IgG antibodies in England using self-testing: the REACT-2 study. *Am J Public Health*. 2023;113(11):1201–1209.

Acceptance Date: June 28, 2023.

DOI: https://doi.org/10.2105/AJPH.2023.307381

CONTRIBUTORS

H. Ward and P. Elliott drafted the article. The other authors critically reviewed the article and provided comments. All authors agreed to submission for publication.

ACKNOWLEDGMENTS

This study was funded by the Department of Health and Social Care in England. H. Ward acknowledges support from the National Institute for Health and Care Research (NIHR) Imperial Biomedical Research Centre, and the NIHR Applied Research Collaboration Northwest London. C. A. Donnelly acknowledges support from the Medical Research Council Centre for Global Infectious Disease Analysis, the NIHR Health Protection Research Unit in Emerging and Zoonotic Infections, and the NIHR-funded Vaccine Efficacy Evaluation for Priority Emerging Diseases (grant PR-OD-1017-20007). M. Chadeau-Hyam acknowledges support from Cancer Research UK (grant 22184), H2020-EXPANSE (Horizon 2020 grant 874627), and H2020-LongITools (Horizon 2020 grant 874739). G. S. Cooke is supported by an NIHR professorship. P. Elliott acknowledges support from Health Data Research UK, the NIHR Imperial

Biomedical Research Centre, NIHR Health Protection Research Units in Chemical and Radiation Threats and Hazards (grant NIHR-200922), and Environmental Exposures and Health (grant NIHR-200880), the British Heart Foundation Centre for Research Excellence at Imperial College London (grant RE/18/4/34215), and the UK Dementia Research Institute at Imperial College London (grant MC_PC_17114).

We thank key collaborators on this work: K. Beaver, S. Clemens, G. Welch, N. Gilby, K. Ward, G. Pantelidou, and K. Pickering at Ipsos; G. Fontana and J. Alford at the Institute of Global Health Innovation at Imperial College London; E. Johnson, R. Elliott, G. Blakoe, M. Piggin, and H. Johnson at the School of Public Health, Imperial College London, UK. We also thank the REACT Public Advisory Panel and all participants in the study. We thank the National Health Service for access to the patient register, and the Department of Health and Social Care for logistical support.

Note. The funders had no role in the design and conduct of the study; collection, management, analysis, and interpretation of the data; or preparation, review, or approval of this article.

CONFLICTS OF INTEREST

The authors have no conflicts of interest to declare.

HUMAN PARTICIPANT PROTECTION

The REACT-2 study received ethical approval from the South Central Berkshire B Research Ethics Committee, UK. Participants gave individual consent to participate either online or by telephone.

REFERENCES

1. Flower B, Brown JC, Simmons B, et al. Clinical and laboratory evaluation of SARS-CoV-2 lateral flow assays for use in a national COVID-19 seroprevalence survey. *Thorax.* 2020;75(12):1082–1088. https://doi.org/10.1136/thoraxjnl-2020-215732
2. Moshe M, Daunt A, Flower B, et al. SARS-CoV-2 lateral flow assays for possible use in national COVID-19 seroprevalence surveys (REACT 2): diagnostic accuracy study. *BMJ.* 2021;372(423):n423. https://doi.org/10.1136/bmj.n423
3. Khan M, Rosadas C, Katsanovskaja K, et al. Simple, sensitive, specific self-sampling assay secures SARS-CoV-2 antibody signals in sero-prevalence and post-vaccine studies. *Sci Rep.* 2022;12(1):1885. https://doi.org/10.1038/s41598-022-05640-x
4. Davies B, Araghi M, Moshe M, et al. Acceptability, usability, and performance of lateral flow immunoassay tests for severe acute respiratory syndrome coronavirus 2 antibodies: REACT-2 study of self-testing in nonhealthcare key workers. *Open Forum Infect Dis.* 2021;8(11):ofab496. https://doi.org/10.1093/ofid/ofab496
5. Cann A, Clarke C, Brown J, et al. Severe acute respiratory syndrome coronavirus 2 (SARS-CoV-2) antibody lateral flow assay for antibody prevalence studies following vaccination: a diagnostic accuracy study. *Wellcome Open Res.* 2021;6:358. https://doi.org/10.12688/wellcomeopenres.17231.1
6. Atchison CJ, Moshe M, Brown JC, et al. Validity of self-testing at home with rapid severe acute respiratory syndrome coronavirus 2 antibody detection by lateral flow immunoassay. *Clin Infect Dis.* 2023;76(4):658–666. https://doi.org/10.1093/cid/ciac629
7. Atchison C, Pristerà P, Cooper E, et al. Usability and acceptability of home-based self-testing for severe acute respiratory syndrome coronavirus 2 (SARS-CoV-2) antibodies for population surveillance. *Clin Infect Dis.* 2021;72(9):e384–e393. https://doi.org/10.1093/cid/ciaa1178
8. UK Department of Health and Social Care. UK COVID-19 vaccines delivery plan. January 13, 2023. Available at: https://www.gov.uk/government/publications/uk-covid-19-vaccines-delivery-plan/uk-covid-19-vaccines-delivery-plan. Accessed August 19, 2023.
9. UK Prime Minister's Office. Prime minister's statement on coronavirus (COVID-19): 23 March 2020. January 23, 2020. Available at: https://www.gov.uk/government/speeches/pm-address-to-the-nation-on-coronavirus-23-march-2020. Accessed August 19, 2023.
10. Diggle PJ. Estimating prevalence using an imperfect test. *Epidemiol Res Int.* 2011;608719. https://doi.org/10.1155/2011/608719
11. Sharot T. Weighting survey results. *J Mark Res Soc.* 1986;28(3):269–284.
12. McLennan D, Noble S, Noble M, Plunkett E, Wright G, Gutacker N. *The English Indices of Deprivation 2019.* September 2019. Available at: https://assets.publishing.service.gov.uk/government/uploads/system/uploads/attachment_data/file/833951/IoD2019_Technical_Report.pdf. Accessed August 19, 2023.
13. Elliott P, Whitaker M, Tang D, et al. Design and implementation of a national SARS-CoV-2 monitoring program in England: REACT-1 study. *Am J Public Health.* 2023;113(5):545–554. https://doi.org/10.2105/AJPH.2023.307230
14. Public Health England. Excess mortality in England, week ending 17 July 2020. October 29, 2020. Available at: https://fingertips.phe.org.uk/static-reports/mortality-surveillance/excess-mortality-in-england-week-ending-17-Jul-2020.html. Accessed August 19, 2023.
15. Ward H, Atchison C, Whitaker M, et al. SARS-CoV-2 antibody prevalence in England following the first peak of the pandemic. *Nat Commun.* 2021;12(1):905. https://doi.org/10.1038/s41467-021-21237-w
16. Wong NCK, Meshkinfamfard S, Turbé V, et al. Machine learning to support visual auditing of home-based lateral flow immunoassay self-test results for SARS-CoV-2 antibodies. *Commun Med (Lond).* 2022;2:78. https://doi.org/10.1038/s43856-022-00146-z
17. Ward H, Cooke GS, Atchison C, et al. Prevalence of antibody positivity to SARS-CoV-2 following the first peak of infection in England: serial cross-sectional studies of 365,000 adults. *Lancet Reg Health Eur.* 2021;4:100098. https://doi.org/10.1016/j.lanepe.2021.100098
18. Riley S, Atchison C, Ashby D, et al. REal-time Assessment of Community Transmission (REACT) of SARS-CoV-2 virus: study protocol. *Wellcome Open Res.* 2021;5:200. https://doi.org/10.12688/wellcomeopenres.16228.1
19. Ward H, Atchison C, Whitaker M, et al. Increasing SARS-CoV-2 antibody prevalence in England at the start of the second wave: REACT-2 round 4 cross-sectional study in 160,000 adults. *medRxiv.* [Posted July 22, 2021]. https://doi.org/10.1101/2021.07.21.21260926
20. Ward H, Cooke G, Whitaker M, et al. REACT-2 round 5: increasing prevalence of SARS-CoV-2 antibodies demonstrate impact of the second wave and of vaccine roll-out in England. *medRxiv.* [Posted March 1, 2021]. https://doi.org/10.1101/2021.02.26.21252512
21. Ward H, Whitaker M, Flower B, et al. Population antibody responses following COVID-19 vaccination in 212,102 individuals. *Nat Commun.* 2022;13(1):907. https://doi.org/10.1038/s41467-022-28527-x
22. Choe PG, Kang CK, Suh HJ, et al. Waning antibody responses in asymptomatic and symptomatic SARS-CoV-2 infection. *Emerg Infect Dis.* 2021;27(1):327–329. https://doi.org/10.3201/eid2701.203515
23. Budd J, Miller BS, Weckman NE, et al. Lateral flow test engineering and lessons learned from COVID-19. *Nat Rev Bioeng.* 2023;1:13–31. https://doi.org/10.1038/s44222-022-00007-3

Extending an Antiracism Lens to the Implementation of Precision Public Health Interventions

Caitlin G. Allen, PhD, MPH, Dana Lee Olstad, PhD, MSc, RD, Anna R. Kahkoska, PhD, MD, Yue Guan, PhD, Paula S. Ramos, PhD, Julia Steinberg, PhD, Stephanie A. S. Staras, PhD, Crystal Y. Lumpkins, PhD, Laura V. Milko, PhD, Erin Turbitt, PhD, Alanna K. Rahm, PhD, Katherine W. Saylor, PhD, Stephanie Best, PhD, Ashley Hatch, MPH, Isabella Santangelo, BS, and Megan C. Roberts, PhD

See also Choate, p. 1141.

Precision public health holds promise to improve disease prevention and health promotion strategies, allowing the right intervention to be delivered to the right population at the right time.

Growing concerns underscore the potential for precision-based approaches to exacerbate health disparities by relying on biased data inputs and recapitulating existing access inequities. To achieve its full potential, precision public health must focus on addressing social and structural drivers of health and prominently incorporate equity-related concerns, particularly with respect to race and ethnicity.

In this article, we discuss how an antiracism lens could be applied to reduce health disparities and health inequities through equity-informed research, implementation, and evaluation of precision public health interventions. (*Am J Public Health*. 2023;113(11):1210–1218. https://doi.org/10.2105/AJPH.2023.307386)

AJPH November 2023, Vol 113, No. 11

Precision public health (PPH) has emerged as a population-level approach that seeks to tailor disease prevention and health promotion strategies to provide the right intervention to the right populations or subpopulations at the right time.[1–3] PPH interventions are defined here as any product, program, or policy delivered to a population to improve its health that includes components tailored to specific biological, social-behavioral, or environmental characteristics of the individuals in the population. Considering heterogeneity both within and across populations, PPH interventions may be more effective for disease prevention and health promotion than its preceding "one size fits all" approach.

Despite its promise, concerns have been raised about whether PPH interventions may exacerbate health inequalities. For example, universal genetic screening for hereditary breast and ovarian cancer, Lynch syndrome, and familial hypercholesterolemia can help tailor disease prevention approaches and, if equitably implemented, has the potential to reduce health disparities and health inequities. However, implementation of screening programs for these conditions remains suboptimal, with significant challenges in uptake among racial and ethnic minority groups, rural communities, uninsured or underinsured people, and those with lower education and income.[4] The COVID-19 pandemic similarly highlighted equity challenges for public health caused by inequitable infrastructure for data collection and interventions. Data on infections, hospitalizations, COVID-19–related deaths, and vaccinations were essential to tailoring infection control efforts. Specifically, structural racism had a negative impact on data collection from racial and ethnic minority groups, exacerbating disparities as well as limiting the effectiveness of PPH in reducing disease burden.[5]

In discussions surrounding the risks and benefits of PPH, much of the literature has focused on approaches that may affect individual agency, with fewer explicit conversations to center other fundamental, structural drivers of health, including racism.[6] Race and ethnicity are social constructs and serve as proxies for numerous social determinants of health because of historic and ongoing structural and experienced racism.[7–9] Racism can be experienced in many forms simultaneously, including internalized, interpersonal, cultural, and structural.[7–9] However, no matter the form, a vast literature confirms that racism is associated with poor physical and mental health, lower access to health interventions, and limited opportunities to participate in research.[8] Thus, without explicitly incorporating equity-related considerations prominently within PPH research, PPH interventions could exacerbate health inequities and the effects of racism.

Recently, Shelton et al.[10] outlined how an antiracism lens could be applied within the field of implementation science (Table A, available as a supplement to the online version of this article at http://www.ajph.org). Implementation science offers theoretical frameworks and strategies to promote the adoption and integration of evidence-based interventions by supporting the delivery of these interventions into various settings. The field of implementation science is thus deeply connected to PPH intervention delivery in that it comprises the key methodologies for implementing and sustaining tailored evidence-based practices, at scale. According to Shelton et al., selecting frameworks, methods, and interventions that are agnostic to the impacts of structural racism can inadvertently exacerbate inequities. Intentionally collecting and analyzing data related to racial and ethnic equity over the life course of a PPH intervention is essential for incorporating an antiracist lens into its implementation. Ongoing work incorporating health equity considerations into implementation science frameworks has examined how to contextualize implementation science evaluations by examining multilevel factors that are integral to successful, equitable implementation. In return, implementation science frameworks can help operationalize evidence-based practices to address health equity and racism within PPH.

Addressing structural drivers of health, including race and racism, must be fundamental to the implementation of PPH interventions. To facilitate PPH in achieving its goal of effective and equitable disease prevention, we focus this article on the intersection of the implementation of PPH interventions and the key social dimension of race and ethnicity. We consider a series of case studies that apply an antiracism lens to the implementation of PPH interventions in the following recommended focus areas:

1. stakeholder engagement;
2. conceptual frameworks and models;
3. development, selection, or adaptations of evidence-based interventions;
4. evaluation approaches;
5. implementation strategies; and
6. individual researcher and research context.[10]

We conclude by summarizing recommendations to guide researchers on how to address the impacts of racism at all stages of the research process, thereby moving the field of PPH in an explicitly equity-oriented direction (Box 1).

STAKEHOLDER ENGAGEMENT

Cocreation and the incorporation of representative stakeholder perspectives are critically important for addressing racism in PPH research and the implementation of PPH interventions.[10,11] Stakeholder engagement offers a process of cocreation to incorporate informed community perspectives on complex topics such as data privacy, novel interventions, emerging genomic discoveries, and allocation of limited resources. In turn, this approach can maximize the likelihood that programs and policies will be relevant, acceptable, and successful for diverse communities.[12] A recent review examining public involvement in genomics research underscored the need for sustainable stakeholder involvement throughout various stages of the project life cycle, given the potential long-term impact of certain genomics research studies.[13]

Democratic deliberation is one strategy to foster colearning among researchers and communities that could be applied to gain informed public input on the implementation of PPH interventions. Democratic deliberation refers to a collective stakeholder engagement process conducted rationally and fairly among a deliberation group that reflects the diversity of community views and life experiences.[14] As part of this process, participants are provided with nonpersuasive neutral information about a topic, after which they collaboratively generate and prioritize the pros and cons of the policy or program under discussion. Groups subsequently come to a consensus opinion that, in theory, would maximize the common good. This approach may be particularly useful when considering PPH interventions for marginalized groups whose perspectives may be missing from other decision processes. Enlisting members of marginalized groups to generate and thoughtfully consider potential pros and cons of health policies and programs through the lens of personally experienced inequities can be an act of empowerment. Previous literature has found that democratic deliberation methods could provide inclusive and informed stakeholder opinions.[15]

In many cases, little attention is given to the appropriateness and standards of the methods used to engage stakeholders in PPH interventions. As a result, approaches for public involvement proliferate with little systematic evidence regarding the quality of these approaches. Several recent studies suggest frameworks to evaluate the quality of public engagement. For example, the Findable, Accessible, Interoperable, Reproducible, Equitable, and Responsible (FAIRER) framework, specifically developed to guide genomic activities, uses 4 themes for deliberative reflection: fairness, context, heterogeneity, and recognizing tensions and conflict.[16] Another important quality consideration is the application of an antiracism lens to stakeholder recruitment. For a recent study with communities of African ancestry in Georgia, the research team partnered with local community organizations to identify characteristics specific to their area that would indicate viewpoint diversity and experiences that required consideration of the common good.[17] The research team used these indicators when considering potential participants through a structured interview process, to ensure that a diversity of views was captured that would encourage a well-rounded discussion centered on the common good.[17] Thoughtful and focused stakeholder recruitment would enable members of communities often excluded from PPH policy decision-making, such as racial and ethnic minorities, to participate in implementation research in accordance with their communities' values and priorities, enabling these values and priorities to be incorporated into the research and future policies.

As stakeholder engagement approaches become more sophisticated, researchers can address PPH implementation issues with more informed and considered community input. Innovative and effective public engagement methods warrant more attention. This can begin by researchers challenging themselves to operationalize higher-intensity strategies (e.g., democratic deliberation) to ensure that interventions and policies align with community perspectives.

CONCEPTUAL FRAMEWORKS AND MODELS

Implementation science theories, models, and frameworks can be used deliberately and in multiple ways in the design, implementation, and evaluation of PPH interventions to address and reduce inequities that disproportionately harm historically excluded and marginalized groups, such as racial and ethnic minorities.[10,18,19] In the preimplementation phase, determinant frameworks such as the Consolidated Framework for Implementation Research (CFIR) can help inform the design of responsive interventions and implementation strategies by identifying barriers and facilitators that affect implementation efforts. Other models and frameworks, such as Reach, Effectiveness, Adoption, Implementation, and Maintenance (RE-AIM), can guide the planning and conduct of implementation as well as the evaluation of multilevel outcomes in implementation and maintenance phases. The following are 3 examples of implementation science frameworks with different approaches to incorporating health equity and how they could be used for PPH.[20]

The Health Equity Implementation Framework (HEIF) is a new determinants framework that modifies and combines components of the integrated-Promoting Action on Research Implementation in Health Services (i-PARIHS) framework and the Health Care Disparities Framework, allowing for the assessment of both implementation and health equity determinants simultaneously.[21] Researchers have used the HEIF to identify and address factors that stimulate or impair the equitable implementation of PPH interventions. For example, Harkness et al. used the HEIF to refine implementation strategies to equitably deliver PPH interventions such as preexposure prophylaxis and HIV treatment to marginalized groups most affected by HIV and AIDS.[22] This approach found that implementation of these programs should address culturally specific factors, leverage networks, tailor resources, and facilitate service navigation.

Another approach has been to incorporate health equity considerations into existing frameworks. For example, the updated CFIR 2.0 has been supplemented with new constructs and subconstructs highlighting barriers and facilitators to health equity. The authors also recommend broadening the lens beyond local determinants to identify and address upstream sources of health inequity that are embedded in the public policies, institutional practices, and cultural norms that sustain structural racism.[23]

Similarly, health equity considerations have been integrated into implementation science frameworks for planning and evaluation. The extended RE-AIM framework provides instructions for applying its health equity considerations to the development, implementation, and maintenance of a PPH intervention. Considering health equity in the planning and evaluation stages of implementation science contributes to long-term sustainability and successful adaptation of evidence-based

BOX 1— Recommendations for Implementing an Antiracist Framework in Precision Public Health Interventions

Implementation Science Components[10]	Recommendations
Stakeholder engagement	Obtain input from communities, particularly those from racial and ethnic minority groups.
	Ensure interventions and policies are aligned with community perspectives.
	Implement higher-engagement strategies for greater community involvement in decision-making.
Conceptual frameworks and models	Seek out and use implementation tools to advance antidiscrimination and antiracism efforts.
	Incorporate structural racism and other contextual factors into conceptual models.
	Measure perceived racism and racial discrimination and recognize their impact on implementation.
	Use transdisciplinary theories to understand the mechanisms that perpetuate health disparities.
Development, selection, or adaptations of evidence-based interventions	Involve communities in identifying and prioritizing evidence-based interventions.
	Include evidence-based strategies to address the impact of racism on implementation of precision public health programs.
Evaluation approaches	Assess the effectiveness of precision public health approaches by race and ethnicity.
	Use validated measures and self-report to assess racial equity and racism, including qualitative methods to amplify the voices of those with lived experiences of racism.
Implementation strategies	Focus on multilevel implementation strategies that address structural racism.
Individual research and research context	Ensure responsible training and engagement of researchers grounded in Public Health Critical Race Praxis.
	Support and advocate for policies, systems, and structures that promote and sustain diversity in precision public health teams.

interventions to diverse contexts. Health equity is therefore centered in each of the 5 recently extended dimensions of the RE-AIM framework.[24] Integrating equity-focused partnerships wherever possible at all stages of PPH implementation is crucial to developing and prioritizing outcomes and measures that reflect whether, how, and why an intervention is being equitably adopted and sustained.

As implementation science increasingly plays an integral role in the development, implementation, and sustainment of PPH interventions, researchers and practitioners must commit to seeking out and using available implementation tools to dismantle discrimination and racism at every opportunity.[4] Although structural racism continues to underpin pervasive inequities in access to preventative and diagnostic health care, multilevel consideration of health equity-oriented constructs remains a top priority and a moral imperative for implementation science. As Shelton et al. emphasize, structural discrimination and racism are deeply embedded contextual factors that must be considered throughout all aspects of implementation. Furthermore, transdisciplinary theories, such as intersectionality and structural violence, can offer insight into important and overlapping dimensions of inequity, such as racism, sexism, and classism. These complementary theoretical perspectives are not as commonly examined in implementation science but may serve to guide and enhance the pursuit of health equity goals for the implementation of PPH.[25]

DEVELOPMENT AND SELECTION OF EVIDENCE-BASED INTERVENTIONS

Shelton et al. emphasize that the development and selection of evidence-based interventions that are devoid of stakeholder involvement and engagement have limited applicability to specific contexts and settings and may reinforce structural barriers that have systematically perpetuated health inequities and will ultimately undermine efficacy and effectiveness in racial and ethnic minority groups. Of particular concern for PPH interventions that rely on large-scale data to inform intervention design is underreporting, inadequate reporting, and defective collection of data from racial and ethnic minority groups; if the underlying data used to tailor PPH approaches is biased, it may replicate existing discrimination. There are also concerns about the potential impact on the development and utility of the intervention itself.[5] These issues were manifested in the development of PPH interventions to address COVID-19 among racial and ethnic minority groups. Intentional integration of data sources and regular testing, refinement, and retesting of

COVID-19 prevention and treatment interventions among racial and ethnic minority groups would have allowed for modifications of interventions based on how participants responded.[26] Collaborating with health equity researchers in the use of qualitative methods, quasi-experimental designs, pragmatic trials, and hybrid effectiveness-implementation study designs is recommended as new PPH interventions are being developed and tested among racial and ethnic minority groups.

Context-specific adaptations to PPH interventions may help enhance health equity. Much of the premise of PPH is to adapt interventions to the specific individual and population to help increase the uptake and effectiveness of these approaches. Further tailoring of these interventions to ensure they are inclusive of the local culture, history, and strengths of the community can support antiracism in the implementation of PPH interventions. By working alongside community partners, researchers could study the impact of adapting a PPH intervention to meet the needs of racial and ethnic minority groups on the acceptability, practicality, feasibility, and integrability of PPH interventions.[27]

EVALUATION APPROACHES

Another tenet of Shelton et al.'s framework is the explicit inclusion of measures that assess health equity. Several implementation evaluation frameworks have already been adapted to consider health equity.[28,29] These frameworks can inform the evaluation of the implementation of PPH interventions as well as guide the selection of key effectiveness, implementation, and health equity outcomes across stages of implementation. Additionally, the use of mixed methods data collection in evaluation of PPH initiatives allows for both breadth and depth in our understanding of the complexities in operationalizing implementation science measures to understand the implementation of PPH across representation populations.[30,31]

The extended RE-AIM framework expands beyond measures of reach and representativeness by explicitly examining whether race and ethnicity—as well as individual, social, and structural determinants for which race is a proxy—influence willingness to participate in a PPH intervention. It can also assess whether participants reflect the catchment area and national population in terms of race and ethnicity, socioeconomic position, educational attainment, primary language, rurality, and other known contributors to health care utilization.

Although measuring race-related outcomes is important for dismantling racial inequity, any studies capturing race should specify the reason within a sociopolitical framework that explicitly acknowledges the relevant social, environmental, and structural factors for which race may serve as a proxy measure.[9] Understanding why individuals decline to participate in a PPH intervention can provide a better understanding of barriers to reaching a representative population. These data can then inform new outreach and enrollment strategies to improve the representativeness of PPH interventions, which can be tested and optimized iteratively.

Key implementation measures, such as tracking of adaptations of PPH, can help to contextualize differential site-level adoption and patient representativeness (Table B, available as a supplement to the online version of this article at https://www.ajph.org). Adoption could be measured to identify potential inequities in the adoption of PPH interventions by key site characteristics (e.g., low-resourced settings) that may affect representative access to PPH. In addition, measuring fidelity can help determine the quality of implementation of a PPH intervention's core components by site characteristics to understand whether variable fidelity could contribute to inequities among patient populations served by these sites. Understanding how PPH interventions are implemented with fidelity and adaptation can provide insights into needed resources and support (e.g., to promote fidelity to core components) as well as the development of local strategies (e.g., to attend to the local context and promote equitable implementation across settings and participant populations). Determinant frameworks such as the HEIF or CFIR 2.0 can provide an understanding of contextual factors that may be associated with implementation outcomes across phases of implementation, pointing to effective strategies for implementation improvement, discussed in the next section. Further, determinant frameworks such as the HEIF or CFIR 2.0 can guide the assessment of important contextual factors that may be associated with implementation outcomes across phases of adoption, implementation, and maintenance by social determinants of health, including site characteristics and patient sociodemographics. Collecting these data can inform implementation strategies and resources (costs, effort, infrastructure) to optimize and sustain equitable delivery of PPH interventions, as discussed in the next section.

Finally, evaluation frameworks demonstrate the importance of collecting both effectiveness and implementation outcomes. As evidence is generated for PPH interventions, understanding not only implementation but also effectiveness at a population level will be critical. Examining key short- and long-term effectiveness outcomes may require pooling data across implementation sites to have the power needed to more fully understand important differences in delivery of PPH interventions and outcomes by race and ethnicity in the United States. Sustained evaluation and iteration are necessary as implementation barriers may change over time.

IMPLEMENTATION STRATEGIES

Shelton et al. highlight the connection between existing implementation strategies and promoting equity and antiracist policies and practices.[32] Implementation science and PPH researchers infrequently focus on and explicitly test the influence of implementation strategies on reversing health disparities caused by racism. Furthermore, implementation science and PPH researchers often do not highlight their use of equity-focused implementation strategies in searchable ways, leaving strategies buried in the literature. Consequently, there is little information to guide researchers on which strategies will be most effective at increasing health equity (Table B).[10]

Health equity suggests that implementation strategies should be selected with community members identifying underlying assumptions and identifying potential barriers faced by vulnerable populations, and adapting the intervention and implementation strategies accordingly.[21,33,34] PPH researchers commonly evaluate disparities, frequently using big data to identify disparities in health outcomes (e.g., opioid use, vaccination) by geography, socioeconomic factors, and health characteristics.[26,35] Less commonly, researchers have used this information to adapt their strategies. For example, upon recognizing that their genetic screening programs were primarily reaching White, wealthier, and urban families, researchers engaged community stakeholders to adapt their strategies to address differential barriers experienced by vulnerable populations.[36]

Shelton et al. note the need for research to compare implementation strategies by their impact on health equity.[10] Comparing 2 PPH studies highlights the potential impact of the level of stakeholder involvement on equitable implementation. First, researchers in 1 PPH study who engaged stakeholders by having a community advisory board review recruitment materials and recontact strategies reported substantial difficulty in implementation and inequity in recontacting participants.[37] By contrast, PPH researchers who involved stakeholders in all study aspects to create patient-centered approaches (e.g., creation of materials by community members) and minimize logistic barriers (e.g., flexible hours) had equitable participant recontact across underrepresented groups.[38]

Another evidence-based implementation strategy, using community health workers to implement interventions, is suggested to identify procedures that limit the effects of inequities on research participation, create and disseminate health information that is culturally and linguistically tailored, and build community trust.[39,40] A model PPH study used community health workers and stakeholder interviews with cancer patients, caregivers, community leaders, and clinicians to identify opportunities to enhance health equity, including tailoring the strategies by allowing multiple modes of interaction (e.g., in-person, telehealth, or telephone), incorporating education, and integrating Spanish language materials.[41] Although research is needed to evaluate the best implementation strategies to increase health equity, 3 traditional implementation strategies—evaluating disparities, stakeholder engagement, and community health workers—stand out as the most promising approaches.[10]

INDIVIDUAL RESEARCHER AND RESEARCH CONTEXT

Equitable implementation of PPH interventions is inextricable from individual perspectives, team diversity, and research infrastructures. It is also threatened by systemic racism, which remains ingrained in science and therefore in the PPH research enterprise.[42] Within individual researcher and research contexts, this appears through the ongoing use of "Whites" as a reference group to which others are compared, by implying that racial groups map to discrete genetic groups, by overemphasizing the role of genetics and genomics as the major explanatory factor in health disparities, or by focusing on recruitment as the end point for community engagement. Some of these racist legacies are current topics of discussion in the PPH field. For example, PPH should move away from the crude racial, ethnic, or ancestral labels it still uses, to embrace all human diversity.[43] Shelton et al.'s antiracism framework includes self-reflection among researchers to ensure the employment of antiracist approaches.

A well-voiced consequence of structural racism is the inequities in representation across the research workforce, which limit scientific innovation.[44,45] Increasing diversity and inclusion across the biomedical research enterprise is an imperative of the US National Institutes of Health.[46] Given that PPH is a field of multidisciplinary collaboration aiming to target diverse individuals, equitable diversification of PPH teams is important. A recent study focused on precision medicine research teams found that (1) existing hierarchies and power structures in the research ecosystem compound challenges for equitable diversification, (2) tokenism and instrumental diversity jeopardize goals to diversify research teams and risk merely transient and superficial diversification, and (3) the siloing of the expertise of underrepresented team members to frontline and diversity-only activities may also perpetuate a turnstile effect. Because diversification of patient populations is interconnected with the diversification of the research workforce, who conducts the research, and how it is implemented, commitments to equity and structural reform are needed to increase the diversity of research teams.[44] Collectively, researchers should adopt an antiracism approach to build diverse teams by (1) being intentional, (2) being critically introspective, and (3) sitting with discomfort. This includes, for example, listening to the experiences of the many scientists who are directly and indirectly affected by structural racism, and creating space for all team members to speak (and reflect) on how race and racism in the research enterprise affect their lived experiences.[45] Commitments to equity and structural reform are needed. Without considering an ecosystem framework that addresses the conditions that structure power within research teams, tokenism can be misrecognized as inclusion.[44]

To mitigate disparities in the implementation of PPH interventions, the responsible training and engagement of researchers is also imperative. Key topics for individual researchers to focus on include the history of the eugenics movements and race-based medicine, the health consequences of the multiple forms of individual and structural racism (e.g., residential segregation, redlining, environmental injustice, police violence), researcher's harms to communities (e.g., the Havasupai Native Americans), and best approaches to transition from transactional community engagement and toward community empowerment when partnering with community members in research.[47]

NEXT STEPS

Looking ahead, the implementation of PPH interventions should incorporate an antiracism lens to address health equity through stakeholder engagement, conceptual models and frameworks, development and selection of evidence-based interventions, evaluation approaches, implementation strategies, and our own individual researcher contexts. Conversations around antiracism at each step of implementation, dissemination, and evaluation can help support the next generation of PPH interventions focused on increasing racial and ethnic health equity (Table B). To support these priorities in the context of a dynamic, evolving research field, we suggest that funders and research institutions aiming to invest in equitable PPH should create new initiatives to advance the study and methods development of best practices for outcomes evaluation with an eye toward structural drivers of health and racism. Multidisciplinary advisory groups could be assembled to lead the periodic reevaluation of these frameworks and best practices. Explicitly addressing racism and ongoing evaluation of the extent to which PPH studies are improving population health is critical to the successful, equitable implementation of PPH interventions to achieve the promise of PPH for all. AJPH

ABOUT THE AUTHORS

Caitlin G. Allen and Ashley Hatch are with the Department of Public Health Sciences, College of Medicine, and Paula S. Ramos is with the Departments of Medicine and Public Health Sciences, Medical University of South Carolina, Charleston. Dana Lee Olstad is with the Department of Community Health Sciences, Cumming School of Medicine, University of Calgary, Calgary, Alberta, Canada. Anna R. Kahkoska is with the Department of Nutrition, Laura V. Milko is with the Department of Genetics, and Megan C. Roberts is with the Eshelman School of Pharmacy, University of North Carolina, Chapel Hill. Yue Guan and Isabella Santangelo are with the Department of Behavioral, Social, and Health Education Sciences, Rollins School of Public Health, Emory University, Atlanta, GA. Julia Steinberg is with The Daffodil Centre, The University of Sydney, a joint venture with Cancer Council NSW, Sydney, Australia. Stephanie A. S. Staras is with the Department of Health Outcome and Biomedical Informatics, College of Medicine, and Institute for Child Health Policy, University of Florida, Gainesville. Crystal Y. Lumpkins is with the Department of Communication, Huntsman Cancer Institute, University of Utah, Salt Lake City. Erin Turbitt is with the Graduate School of Health, University of Technology Sydney, Ultimo, NSW, Australia. Alanna K. Rahm is with the Department of Genomic Health, Geisinger Medical Center, Danville, PA. Katherine W. Saylor is with the Department of Medical Ethics and Health Policy, Perelman School of Medicine, University of Pennsylvania, Philadelphia. Stephanie Best is with the Peter MacCallum Cancer Centre, Melbourne, VIC, Australia.

CORRESPONDENCE

Correspondence should be sent to Caitlin G. Allen, Medical University of South Carolina, 22 West Edge St, Suite 213, Charleston, SC 29403 (e-mail: allencat@musc.edu). Reprints can be ordered at http://www.ajph.org by clicking the "Reprints" link.

PUBLICATION INFORMATION

Full Citation: Allen CG, Olstad DL, Kahkoska AR, et al. Extending an antiracism lens to the implementation of precision public health interventions. *Am J Public Health*. 2023;113(11):1210–1218.

Acceptance Date: July 6, 2023.

DOI: https://doi.org/10.2105/AJPH.2023.307386

CONTRIBUTORS

C. G. Allen and M. C. Roberts conceptualized the article. C. G. Allen oversaw all aspects of article development. D. L. Olstad, A. R. Kahkoska, Y. Guan, P. S. Ramos, S. A. S. Staras, C. Y. Lumpkins, L. V. Milko, and M. C. Roberts drafted specific sections of the article. J. Steinberg, E. Turbitt, A. K. Rahm, K. W. Saylor, and M. C. Best provided critical feedback to support the cohesiveness of each section. C. G. Allen compiled author feedback and completed revisions with support from A. Hatch and I. Santangelo. All authors reviewed the article, provided revisions, and approved the final version.

ACKNOWLEDGMENTS

The concept for this article was developed during the Transdisciplinary Conference for Future Leaders in Precision Public Health, which was supported through the National Cancer Institute (1R13CA261073-01). C. G. Allen receives support through 5K00CA253576-04.

CONFLICTS OF INTEREST

The authors have no conflicts of interest to disclose.

HUMAN PARTICIPANT PROTECTION

No human participants were part of this article.

REFERENCES

1. Allen CG, Fohner AE, Landry L, et al. Early career investigators and precision public health. *Lancet.* 2019;394(10196):382–383. https://doi.org/10.1016/S0140-6736(19)30498-2
2. Khoury MJ, Iademarco MF, Riley WT. Precision public health for the era of precision medicine. *Am J Prev Med.* 2016;50(3):398–401. https://doi.org/10.1016/j.amepre.2015.08.031
3. Allen CG, Fohner AE, Landry L, et al. Perspectives from early career investigators who are "staying in the game" of precision public health research. *Am J Public Health.* 2019;109(9):1186-1187. https://doi.org/10.2105/AJPH.2019.305199
4. Khoury MJ, Bowen S, Dotson WD, et al. Health equity in the implementation of genomics and precision medicine: a public health imperative. *Genet Med.* 2022;24(8):1630–1639. https://doi.org/10.1016/j.gim.2022.04.009
5. Geneviève LD, Martani A, Wangmo T, Elger BS. Precision public health and structural racism in the United States: promoting health equity in the COVID-19 pandemic response. *JMIR Public Health Surveill.* 2022;8(3):e33277. https://doi.org/10.2196/33277
6. Taylor-Robinson D, Kee F. Precision public health—the emperor's new clothes. *Int J Epidemiol.* 2019;48(1):1–6. https://doi.org/10.1093/ije/dyy184
7. Williams DR, Mohammed SA. Racism and health I: pathways and scientific evidence. *Am Behav Sci.* 2013;57(8):1152–1173. https://doi.org/10.1177/0002764213487340
8. Williams DR, Lawrence JA, Davis BA. Racism and health: evidence and needed research. *Annu Rev Public Health.* 2019;40(1):105–125. https://doi.org/10.1146/annurev-publhealth-040218-043750
9. Flanagin A, Frey T, Christiansen SL, AMA Manual of Style Committee. Updated guidance on the reporting of race and ethnicity in medical and science journals. *JAMA.* 2021;326(7):621–627. https://doi.org/10.1001/jama.2021.13304
10. Shelton RC, Adsul P, Oh A, Moise N, Griffith DM. Application of an antiracism lens in the field of implementation science: recommendations for reframing implementation research with a focus on justice and racial equity. *Implement Res Pract.* 2021;2:1–19. https://doi.org/10.1177/26334895211049482
11. Burton H, Adams M, Bunton R, Schröder-Bäck P. Developing stakeholder involvement for introducing public health genomics into public policy. *Public Health Genomics.* 2009;12(1):11–19. https://doi.org/10.1159/000153426
12. Lemke AA, Esplin ED, Goldenberg AJ, et al. Addressing underrepresentation in genomics research through community engagement. *Am J Hum Genet.* 2022;109(9):1563–1571. https://doi.org/10.1016/j.ajhg.2022.08.005
13. Nunn JS, Tiller J, Fransquet P, Lacaze P. Public involvement in global genomics research: a scoping review. *Front Public Health.* 2019;7:79. https://doi.org/10.3389/fpubh.2019.00079
14. Abelson J, Forest PG, Eyles J, Smith P, Martin E, Gauvin FP. Deliberations about deliberative methods: issues in the design and evaluation of public participation processes. *Soc Sci Med.* 2003;57(2):239–251. https://doi.org/10.1016/S0277-9536(02)00343-X
15. Sullivan G, Cheney A, Olson M, et al. Rural African Americans' perspectives on mental health: comparing focus groups and deliberative democracy forums. *J Health Care Poor Underserved.* 2017;28(1):548–565. https://doi.org/10.1353/hpu.2017.0039
16. Murtagh MJ, Machirori M, Gaff CL, et al. Engaged genomic science produces better and fairer outcomes: an engagement framework for engaging and involving participants, patients and publics in genomics research and healthcare implementation. *Wellcome Open Res.* 2021;6:311. https://doi.org/10.12688/wellcomeopenres.17233.1
17. Guan Y, Pathak S, Ballard D, et al. Testing a deliberative democracy method with citizens of African ancestry to weigh pros and cons of targeted screening for hereditary breast and ovarian cancer risk. *Front Public Health.* 2022;10:984926. https://doi.org/10.3389/fpubh.2022.984926
18. Roberts MC, Mensah GA, Khoury MJ. Leveraging implementation science to address health disparities in genomic medicine: examples from the field. *Ethn Dis.* 2019;29(suppl 1):187–192. Available at: https://www.ncbi.nlm.nih.gov/pmc/articles/PMC6428174. Accessed October 21, 2022.
19. Miranda J, Duan N, Sherbourne C, et al. Improving care for minorities: can quality improvement interventions improve care and outcomes for depressed minorities? Results of a randomized, controlled trial. *Health Serv Res.* 2003;38(2):613–630. https://doi.org/10.1111/1475-6773.00136
20. Saylor KW, Roberts MC. Implementation science can do even more for translational ethics. *Am J Bioeth.* 2020;20(4):83–85. https://doi.org/10.1080/15265161.2020.1730511
21. Woodward EN, Matthieu MM, Uchendu US, Rogal S, Kirchner JE. The health equity implementation framework: proposal and preliminary study of hepatitis C virus treatment. *Implement Sci.* 2019;14(1):26. https://doi.org/10.1186/s13012-019-0861-y
22. Harkness A, Weinstein ER, Lozano A, et al. Refining an implementation strategy to enhance the reach of HIV-prevention and behavioral health treatments to Latino men who have sex with men. *Implement Res Pract.* 2022;3:26334895221096293. https://doi.org/10.1177/26334895221096293
23. Damschroder LJ, Reardon CM, Widerquist MAO, Lowery J. The updated Consolidated Framework for Implementation Research based on user feedback. *Implement Sci.* 2022;17(1):75. https://doi.org/10.1186/s13012-022-01245-0
24. Shelton RC, Chambers DA, Glasgow RE. An extension of RE-AIM to enhance sustainability: addressing dynamic context and promoting health equity over time. *Front Public Health.* 2020;8:134. https://doi.org/10.3389/fpubh.2020.00134
25. Snell-Rood C, Jaramillo ET, Hamilton AB, Raskin SE, Nicosia FM, Willging C. Advancing health equity through a theoretically critical implementation science. *Transl Behav Med.* 2021;11(8):1617–1625. https://doi.org/10.1093/tbm/ibab008
26. Rasmussen SA, Khoury MJ, Del Rio C. Precision public health as a key tool in the COVID-19 response. *JAMA.* 2020;324(10):933–934. https://doi.org/10.1001/jama.2020.14992
27. Alvidrez J, Nápoles AM, Bernal G, et al. Building the evidence base to inform planned intervention adaptations by practitioners serving health disparity populations. *Am J Public Health.* 2019;109(suppl 1):S94–S101. https://doi.org/10.2105/AJPH.2018.304915
28. Woodward EN, Singh RS, Ndebele-Ngwenya P, Melgar Castillo A, Dickson KS, Kirchner JE. A more practical guide to incorporating health equity domains in implementation determinant frameworks. *Implement Sci Commun.* 2021;2(1):61. https://doi.org/10.1186/s43058-021-00146-5
29. Allen CG, Judge DP, Levin E, et al. A pragmatic implementation research study for In Our DNA SC: a protocol to identify multi-level factors that support the implementation of a population-wide genomic screening initiative in diverse populations. *Implement Sci Commun.* 2022;3(1):48. https://doi.org/10.1186/s43058-022-00286-2
30. Allen CG, Lenert L, Hunt K, et al. Lessons learned from the pilot phase of a population-wide genomic screening program: building the base to reach a diverse cohort of 100,000 participants. *J Pers Med.* 2022;12(8):1228. https://doi.org/10.3390/jpm12081228
31. Jones LK, Strande NT, Calvo EM, et al. A RE-AIM framework analysis of DNA-based population screening: using implementation science to translate research into practice in a healthcare system. *Front Genet.* 2022;13:883073. https://doi.org/10.3389/fgene.2022.883073
32. Proctor EK, Powell BJ, McMillen JC. Implementation strategies: recommendations for specifying and reporting. *Implement Sci.* 2013;8(1):139. https://doi.org/10.1186/1748-5908-8-139
33. Gaias LM, Arnold KT, Liu FF, Pullmann MD, Duong MT, Lyon AR. Adapting strategies to promote implementation reach and equity (ASPIRE) in school mental health services. *Psychol Sch.* 2021;59(12):2471–2485. https://doi.org/10.1002/pits.22515
34. Kerkhoff AD, Farrand E, Marquez C, Cattamanchi A, Handley MA. Addressing health disparities through implementation science—a need to integrate an equity lens from the outset. *Implement*

Sci. 2022;17(1):13. https://doi.org/10.1186/s13012-022-01189-5

35. Staras SAS, Huo T, Rothbard SM, et al. Human papillomavirus vaccination and human papillomavirus-associated cancer rates within Florida counties. *Am J Prev Med.* 2021;61(6):812–820. https://doi.org/10.1016/j.amepre.2021.05.016
36. Senier L, Tan C, Smollin L, Lee R. Understanding the potential of state-based public health genomics programs to mitigate disparities in access to clinical genetic services. *Genet Med.* 2019;21(2):373–381. https://doi.org/10.1038/s41436-018-0056-y
37. Shaibi GQ, Kullo IJ, Singh DP, et al. Returning genomic results in a federally qualified health center: the intersection of precision medicine and social determinants of health. *Genet Med.* 2020;22(9):1552–1559. https://doi.org/10.1038/s41436-020-0806-5
38. Horowitz CR, Sabin T, Ramos M, et al. Successful recruitment and retention of diverse participants in a genomics clinical trial: a good invitation to a great party. *Genet Med.* 2019;21(10):2364–2370. https://doi.org/10.1038/s41436-019-0498-x
39. Valeriani G, Sarajlic Vukovic I, Bersani FS, Sadeghzadeh Diman A, Ghorbani A, Mollica R. Tackling ethnic health disparities through community health worker programs: a scoping review on their utilization during the COVID-19 outbreak. *Popul Health Manag.* 2022;25(4):517–526. https://doi.org/10.1089/pop.2021.0364
40. Kim K, Choi JS, Choi E, et al. Effects of community-based health worker interventions to improve chronic disease management and care among vulnerable populations: a systematic review. *Am J Public Health.* 2016;106(4):e3–e28. https://doi.org/10.2105/AJPH.2015.302987
41. Wood EH, Leach M, Villicana G, et al. A community-engaged process for adapting a proven community health worker model to integrate precision cancer care delivery for low-income Latinx adults with cancer. *Health Promot Pract.* 2023;24(3):491–501. https://doi.org/10.1177/15248399221096415
42. Nobles M, Womack C, Wonkam A, Wathuti E. Ending racism is key to better science: a message from *Nature's* guest editors. *Nature.* 2022;610(7932):419–420. https://doi.org/10.1038/d41586-022-03247-w
43. Martschenko DO, Young JL. Precision medicine needs to think outside the box. *Front Genet.* 2022;13:795992. https://doi.org/10.3389/fgene.2022.795992
44. Jeske M, Vasquez E, Fullerton SM, et al. Beyond inclusion: enacting team equity in precision medicine research. *PLoS One.* 2022;17(2):e0263750. https://doi.org/10.1371/journal.pone.0263750
45. Thomas SP, Amini K, Floyd KJ, et al. Cultivating diversity as an ethos with an anti-racism approach in the scientific enterprise. *HGG Adv.* 2021;2(4):100052. https://doi.org/10.1016/j.xhgg.2021.100052
46. Collins FS, Adams AB, Aklin C, et al. Affirming NIH's commitment to addressing structural racism in the biomedical research enterprise. *Cell.* 2021;184(12):3075–3079. https://doi.org/10.1016/j.cell.2021.05.014
47. Braveman PA, Arkin E, Proctor D, Kauh T, Holm N. Systemic And structural racism: definitions, examples, health damages, and approaches to dismantling. *Health Aff (Millwood).* 2022;41(2):171–178. https://doi.org/10.1377/hlthaff.2021.01394

Conducting Health Research with Native American Communities

Edited by Teshia G. Arambula Solomon, PhD and Leslie L. Randall, RN, MPH, BSN

The current research and evaluation of the American Indian and Alaska Native (AIAN) people demonstrates the increased demand for efficiency, accompanied by solid accountability in a time of extremely limited resources. This environment requires proficiency in working with these vulnerable populations in diverse cross-cultural settings. This timely publication is the first of its kind to provide this information to help researchers meet their demands.

This book provides an overview of complex themes as well as a synopsis of essential concepts or techniques in working with Native American tribes and Alaska Native communities. *Conducting Health Research with Native American Communities* will benefit Native people and organizations as well as researchers, students and practitioners.

APHA PRESS
AN IMPRINT OF AMERICAN PUBLIC HEALTH ASSOCIATION

2014, 340 pp., softcover, ISBN 978-0-87553-2028
Available as an eBook and softcover
ORDER ONLINE at www.aphabookstore.org

Examining Excess Mortality Among Critical Workers in Minnesota During 2020–2021: An Occupational Analysis

Harshada Karnik, PhD, MS, MPP, Elizabeth Wrigley-Field, PhD, Zachary Levin, PhD, Yea-Hung Chen, PhD, Erik W. Zabel, PhD, MPH, Marizen Ramirez, PhD, and Jonathon P. Leider, PhD

Objectives. To understand the occupational risk associated with COVID-19 among civilian critical workers (aged 16–65 years) in Minnesota.

Methods. We estimated excess mortality in 2020 to 2021 for critical occupations in different racial groups and vaccine rollout phases using death certificates and occupational employment rates for 2017 to 2021.

Results. Excess mortality during the COVID-19 pandemic was higher for workers in critical occupations than for noncritical workers. Some critical occupations, such as transportation and logistics, construction, and food service, experienced higher excess mortality than did other critical occupations, such as health care, K–12 school staff, and agriculture. In almost all occupations investigated, workers of color experienced higher excess mortality than did White workers. Excess mortality in 2021 was greater than in 2020 across groups: occupations, vaccine eligibility tiers, and race/ethnicity.

Conclusions. Although workers in critical occupations experienced greater excess mortality than did others, excess mortality among critical workers varied substantially by occupation and race.

Public Health Implications. Analysis of mortality across occupations can be used to identify vulnerable populations, prioritize protective interventions for them, and develop targeted worker safety protocols to promote equitable health outcomes. (*Am J Public Health*. 2023;113(11):1219–1222. https://doi.org/10.2105/AJPH.2023.307395)

AJPH November 2023, Vol 113, No. 11

Although there is evidence of higher COVID-19 mortality among certain populations (older adults,[1] people of color,[2] and persons with certain preexisting conditions[1]), occupational differences remain underexplored.[3] This variation can be partly attributed to exposure, especially among critical workers exempt from shelter-in-place orders who could not work remotely.[4] We defined critical workers as workers who perform operations or offer services essential to continue critical infrastructure operations as defined by the Cybersecurity and Infrastructure Security Agency.

We measured excess mortality—deaths beyond those expected during usual circumstances—in 2020 and 2021 among workers usually employed in critical occupations in Minnesota. Unlike aggregated death data available from most states, Minnesota makes available individual-level microdata for the entire population of deceased individuals (all death records), allowing us to disaggregate results by race and occupation-based vaccine eligibility.

METHODS

We obtained death certificates for all decedents in Minnesota between 2017 and 2021 from the Minnesota Department of Health that included the decedent's usual occupation in free text format. We coded this into census occupation codes using the National Institute for Occupational Safety and Health's Industry and Occupation Computerized Coding System, which reports the accuracy probability of codes assigned to individual entries.

We excluded 2708 observations with a probability in the bottom fifth percentile (probability < 0.75) and manually coded 2248 observations with a probability between 0.75 and 0.90. We further aggregated census occupation codes into Minnesota's 12 predefined critical occupations and vaccine eligibility groups (listed in Table 1; detailed in Appendix Table A, available as a supplement to the online version of this article at http://www.ajph.org).[5,6]

Critical occupations in Minnesota included health care professionals, emergency and first responders, childcare, K–12 school staff, food processing, agriculture, food service, 2 categories of transportation and logistics (T&L-1, i.e., public transit workers, airport staff, and postal service employees; and T&L-2, i.e., logistics, delivery, and infrastructure transportation), manufacturing, construction, and retail. We audited 20% of aggregated codes, resolved inconsistencies observed in approximately 20 codes (1% audited codes) through discussion, and jointly coded those (n = 50; 10% aggregated codes) that were ambiguous to the coders. Although manually coding specific occupations with moderate match probability, we found that the aggregated occupational grouping we used in this analysis was already accurately assigned in 96.83% of cases, increasing confidence in our matches. We restricted our sample to working-age civilians aged 16 to 65 years.

We estimated the excess mortality rate (EMR) as excess deaths divided by the number of workers in the occupation statewide (Appendix Table B,

TABLE 1— Excess Mortality Rate Among Civilian Workers (Aged 16–65 Years) in Minnesota: 2020–2021

	All, EMR (95% CI)		Non-Hispanic White, EMR (95% CI)		BIPOC, EMR (95% CI)	
Vaccine Phase[a]	2020	2021	2020	2021	2020	2021
All workers[b]	3.0 (3.0, 3.1)	4.5 (4.4, 4.5)	2.7 (2.7, 2.8)	4.4 (4.3, 4.4)	4.6 (4.4, 4.8)	5.6 (5.4, 5.7)
Phase 1A	2.9 (2.7, 3.1)	3.4 (3.3, 3.5)	3.1 (3.0, 3.3)	3.6 (3.4, 3.8)	2.3 (2.1, 2.6)	2.8 (2.7, 2.9)
Health care	3.2 (3.0, 3.3)	3.3 (3.1, 3.4)	3.5 (3.3, 3.7)	3.6 (3.4, 3.8)	2.2 (2.0, 2.5)	2.6 (2.6, 2.7)
First responders	0.4 (0.0, 1.1)	4.6 (3.9, 5.5)	−0.4 (−0.7, 0.2)	4.1 (3.3, 5.2)	3.3 (1.6, 10.1)	7.5 (6.0, 9.3)
Phase 1B Tier 1	1.7 (1.6, 1.8)	2.9 (2.7, 3.0)	2.4 (2.3, 2.6)	3.4 (3.2, 3.6)	−2.1 (−1.7, −2.8)	0.1 (0.2, −0.2)
K–12 school staff	1.0 (0.9, 1.1)	1.4 (1.4, 1.5)	1.5 (1.4, 1.7)	1.9 (1.8, 2.0)	−2.6 (−1.8, −4.2)	−1.7 (−1.2, −2.6)
Childcare	3.6 (3.2, 4.1)	7.2 (6.5, 8.0)	5.2 (4.7, 5.7)	8.2 (7.3, 9.4)	−1.5 (−1.4, −1.2)	3.4 (2.7, 4.6)
Phase 1B Tier 2: food processing	9.2 (7.3, 12.2)	9.6 (8.2, 11.5)	8.6 (6.3, 12.8)	11.0 (8.8, 14.4)	9.2 (6.4, 16.1)	7.5 (5.9, 10.1)
Phase 1B Tier 3	4.9 (4.6, 5.1)	5.5 (5.3, 5.7)	3.0 (2.8, 3.2)	6.1 (5.9, 6.5)	11.0 (10.0, 12.2)	5.8 (5.5, 6.2)
T&L-1[c]	1.6 (1.5, 1.7)	3.0 (2.6, 3.4)	0.9 (0.7, 1.1)	0.7 (0.3, 1.2)	2.2 (1.6, 3.5)	11.6 (8.8, 16.9)
Manufacturing	5.5 (5.0, 6.1)	5.6 (5.3, 5.9)	4.6 (4.0, 5.4)	8.0 (7.5, 8.6)	8.8 (7.6, 10.5)	4.1 (3.9, 4.3)
Food service	8.2 (7.7, 8.8)	7.6 (7.2, 8.1)	5.8 (5.2, 6.4)	7.6 (6.9, 8.3)	15.0 (13.2, 17.4)	8.6 (7.8, 9.6)
Agriculture	−4.0 (−3.9, −4.1)	2.3 (1.6, 3.3)	−5.7 (−5.4, −6.1)	2.8 (2.0, 3.9)	12.3 (7.6, 26.3)	−0.3 (−0.3, −0.2)
Phase 1C	3.6 (3.5, 3.8)	7.7 (7.5, 7.9)	2.9 (2.8, 3.1)	6.8 (6.6, 7.0)	7.1 (6.6, 7.7)	12.0 (11.1, 13.1)
T&L-2[c]	7.3 (7.0, 7.6)	14.0 (13.4, 14.6)	4.8 (4.6, 5.1)	14.5 (13.9, 15.2)	16.9 (14.9, 19.4)	13.7 (12.2, 15.6)
Retail	4.1 (3.8, 4.4)	8.7 (8.2, 9.3)	4.4 (4.0, 4.8)	8.6 (8.1, 9.2)	3.5 (3.1, 4.1)	8.9 (7.4, 11.1)
Construction	2.9 (2.6, 3.2)	8.9 (8.0, 9.8)	0.5 (0.2, 0.8)	6.2 (5.4, 7.1)	17.9 (15.3, 21.6)	24.3 (19.9, 31.2)
Phase 2	1.8 (1.7, 2.0)	2.2 (2.1, 2.3)	2.1 (1.9, 2.2)	2.2 (2.1, 2.3)	1.1 (1.0, 1.2)	2.4 (2.3, 2.4)
Other essential	3.2 (3.0, 3.4)	2.5 (2.3, 2.6)	3.5 (3.3, 3.7)	2.7 (2.5, 2.8)	2.2 (2.0, 2.5)	2.0 (1.9, 2.1)
Nonessential	0.5 (0.3, 0.6)	1.9 (1.8, 2.0)	0.7 (0.6, 0.9)	1.8 (1.7, 1.9)	−0.8 (−0.7, −0.9)	2.9 (2.8, 3.1)

Note. BIPOC = Black people, Indigenous people, and other people of color; CI = confidence interval; EMR = excess mortality rate; T&L = transportation and logistics. The table represents the EMR among White people and BIPOC who usually work in critical occupations in Minnesota. Most of these estimates are significantly different from zero. *P* values are reported in Appendix Table E (available as a supplement to the online version of this article at http://www.ajph.org).

[a]The vaccine eligibility tiers in Minnesota were based on critical occupations, as detailed in Appendix Table A (available as a supplement to the online version of this article at http://www.ajph.org).

[b]All civilian workers aged 16–65 years.

[c]T&L-1 includes public transit workers, airport staff, and postal service employees. T&L-2 includes those who work in logistics, delivery, and infrastructure transportation.

available as a supplement to the online version of this article at http://www.ajph.org).[7] Excess deaths (Appendix Table C, available as a supplement to the online version of this article at http://www.ajph.org) represent differences between observed deaths and expected deaths. To measure expected deaths, we multiplied the average baseline occupation-specific mortality rate by the size of the occupation in 2020 and 2021 to adjust for changes in occupation size.[8] We used the American Community Survey (2017–2021) to estimate year-specific employment.

We also conducted a sensitivity analysis using prepandemic occupation sizes as denominators (presented in Appendix Table D, available as a supplement to the online version of this article at http://www.ajph.org). To compare excess mortality across racial groups, we aggregated non-White and Hispanic decedents into 1 category. This aggregation is warranted because individual Hispanic people and Black people, Indigenous people, and other people of color (BIPOC) subpopulations were too small to disaggregate further, and all BIPOC subpopulations had substantially higher COVID-19 mortality than did White Minnesotans.[7]

RESULTS

Workers experienced increased mortality during the COVID-19 pandemic in Minnesota (EMR = 3.0/10 000 persons in 2020 and 4.5 in 2021). Decedents usually employed in noncritical occupations experienced lower excess mortality than did critical workers. In 2020, the highest EMR was observed in food processing (9.2/10 000 workers) followed by food service and T&L-2. In addition to these occupations, construction and retail experienced high EMR in 2021.

Excess mortality among workers increased from 2020 to 2021. For workers in vaccination phase 1A, EMR increased from 2.9 deaths per 10 000 workers in 2020 to 3.4 in 2021. EMR for occupations in phase 1B, tier 1 increased from 1.7 per 10 000 workers to 2.9. Phase 1B, tiers 2 and 3, and phase 1C also experienced a large increase in excess mortality from 2020 to 2021, with the numbers in phase 1C more than doubling.

BIPOC workers experienced higher EMR (4.6 in 2020 and 5.6 in 2021) than did White workers (2.7 and 4.4, respectively), particularly in food processing, food service, construction, retail, and T&L. When aggregated by vaccine eligibility tiers, BIPOC workers had higher EMR than did White workers, especially in 2020 and in occupations included in the later vaccine eligibility tiers.

DISCUSSION

All critical occupations experienced higher EMR than did noncritical occupations. BIPOC workers experienced higher EMR than did White workers in high-risk occupations. Across occupations, racial groups, and vaccine tiers, EMR increased from 2020 to 2021 (as occurred nationally[9]) even as vaccines started becoming available, and the vaccine tiers were not associated with EMR in 2020 or 2021.

Minnesota determined vaccine eligibility phases based on risks associated with age, occupation, and health conditions. Health care and childcare workers were prioritized for vaccination to reduce transmission to vulnerable populations they work with and to keep critical workers at work. However, from the perspective of allocating limited supplies to workers with the greatest risk of death, our analysis suggests that some vulnerable groups were insufficiently prioritized. Health care workers and first responders had lower EMR despite being at risk, possibly because they were prioritized to receive protective equipment. Some vulnerable occupations (i.e., food service, construction, retail, T&L, food processing) included in vaccine phase 1B-tiers 2 and 3 tend to employ more BIPOC workers and experienced higher EMR than did workers in earlier phases. Those workers' high risk underscores the need to incentivize workplace protections such as improved ventilation, nonpunitive sick leave, and policies promoting booster uptake in such occupations.

The pandemic accentuated existing disparities. Several critical occupations are low-income jobs. High EMR observed among workers in these occupations—particularly BIPOC workers in critical occupations—could stem from socioeconomic disadvantages, including transportation modes, living arrangements,[10] and other factors, such as preexisting health conditions[10] or not having the political influence to advocate workplace safety.[11] Higher EMR among BIPOC Minnesotans employed in key occupations compared with workers in higher-priority, predominantly White occupations suggests that occupation-based vaccination may have prioritized lower-risk White workers above higher-risk BIPOC workers. Similar results were observed in California.[8] These disparities—especially in 2021, when vaccines were becoming available—suggest a failure to identify and prioritize interventions for vulnerable groups and achieve equity goals.

Like other occupational analyses, our results are constrained by the accuracy of occupational data. Death certificates record decedents' usual occupation at the time of their death.[12] This may lead EMR to be overestimated if numerators include, but denominators exclude, people who are ordinarily employed but were out of work during the pandemic. Our sensitivity analysis shows that EMR estimates, mainly for BIPOC workers, are generally higher when using prepandemic occupation sizes as denominators (Appendix Table D) compared with the main results using occupation sizes in 2020 and 2021 (Table 1).

In conclusion, we identified groups of workers facing elevated risk during the pandemic. Although these results may not indicate causal effects of occupations on exposure risk, they are a good proxy to identify vulnerable individuals and locations to implement place-based interventions. In addition to vaccine prioritization, the workplace precautions that some critical occupations, such as health care, implemented to reduce the death toll of COVID-19 could be identified, adapted, and implemented in other occupations to protect critical workers. AJPH

ABOUT THE AUTHORS

Harshada Karnik, Zachary Levin, and Jonathon P. Leider are with the Health Policy and Management Division, University of Minnesota School of Public Health, Minneapolis. Elizabeth Wrigley-Field is with the Department of Sociology and Minnesota Population Center, University of Minnesota. Yea-Hung Chen is with the Department of Epidemiology and Biostatistics, University of California, San Francisco. Erik W. Zabel is with the Center for Occupational Health and Safety, Minnesota Department of Health, St. Paul. Marizen Ramirez was with the Division of Environmental Health Sciences, University of Minnesota School of Public Health, Twin Cities when the study was conducted.

CORRESPONDENCE

Correspondence should be sent to Harshada Karnik, University of Minnesota School of Public Health, 420 Delaware St SE, Minneapolis, MN 55455 (e-mail: harshada@umn.edu). Reprints can be ordered at http://www.ajph.org by clicking the "Reprints" link.

PUBLICATION INFORMATION

Full Citation: Karnik H, Wrigley-Field E, Levin Z, et al. Examining excess mortality among critical workers in Minnesota during 2020–2021: an occupational analysis. *Am J Public Health*. 2023; 113(11):1219–1222.

Acceptance Date: July 15, 2023.

DOI: https://doi.org/10.2105/AJPH.2023.307395

CONTRIBUTORS

H. Karnik wrote the first draft of the article. H. Karnik and Z. Levin conducted the data analysis. E. Wrigley-Field and J. P. Leider secured data and funding. All authors contributed to study design, revised the article critically for intellectual content, and approved the final version submitted.

ACKNOWLEDGMENTS

E. Wrigley-Field was supported by the Eunice Kennedy Shriver National Institutes of Child Health and Human Development via the Minnesota Population Center (grant P2C HD041023).

CONFLICTS OF INTEREST

The authors have no conflicts of interest to disclose.

HUMAN PARTICIPANT PROTECTION

The University of Minnesota institutional review board determined this study to not be human participants research (IRB no. STUDY00012527).

REFERENCES

1. Shahid Z, Kalayanamitra R, McClafferty B, et al. COVID-19 and older adults: what we know. *J Am Geriatr Soc*. 2020;68(5):926–929. https://doi.org/10.1111/jgs.16472
2. Wrigley-Field E, Garcia S, Leider JP, Robertson C, Wurtz R. Racial disparities in COVID-19 and excess mortality in Minnesota. *Socius*. 2020;6:2378023120980918. https://doi.org/10.1177/2378023120980918
3. Zhang M. Estimation of differential occupational risk of COVID-19 by comparing risk factors with case data by occupational group. *Am J Ind Med*. 2021;64(1):39–47. https://doi.org/10.1002/ajim.23199.
4. Lancet. The plight of essential workers during the COVID-19 pandemic. *Lancet*. 2020;395(10237):1587. https://doi.org/10.1016/S0140-6736(20)31200-9
5. Minnesota Department of Health. Minnesota guidance for allocating and prioritizing COVID-19 vaccine—phase 1a. March 10, 2021. Available at: https://www.health.state.mn.us/diseases/coronavirus/vaccine/phase1aguide.pdf. Accessed August 31, 2023.
6. Minnesota Department of Health. Minnesota guidance for allocating and prioritizing COVID-19 vaccine—phases 1b, 1c, 2. March 10, 2021. Available at: https://www.health.state.mn.us/diseases/coronavirus/vaccine/phase1b1c2.pdf. Accessed August 31, 2023.
7. Karaca-Mandic P, Georgiou A, Sen S. Assessment of COVID-19 hospitalizations by race/ethnicity in 12 states. *JAMA Intern Med*. 2021;181(1):131–134. https://doi.org/10.1001/jamainternmed.2020.3857
8. Shiels MS, Almeida JS, García-Closas M, Albert PS, Freedman ND, Berrington de González A. Impact of population growth and aging on estimates of excess US deaths during the COVID-19 pandemic, March to August 2020. *Ann Intern Med*. 2021; 174(4):437–443. https://doi.org/10.7326/M20-7385
9. Centers for Disease Control and Prevention. Provisional mortality data—United States, 2021. *MMWR Morb Mortal Wkly Rep*. 2022;71(17):597–600. https://doi.org/10.15585/mmwr.mm7117e1
10. Khanijahani A, Iezadi S, Gholipour K, Azami-Aghdash S, Naghibi D. A systematic review of racial/ethnic and socioeconomic disparities in COVID-19. *Int J Equity Health*. 2021;20(1):1–30. https://doi.org/10.1186/s12939-021-01582-4
11. Fabreau GE, Holdbrook L, Peters CE, et al. Vaccines alone will not prevent COVID-19 outbreaks among migrant workers—the example of meat processing plants. *Clin Microbiol Infect*. 2022;28(6):773–778. https://doi.org/10.1016/j.cmi.2022.02.004
12. Hawkins D. Understanding the role of work in mortality: making the best use of available US death certificate occupation data and opportunities for improvements. *J Occup Environ Med*. 2021;63(6):503–507. https://doi.org/10.1097/JOM.0000000000002177

Erratum In: "*AJPH* Global News"

In: "*AJPH* Global News"

An incorrect map was published as part of the "Global News" forum for the April through October 2022 issues of *AJPH*. The text is not affected by this change. The following articles are being updated with the appropriate image:

AJPH Global News. *Am J Public Health*. 2022;112(10):1360. https://doi.org/10.2105/AJPH.2022.307055

AJPH Global News. *Am J Public Health*. 2022;112(9):1230. https://doi.org/10.2105/AJPH.2022.306991

AJPH Global News. *Am J Public Health*. 2022;112(8):1080. https://doi.org/10.2105/AJPH.2022.306955

AJPH Global News. *Am J Public Health*. 2022;112(7):952. https://doi.org/10.2105/AJPH.2022.306954

AJPH Global News. *Am J Public Health*. 2022;112(6):815. https://doi.org/10.2105/AJPH.2022.306859

AJPH Global News. *Am J Public Health*. 2022;112(5):694. https://doi.org/10.2105/AJPH.2022.306795

AJPH Global News. *Am J Public Health*. 2022;112(4):534. https://doi.org/10.2105/AJPH.2022.306752

DOI: https://doi.org/10.2105/AJPH.2023.307419 AJPH

Read

AJPH

A PUBLICATION OF THE
AMERICAN PUBLIC HEALTH ASSOCIATION

Earn Continuing Education credits while you learn

Thanks to APHA's program with the ***American Journal of Public Health***, earning continuing education credits is easy.

By reading select articles from *AJPH*, you can get credits for **CHES®**,**CME**, **CNE**, and **CPH**.

SIGN UP TODAY!

Introductory rate:

APHA members: $10 per credit
Non-members: $20 per credit

Online Continuing Education Program

APHA.org/continuing-education

APHA
AMERICAN PUBLIC HEALTH ASSOCIATION
For science. For action. For health.

DISASTERS DON'T PLAN AHEAD.

YOU CAN.

DON'T WAIT. COMMUNICATE.

Talk to your loved ones about how you are going to be ready in an emergency.

VISIT READY.GOV/PLAN.

Ad Council Ready® FEMA

Vaping can
cause irreversible
lung damage.
TalkAbout
Vaping.org
Get the facts
about youth vaping.
American
Lung
Association.
ad
COUNCIL
#DoThe
VapeTalk

GET DOWN
WITH YOUR BLOOD PRESSURE™
1
GET IT
2
SLIP IT
3
CUFF IT
4
CHECK IT
Check it every day. Self-monitoring is power.
ad COUNCIL
American Heart Association.
AMA
AMERICAN MEDICAL ASSOCIATION
Visit: ManageYourBP.org
Or scan code for more.
In partnership with HHS Office of Minority Health and Health Resources and Services Administration under cooperative agreements CPIMP211227 and CPIMP211228.

Adopt US Kids

ad COUNCIL

His first football season, Isaiah told us, 'Wear a jersey with my name on it. I want everyone to know you're here for me.'

Darnell and Denna, adopted 16-year-old Isaiah

LEARN ABOUT ADOPTING A TEEN
YOU CAN'T IMAGINE THE REWARD

ADOPTUSKIDS.ORG

MADDY TURNED HATE
Maddy Park
Founder,
@CafeMaddyCab
INTO HOPE
AND STARTED A MOVEMENT
In 2021, the rise of violence against the Asian community made even the simple act of taking public transportation unsafe. So, Maddy started a fund to pay for cab rides for those in the Asian community that needed it most, including women, the elderly, and the LGBTQ+ community. With over $100,000 raised in just two days, she started a movement based on love that lives on today.
love has no labels
ad COUNCIL
Join Maddy's cause and get the tools to support the Asian community now at
LoveHasNoLabels.com

"Early detection allowed us to take control of the situation and make a plan together."
If you're noticing changes, it could be Alzheimer's. Talk about visiting a doctor together.
ALZ.org/TimeToTalk
ad COUNCIL
ALZHEIMER'S ASSOCIATION

UNITED STATES POSTAL SERVICE®

Statement of Ownership, Management, and Circulation (All Periodicals Publications Except Requester Publications)

1. Publication Title	2. Publication Number	3. Filing Date
American Journal of Public Health	0090-0036	09/30/2023
4. Issue Frequency	**5. Number of Issues Published Annually**	**6. Annual Subscription Price**
Monthly	12	$993–$1445 Online + Print

7. Complete Mailing Address of Known Office of Publication (*Not printer*) (*Street, city, county, state, and ZIP+4®*)
American Public Health Association
800 I St., NW, Washington, DC 20001-3710

Contact Person
Brian Selzer
Telephone (*Include area code*)
202-777-2464

8. Complete Mailing Address of Headquarters or General Business Office of Publisher (*Not printer*)
American Public Health Association
800 I St., NW, Washington, DC 20001-3710

9. Full Names and Complete Mailing Addresses of Publisher, Editor, and Managing Editor (*Do not leave blank*)

Publisher (*Name and complete mailing address*)
American Public Health Association
800 I St., NW, Washington, DC 20001-3710

Editor (*Name and complete mailing address*)
Alfredo Morabia, MD, PhD, Barry Commoner Center for Health and the Environment, Queens College at City University of New York, Remsen #311, 65-30 Kissena Blvd, Flushing, NY 11369

Managing Editor (*Name and complete mailing address*)
Brian Selzer, American Public Health Association
800 I St., NW, Washington, DC 20001-3710

10. Owner (*Do not leave blank. If the publication is owned by a corporation, give the name and address of the corporation immediately followed by the names and addresses of all stockholders owning or holding 1 percent or more of the total amount of stock. If not owned by a corporation, give the names and addresses of the individual owners. If owned by a partnership or other unincorporated firm, give its name and address as well as those of each individual owner. If the publication is published by a nonprofit organization, give its name and address.*)

Full Name	Complete Mailing Address
American Public Health Association	800 I St., NW, Washington, DC 20001-3710

11. Known Bondholders, Mortgagees, and Other Security Holders Owning or Holding 1 Percent or More of Total Amount of Bonds, Mortgages, or Other Securities. If none, check box ☐ None

Full Name	Complete Mailing Address
District of Columbia	Washington, DC

12. Tax Status (*For completion by nonprofit organizations authorized to mail at nonprofit rates*) (*Check one*)
The purpose, function, and nonprofit status of this organization and the exempt status for federal income tax purposes:
☑ Has Not Changed During Preceding 12 Months
☐ Has Changed During Preceding 12 Months (*Publisher must submit explanation of change with this statement*)

13. Publication Title	14. Issue Date for Circulation Data Below
American Journal of Public Health	09/30/2022

15. Extent and Nature of Circulation		Average No. Copies Each Issue During Preceding 12 Months	No. Copies of Single Issue Published Nearest to Filing Date
a. Total Number of Copies (*Net press run*)		8185	7537
b. Paid Circulation (*By Mail and Outside the Mail*)	(1) Mailed Outside-County Paid Subscriptions Stated on PS Form 3541 (*Include paid distribution above nominal rate, advertiser's proof copies, and exchange copies*)	7719	7108
	(2) Mailed In-County Paid Subscriptions Stated on PS Form 3541 (*Include paid distribution above nominal rate, advertiser's proof copies, and exchange copies*)	0	0
	(3) Paid Distribution Outside the Mails Including Sales Through Dealers and Carriers, Street Vendors, Counter Sales, and Other Paid Distribution Outside USPS®	163	158
	(4) Paid Distribution by Other Classes of Mail Through the USPS (e.g., First-Class Mail®)	0	0
c. Total Paid Distribution [*Sum of 15b (1), (2), (3), and (4)*]		7882	7266
d. Free or Nominal Rate Distribution (*By Mail and Outside the Mail*)	(1) Free or Nominal Rate Outside-County Copies included on PS Form 3541	0	0
	(2) Free or Nominal Rate In-County Copies Included on PS Form 3541	0	0
	(3) Free or Nominal Rate Copies Mailed at Other Classes Through the USPS (e.g., First-Class Mail)	0	0
	(4) Free or Nominal Rate Distribution Outside the Mail (*Carriers or other means*)	0	0
e. Total Free or Nominal Rate Distribution (*Sum of 15d (1), (2), (3) and (4)*)		0	0
f. Total Distribution (*Sum of 15c and 15e*)		7882	7266
g. Copies not Distributed (*See Instructions to Publishers #4 (page #3)*)		297	271
h. Total (*Sum of 15f and g*)		0	0
i. Percent Paid (*15c divided by 15f times 100*)		100	100

* If you are claiming electronic copies, go to line 16 on page 3. If you are not claiming electronic copies, skip to line 17 on page 3.

UNITED STATES POSTAL SERVICE®

Statement of Ownership, Management, and Circulation (All Periodicals Publications Except Requester Publications)

16. Electronic Copy Circulation	Average No. Copies Each Issue During Preceding 12 Months	No. Copies of Single Issue Published Nearest to Filing Date
a. Paid Electronic Copies	13437	7537
b. Total Paid Print Copies (Line 15c) + Paid Electronic Copies (Line 16a)	21319	14803
c. Total Print Distribution (Line 15f) + Paid Electronic Copies (Line 16a)	21319	14803
d. Percent Paid (Both Print & Electronic Copies) (16b divided by 16c × 100)	100	100

☑ **I certify that 50% of all my distributed copies (electronic and print) are paid above a nominal price.**

17. Publication of Statement of Ownership
☑ If the publication is a general publication, publication of this statement is required. Will be printed in the 11/01/2023 issue of this publication. ☐ Publication not required.

18. Signature and Title of Editor, Publisher, Business Manager, or Owner
Brian Selzer
Date
9/27/2023

I certify that all information furnished on this form is true and complete. I understand that anyone who furnishes false or misleading information on this form or who omits material or information requested on the form may be subject to criminal sanctions (including fines and imprisonment) and/or civil sanctions (including civil penalties).

AJPH

A PUBLICATION OF THE
AMERICAN PUBLIC HEALTH ASSOCIATION

SUBSCRIBE TODAY!

AJPH publishes the highest quality articles in essential areas of research, policy analysis, and program evaluation. Each monthly issue also features critical commentaries, editorials, and letters to the editor.

Mail orders to:

American Public Health Association
800 I St, NW
Washington, DC 20001

E-mail: apha.subscriptions@apha.org

2024 Institutional Pricing:

Online	Tier 2:	☐ $935 (U.S. and International)	
	Tier 3:	☐ $1160 (U.S. and International)	
	Tier 4:	☐ $1390 (U.S. and International)	
Print + Online	Tier 2:	☐ $1150 (U.S.)	☐ $1240 (International)
	Tier 3:	☐ $1415 (U.S.)	☐ $1505 (International)
	Tier 4:	☐ $1670 (U.S.)	☐ $1765 (International)
Print Only		☐ $855 (U.S.)	☐ $955 (International)

The official version of AJPH *is our online journal. Please note that print-only subscribers will not have online access to any online-only articles and supplements.*

Features of *AJPH* online subscriptions:

- Perpetual access for each year subscribed
- Enhanced search capabilities
- Dynamic PDFs
- Mobile and e-reader options
- Personalization and management tools to view your content
- Access to research online ahead of print
- COUNTER report-availability notification
- Archives dating back to 1911
- Supplement issues

***AJPH* Highlights**

- *AJPH* Global News
- Podcasts in English, Spanish, and Chinese
- E-mail alerts and more
- Special topic collections
- Perspectives from prominent voices in public health
- Book reviews

APHA
AMERICAN PUBLIC HEALTH ASSOCIATION

For more information, visit **www.ajph.org** today!

978-0-87553-340-7, 2023, 450 PP, SOFTCOVER

Black Women's Reproductive Health and Sexuality: A Holistic Public Health Approach

Edited by Regina Moss Davis, PhD, MPH

Reproductive health and sexual well-being are important parts of human health. But for Black women, research and education tend to focus on negative risks and outcomes. *Black Women's Reproductive Health and Sexuality: A Holistic Public Health Approach* offers a comprehensive look at the determinants of Black women's reproductive health and sexuality and shares evidence-based programs, policies, and promising solutions that support Black women in leading healthy and safe lives.

APHABOOKSTORE.ORG

APHA PRESS

AN IMPRINT OF **AMERICAN PUBLIC HEALTH ASSOCIATION**

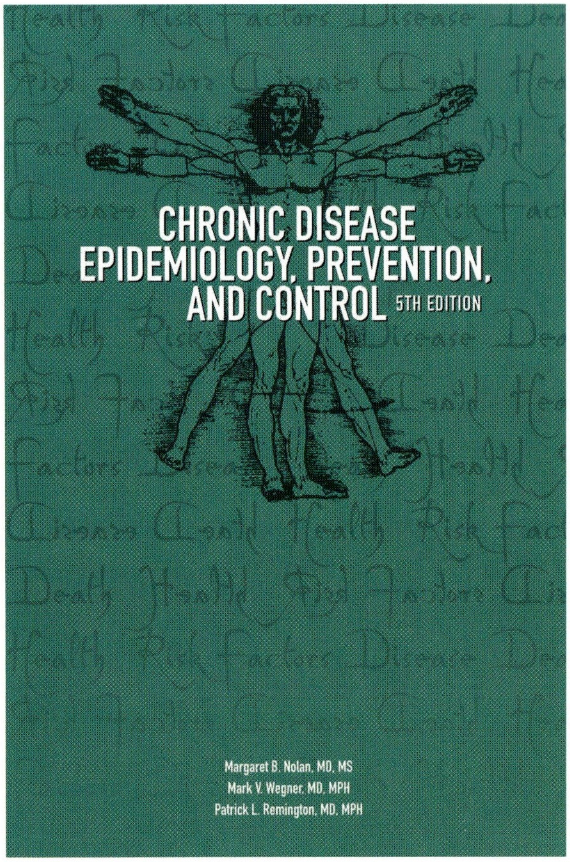

2023, SOFTCOVER, 978-087553-3360

Chronic Disease Epidemiology, Prevention, and Control, 5th edition

Edited by Margaret B. Nolan, MD, MS, Mark V. Wegner, MD, MPH, and Patrick L. Remington, MD, MPH

The fifth edition of *Chronic Disease Epidemiology, Prevention, and Control* has been updated. Its original content has been expanded to include new chapters on often overlooked chronic disease topics such as sleep and oral health. With an enhanced focus on health equity and social determinants of health, as well as the impact of the COVID-19 pandemic on chronic disease prevention and control, this manual is bound to serve as an effective guide for public health practitioners.

APHABOOKSTORE.ORG

APHA PRESS

AN IMPRINT OF **AMERICAN PUBLIC HEALTH ASSOCIATION**